The Underside of
Toronto

The Underside of Toronto

Edited by W. E. Mann

McClelland and Stewart Limited
Toronto/Montreal

The Canadian Publishers
McClelland and Stewart Limited
25 Hollinger Road, Toronto 374

PRINTED AND BOUND IN CANADA

Contents

Preface: The Soft
Underbelly of Toronto

Sociology has many functions – one sometimes despairingly thinks about as many functions as there are sociologists. But this is doubtless a mild exaggeration.

There are those who hold that sociology does – or can, or will – discover general laws governing the realm of the social, essentially similar to the physical laws that are held to govern the domain of the physical.

A second, more modest, but doubtless more vicious, function of sociology is essentially to furnish "intelligence" to those who already have power and goods for use in defeating the aims of those who seek their share of these. It is difficult to believe that the greater part of sociology today does not have this effect, and a great deal of it, especially as practised by the bearers of the "great names" (thus *made* great), clearly has this intent. The study of "insurgency" permits the government of the United States to take more effective measures to advance its most crass and material interests abroad or at home against all whose needs for goods, justice, or dignity require them even faintly to tread upon those "interests." But this is the most blatant and notorious case. Most of the evil done by sociology is banal, as Eichmann's monstrous evil was banal: one simply loyally follows the path of least resistance. This means that one studies the weak and powerless because they do not have the defences against being studied that are part of the power of the strong. One also treats the weak as somehow being (or having) "the problem," thus arbitrarily predetermining who is, in effect, plaintiff and who is defendant, or who is to control and who is to be controlled in a society which, whatever else it is, is a conflict-system. To supply "intelligence" about one side in a struggle to the other side – even if publication is "open," the sides are unevenly matched in their abilities to read, digest, and use data – may well be more decisive than supplying arms.

7

A third function of sociology (though I should prefer to call it "sociography") is to hold up a mirror to society. The motive and effect may be dualistic. One motive and effect combination is more artistic than moral or political: the object here is to permit people to see and appreciate the vast panorama of shared human behaviour in all its fascinating variety, in contrast with the limited view of human life visible from any one person's particular social position or the utterly distorted view derived from the official account of the society. Such sociography is an invitation to appreciate and enjoy the remarkable mosaic that a society like ours presents – and perhaps, in so doing, to enlarge mind and heart. These are essentially humanistic objectives. Similar in method, but different in tone, motive, and effect, is the holding of the mirror so that society *must* confront what it never wants to confront: its true image as opposed to the image which its dominant (that is, power-backed) myths attempt to project. The objects here are moral and political: to make self-deceit harder come by, to reveal what the comfortable would rather conceal, and thus to create a crack in the armour for the entering wedge of justice and decency, whether powered by greater pressure for reform or the threat or actuality of revolution.

The book at hand clearly falls in the category of sociography as defined, though it shares (perhaps necessarily, since its contributors are so various) in both the humanistic-appreciative tradition and in the moral-political one. Most of it can be read as a travelogue (which might have been called *Toronto the Unknown)* or as an indictment of or admonition to a society that can blandly let such things be and callously allow them to continue. The contents of this book describe the soft underbelly of Toronto the Good, and that description seems to indicate the author's intent: the reason for mapping the soft underbelly, whether in Churchill's war or in deadly animal combat, is to find the most vulnerable area for the destruction or defeat of whatever the belly belongs to.

The book has, of course, a bias, doubtless forced upon it by the previously mentioned ability of the strong to preserve secrecy and prevent their being studied – that is, the differential power effectively to conspire. Otherwise, surely, among "Hidden Social Worlds," we should have found the University Club and the York Club (cultural equivalents of the Pentagon's War Room or the C.I.A.'s top echelon councils), the meetings among the city's university "administrators," the conferences in corporate boardrooms and those "hidden social worlds" where politicians and big businessmen meet to determine how best (with the greatest safety, stability, and profit) to sell the Canadian heritage and future to foreign power, public and private. Similarly, among "Little Known Groups and Their Behaviour," we should expect to find advertising agencies where, with the aid of social scientists ("motivation researchers"), the schemes are laid to play upon the less aware functions of men's minds in order to make them "want" what they could not reasonably desire – thus separating such engineered fools from their money in the way least likely to lead to immediate reprisals. And one might add meetings of teachers and educators with one eye on maximizing their own comfort and convenience (their private duty) and the other eye on more effectively chopping the living child into a potential slot-filler for somebody's "manpower needs" or "table of organization" (their public duty).

It is particularly apt that the articles in this anthology should have one geographic locus, and that that locus should be Toronto. Every city has a self-image, and every city's self-image is almost precisely a representation of what it is *not*, what it is *least*. In Indianapolis, for instance, a city I studied for three years, the "Hoosier image" was one of moderation and common-sense, both of which were most notably absent in nearly all spheres of life. Toronto's self-image, "Toronto the Good," "Toronto, the city of homes and churches," leads it to think (or, until recently, led it to think) of itself as a bastion of British moderation and Calvinist right-doing. Whatever Toronto now is, these images once rationalized, at best, dullness, mediocrity, self-righteousness, and the cut-throat competition and mutual antagonism and suspicion that characterized the much despised American way, disguised – and, therefore, made better or worse, depending on how you view it – by a sheen of good manners and decorum. To the degree that this book reveals what is not compatible with that self-deceit, it is most useful.

Perhaps one more word should be said. The soft underbelly sketched here is only underbelly to the official Toronto. If we were to search for the city's *real* underbelly, that point of vulnerability at which it is most likely to be destroyed, then we should have to look at the places where high policy is made and big deals are perpetrated. Gambling, nudity, pornography, homosexuality will never destroy or seriously threaten either the goodness of a society's life or the viability of the society itself; only the routine immorality and banality of its élite and the institutions of the establishment can do that. And they are well on their way.

If I were looking for the real underbelly with any hostile intent, I would look in Toronto the Good, among the *officially* good. And their defences against being studied fill out the figure – the animal attacked, unless it wants to signal it will yield, turns and manoeuvres to keep its underbelly out of sight and out of reach.

This is, in part, preface to a book which has not yet been written, a book about that other underbelly. I look hopefully for future studies – directed there.

JOHN R. SEELEY
January, 1970

Introduction

We are living now in the metropolitan era, that period when cities of great size, complexity, power, and technological interdependence both shape the significant activities of mankind and provide the launching pad for humankind's future on this planet. The metropolises constitute, in effect, the basic social units of the global village. In them, the formative ideas, the new styles of life, and the new directions of the "village" are developed, questioned, refined, and transmitted to their dependent hinterlands. What is significant in the metropolises is significant for mankind.

One of the truly impressive metropolises of the global village is Toronto, Canada. In the Huron language, Toronto means "the meeting place," and this name is especially appropriate today. Dhalla notes:

> Reaching into and out of Toronto are ten railway lines and twelve major highways. Five scheduled airlines (Air Canada, C.P.A., B.O.A.C., American, Mohawk) serve Toronto International Airport. With the completion of the St. Lawrence Seaway, the city has acquired the status of an international seaport. Just as Toronto was in a bygone era a meeting place for Indian tribes, it is today the meeting place for all Canada. . . . In fact, its influence as a financial, industrial, transportation and commercial centre is so great that mere distance from Toronto has become a major fact in the economic geography of the country.[1]

Boom city of Canada in the '60's, centre of the dynamic Golden Horseshoe that lies at the base of the rich province of Ontario, Toronto has nowhere to go but up. With an annual population increase of 80,000 to 90,000, an increasing share of the industry and talent of English-speaking Canada, and boasting frequent air links with all the major world centres, Toronto in 1970 is a city whose fame and glamour are certain to grow. Some of the impressive story of Toronto's last twenty years has been described in print and picture book. Especially since the building of its

11

famous circular, twenty-five-storey city hall and the impressive success of its metropolitan form of government, it has received increasing coverage in print. Each month now, a new magazine, *Toronto Life*, depicts novelties on the social and cultural scene. A weekly catalogue of coming events is now being made available in another new publication, *Toronto Calendar*. Thus, as the population of this fast-growing child of the Technopolitan Age rapidly approaches a population of over two million, media of various kinds attempt to record its myriad creations and speculate on its future.

> During the last two decades Toronto has undergone the most sweeping and rapid change in its 175-year history. Within the city limits proper, largely because of postwar immigration, every second Torontonian is at present a Roman Catholic. Half of all the immigrants arriving in Canada come to Ontario, and about 50% of these settle down in Toronto. The outlanders whose mother tongue is Italian, Slavic or German can by themselves constitute medium-sized cities. As a result the old Toronto (strongly traditional, puritanical, and predominantly Anglo-Saxon and Protestant) is now largely a piece of the past. This town of quiet homes and quiet Sundays, this primary outpost of Victorian culture, has somehow exploded into something dramatically different.[2]

This new Toronto of 1970 is withal a much more vital and dynamic place. It boasts its Bohemia (in Yorkville), its poets and artists, and its clever satirists. It is fast acquiring touches of European sophistication; attractive bars, coffee houses, and foreign restaurants are blossoming, and there are even sidewalk cafés in the summer. Downtown newsstands are overflowing with foreign language papers and magazines, many of the former published locally. In the ethnic areas, stores sell exotic imported foods, and druggists advertise their wares in half a dozen languages. Old "Hogtown" Toronto now advertises avant-garde plays, ragtime bands, Italian song festivals, pizza carnivals, motoramas, pop festivals, stripperamas, and numerous attic and cellar clubs where one can listen to poetry, jazz, and folk music until late into the night.

In short, Toronto has begun to mirror every sophisticated metropolis in the world as a centre of many facets. Thus, Hugh Garner, Toronto's leading novelist, claims the city "is a score of cities joined together by geographical propinquity which has resulted in a bizarre incestuous relationship between the Junction and Rosedale, Cabbagetown and Forest Hill, etc., etc." It is a city of literally hundreds of separate social worlds, some more and others less hidden from conventional public inspection or appreciation.

It is typical for a city to be socially differentiated; in fact, it is the very genius of the big city to create ever new social and cultural worlds, or sub-worlds, which offer to its citizenry an ever increasing richness of personal and social experience and discovery. As Jane Jacobs has recently pointed out, it is the nature of the urban economy to encourage and promote intellectual and technological innovation and creativity – to be the prime mover for society's great leaps forward.

To a certain extent, geographic distinctions may aid or encourage the co-existence of a rich variety of different worlds or subcultures within the big city. This seems to have been the case with Toronto. Two river systems, the Don and the Humber, along with several extensive and well-preserved ravines, have doubtless helped preserve the integrity of specific social worlds, and these have evolved distinctive neighbourhood names and styles of life. The rivers or ravines have long acted as protective walls, so that when outsiders venture in, they sense a distinctive atmosphere, a hidden world awaiting discovery and understanding. Such, for example, is old Cabbagetown, a section of lower- and working-class homes and institutions lying just west of the Don River and south of Bloor. Just north of Bloor and its adjacent ravine is Rosedale, a centre of large homes and estates. East of the Don lies Riverdale, a still different section of modest working-class homes. West of Yonge, the rise of land a bit north of Bloor attracted certain wealthier elements and helps explain that secluded, exclusive enclave, Wychwood Park.

On the west side of Toronto, other distinct districts have evolved, often assisted by locational factors. For instance, lying a bit north of the sunken railway tracks and west of the broad expanse of University Avenue is the Lower Ward, a lower-class enclave that stretches for perhaps a mile below old Queen Street. Above Queen and near the ethnically famous Spadina Avenue is the now famous Kensington Market, which preserves many attributes of a European farmer's market. Not far north and east of Casa Loma, one comes upon another now-famous sub-area, Forest Hill, a predominantly wealthy Jewish residential area, described in such detail in that widely known study, *Crestwood Heights*.

These are but a few of the more well-known of Toronto's many neighbourhoods, most of which can still lay claim to a distinctive style of life – much of it hidden to the outsider. Besides geographical factors, their separateness and cultural cohesion may be attributed in part to historical accident – the early claiming of a certain district by adventuresome home or industry builders – and to the rich ethnic diversity of Toronto. As early immigrants of a group like the Jews or Italians settled in a certain neighbourhood and developed specific supportive institutions in stores, clubs, or churches, late-comers found it convenient to move close by and enjoy these facilities and the protection they offered to a traditional and cherished way of life. In other cases, status differences may account for the continuing integrity of both lower- and upper-class enclaves.

Yonge Street, which bisects Toronto into east and west, supports other little-known social worlds. Below Bloor Street, one finds the taverns that cater to the homosexual trade, the bars featuring go-go girls, and the small stores that sell pornography. These are only three of the socially-deviant behaviour patterns that seem focussed on or near downtown Yonge Street. A half-mile to the west, Spadina Street runs Yonge a close second for sponsoring hidden worlds or groups; here is located the city's only burlesque house, the Victory, and one of the biggest enterprises caring for the men on skid row, the Scott Mission. A few blocks west and north, around Bathurst and just above Bloor, is another fascinating neighbourhood, the Annex, now a melting-pot area housing many Asiatics and blacks. Such is the geography of Metro Toronto that exotic and unusual groups or behaviour patterns may be observed throughout much of its 150-square-mile area.

Up until now there have been distressingly few book-length studies of boom-city Toronto which can claim sociological standing. In the mid-'50's, John R. Seeley and his colleagues produced the thoughtful and fascinating *Crestwood Heights*, examining life in the "suburb" of Forest Hill. In *The Suburban Society*, S. D. Clark of the University of Toronto questioned the assumptions of certain American writers regarding suburban values and life-styles. This was a rather discursive study that included areas many miles north of Metro Toronto's boundaries. Neither of these two books, nor Clark's earlier anthology (curiously entitled *Urbanism in the Changing Canadian Society)*, focussed on Toronto. In fact, neither professional nor amateur sociologists have attempted book-length descriptions of the over-all life of the metropolis. The closest to any such attempt is *Urban Political Systems: A Functional Analysis of Metro Toronto*, written by Harold Kaplan, a York University political scientist, who sociologically examined the operation of the metropolitan government during the administration of Frederick G. Gardiner. This lack of over-all studies or monographs on specific areas or subcultures is a rather curious phenomenon.

By comparison, Chicago, in the 1920's and 1930's, produced at least ten good monographs depicting and analysing its major "ghetto" groups, particularly its social deviants.[3] Thus Toronto's backwardness in self-study represents not the usual lag of twenty years behind the United States, but something like thirty or forty years. (It might be noted that Montreal and Vancouver are no better represented by good sociological studies.) Some of this lag may be explained by the typical conservatism and reluctance of Canadians to take their own work and culture seriously. But the fault must also be attributed in part to the slowness of sociology's acceptance in Canada, particularly to the retarded growth of that social science at the University of Toronto from 1945-1960 and the paucity of Canadians (especially Torontonians) on the faculty during that period.[4]

Since the opening of York University and the several community colleges in the city, the picture has slowly begun to improve. Much more interest is now being shown at these institutions, as well as at the University of Toronto, in field investigations of the city's rich and complex social life. Now under way are a number of significant studies which in due course should enrich our understanding of Toronto. Among these are Dr. Donald Coates' study of community mental health in Leaside and East York, Professor Anthony Richmond's investigations into the integration of the city's ethnic groups, Professor Stewart Crysdale's three-year survey of working-class youth in Riverdale, and several studies being directed by Dr. Wilson Head of the Metro Social Planning Council. Also, early in 1970, the Ontario Government's Commission on the Healing Arts will be releasing a volume written by Dr. John Lee on healing cults, many of which are located in Toronto.

Owing to the current lack of strong, book-length studies, however, it has not been an easy task to put together this anthology. In searching for articles on the hidden or little-known social worlds and subcultures of Toronto, including deviant and unconventional institutions and behaviour patterns, it was necessary to search through many sources and to use some articles written by social observers not formally trained in sociology. Naturally, the majority of the articles chosen consists of writings by professional sociologists; these were mainly written by teachers drawn from the city's two universities and three community colleges. Thus, two of the authors are on the faculty of the University of Toronto, and two others were on it until quite recently. Four articles are by York University faculty members. Three others are by Community College teachers, one apiece from Centennial, Seneca, and Humber Community Colleges; another three are from the pens of sociologists not presently teaching full-time. Among those writers not trained in social science, it is especially gratifying to include pieces done by such nationally known journalists and literary figures as Pierre Berton, Robert Fulford, June Callwood, and Elizabeth Kilbourn. These and other well-trained journalists, describing social phenomena with which they usually have a particular acquaintance, make a fine contribution to our volume.

A few rather obvious criteria governed the selection of articles. Was the writer well-acquainted with his data and did he assume an objective posture in his report? Does the piece contribute to an over-all understanding of the many-sided mosaic of Toronto's social life? Is it readable, does it make its points succinctly? Occasionally some studies were abridged to achieve this last goal. In general, the aim was to include articles neither too long (over 8,000 words) nor too short and slight (under 2,000 words); preference was also given to those no more than five years old.

The over-all purpose of this collection is threefold: firstly, to describe and analyse "underground" or hidden or unconventional aspects of Toronto's society, phenomena commonly unreported in the usual books about the big city's life; secondly, to create a collection of some of the most interesting and valuable studies of sub-areas of the city's complex social structure, places like Little Italy, the Lower Ward, and Yorkville; and thirdly, to illuminate the vast complexity and variety of social behaviour in the city, so that students and the public can realize something of the maturity, the social problems, and the cultural trends that make up this booming metropolis at its entrance into the '70's.

While touching on many fascinating subcultures and deviant groupings, this anthology makes no claim to be either fully representative or comprehensive. Limitations of space – and of available articles – have forced a selection which is aimed at a broad understanding of Toronto's complexity; in the last analysis, the editor must take responsibility for the choice. In a very few instances, articles were commissioned to try to cover what seemed to be significant gaps. But many fascinating topics, generally as interesting and valuable as those dealt with here, had to be ignored since space was lacking or no usable article was available. Among the fascinating topics that might have been included are: 1) such racial groups as the Indians, the Chinese, and the Japanese; 2) deviant groups like the labour racketeers, the Mafia, call-girls, phony bankruptcy "artists," stock market gamblers, rich playboys, and draft dodgers; and 3) unusual or marginal groups like religious cults, political reform groups like C.I.V.A.C., the sex specialists of the Sex Information and Educational Association of Canada, and the single "swingers" of the ritzy St. James Town apartments. Hopefully, students and teachers of sociology will tackle at least some of these topics in the future and will add to our understanding of the Toronto scene.

In spite of the many limitations of this anthology, it is hoped that it will enable the reader to gain some appreciation of the exciting, ever-increasing variety, complexity, and uniqueness of the Metro Toronto community in the period 1965-1970. In addition, he should gain some further grasp of Toronto as an extraordinary organism, trying to come of age and shedding much of its hidebound past in the process. Of course, bits and pieces of the old Hogtown Toronto still remain, and they necessarily receive occasional mention. By no means all of the city's Family Compact, Anglican, part-United-Empire-Loyalist, part-Orange-Order past has been superseded. So our collection includes some hearkening back as well as looking ahead. No study of the contemporary scene can ignore the influence of the past or the challenge of the future. But above all, we attempt to depict the extraordinary mosaic that is Toronto in 1970; no doubt this will change under the pressure of events, and another and perhaps quite different volume will be needed in five or ten years.

W. E. MANN
York University
January, 1970

Part One:

Hidden
Social
Worlds

1

Anthropology on the Town

Charles Tilly

What are the differences between common-sense notions, usually linked to casual, untrained observations, and the ideas and observations made by social scientists? How does a social anthropologist or sociologist – in terms, aims, and general methodology, the disciplines are much the same – go about studying an urban area? For many people, these are basic questions which need both general and specific answers, the sort of answers which are provided in this essay by Professor Charles Tilly. And since all of these questions lead up to a more complete sociological understanding of the city of Toronto, this piece is located at the beginning of our anthology.

Professor Tilly, the author of *La Vendée,* a brilliant study of a French rebellion, was, until recently, a senior professor of sociology at the University of Toronto. He is now at the University of Michigan at Ann Arbor. This article first appeared in *Habitat,* Volume 10, No. 1.

Once upon a time, anthropologists were supposed to spend all their time out in the bush, smoking hemp with primitive people. Not any more! Some of them may still be smoking hemp, but the old, ethnocentric division between "primitive" and "civilized" peoples has fallen by the wayside. No one is sure which is which now. And many anthropologists have come to town. Some have followed their subject matter from tribal areas to cities, while others have simply realized that their methods apply to city dwellers as well as to inhabitants of tiny villages.

As an urban sociologist, I greet them with mixed feelings. Have they come to fight for my turf, my city? Yet, as a student of cities, I have to admit they have something: a style of disciplined, direct observation which gets at the experience of living in different nooks and crannies of big cities.

Now, everyone knows what life is like in his own cranny. The trouble is that we don't know enough about each other's worlds – how they overlap, how they differ, how they add up. Sociologists have done fairly well at adding up pieces of individual lives to get the big picture of land use, or the location of different nationalities within a city, or the distribution of crime. Their development of the sample survey has provided a convenient way of detecting the main trends and major subdivisions in big-city population. They have helped design the biggest survey of them all – the census – and have invented some ingenious ways of using numbers from the census to find out where the city is going. The urban sociologists are great at averaging, at finding the main line. That helps in learning whether the population is getting more mobile, or if one national group is sending more of its children to college, or who is getting what during a general rise in prosperity. It is important to know the averages.

Yet once we know the averages, the deviations from the average begin to matter; so does the way it feels to be at the average, or far away from it. That is where the urban anthropologist shines.

We can see the difference in the study of urban poverty in North America. The sociologists and economists have not done a bad job of finding out how many poor people there are by various definitions of poverty, how the proportions have been changing, and roughly who they are. Where they have often fallen down is in analysing how people got into their various categories, and what it is like to be there.

Three non-sociologists – an anthropologist, a city planner, and a free-lance writer – played a large part in turning students of cities back towards greater attention to the ways poor people face life in the city. Oscar Lewis, an anthropologist, began his work by studying everyday life in a Mexican village. Later, he followed his villagers to the slums of Mexico City. There he lived with them and let them tell their own stories while his tape recorder turned. The results were a new kind of book, built almost entirely on the oral autobiographies of the people under study, and a new understanding of the distinct way of life Lewis called the "culture of poverty." Since then, the ideas and techniques Oscar Lewis put into such books as *Five Families* and *The Children of Sanchez* have turned up more and more in the study of North American cities.

The city planner was Herbert Gans, who went and lived in the West End of Boston. The West End was a low-income, Italian-family section, slated for razing and replacement by a tall complex of expensive apartments. His book, *The Urban Villagers*, reporting what he learned, did not appear in time to save the West End from destruction. But it raised prickly questions about outsiders' assumptions that the West End was "disorganized" and a "slum," that it was therefore good only for clearance and that its residents had everything to gain through relocation. Since then, planners in Boston and elsewhere have taken their responsibility for learning what kinds of communities they are proposing to renew much more seriously.

Michael Harrington, the writer, tells us himself how he went from a useful, but distant, statistical analysis of poverty to a first-hand exploration of its labyrinths:

> After I wrote my first article on poverty in America, I had all the statistics down on paper. I had proved to my satisfaction that there were around 50 million poor in this country. Yet, I realized that I did not believe my figures. The poor existed in the Government reports; they were percentages and numbers in long, close columns, but they were not part of my experience. I could prove that the other America existed, but I had never been there.[1]

Then he went to the streets of New York and other cities to live with the poor. Harrington laid out the results of his inquiry in a powerful book, *The Other America*. And the American government listened as it established its anti-poverty program.

It happens that Lewis, Gans, and Harrington all wrote influential books. But writing books is not all that comes of the anthropological approach to the city. When the group building the big new city of Guayana, in Venezuela, asked Lisa Redfield Peattie to join them as staff anthropologist, they probably thought she would work mainly at feeding back information about sore spots in people's adaptation to the city, and at explaining what was going on to the natives. With her wide experience in rural Latin America, she certainly could have done this. In fact, she did become a good source of information about what was going on in the poor people's neighbourhoods in Guayana, but she did it by settling with her family in the local shack-town and helping its residents organize a successful protest against living conditions there. Now she is teaching city planners at Massachusetts Institute of Technology and once again helping poor people – this time in Boston – articulate their demands for planning which will take their needs into account.

It is easy to see the implications for urban action in these investigations of poverty. It may not be so obvious that they contribute to our general understanding of how cities work. The very title of Gans' book, for example, states an important idea: the similarity between the social organization of many of the city's ethnic enclaves – urban villages – and of the small communities from which their members or their members' forebears came. People have been noticing the diversity of cultures in North American cities for a century, but usually under the impression that they were transient residues of old-country customs. Gans establishes the durability of some of these village cultures and helps explain that durability. Thus a piece of work with direct practical applications contributes to the theory of the city as well.

What do these urban anthropologists do besides settling down in slums? Well, that in itself is an important beginning. It is a way of sharing an important experience and gaining acceptance at the same time. The trained participant observer has a chance to see people when they take off their business faces, to accompany them through the full daily, weekly, or monthly round. He makes sure he establishes some contact with all parts of the population he is dealing with, not just the talkative élite. He records what

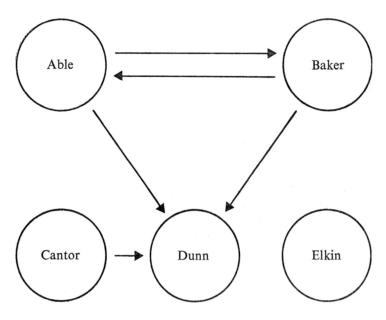

he sees in a systematic way – in classified field notes, in a journal, or perhaps on cards representing different individuals or groups. He may very well take a "sociometric" approach, concentrating on the frequencies and kinds of contact among pairs of members of the group. Those observations he can sum up in diagrams of group structure like this hypothetical, but realistic, representation of visiting patterns among a group of housewives in adjoining houses.

Here, Mrs. Able and Mrs. Baker regularly exchange visits; Mrs. Able, Mrs. Baker, and Mrs. Cantor regularly visit Mrs. Dunn; and Mrs. Elkin stays by herself. We can do the same diagramming for other members of the families, or for different kinds of contact, like giving help, borrowing tools, or going shopping together.

The people actually involved do not need a diagram to tell them that A and B are close, that D is a centre of attraction, or that E is an isolate. However, where the observer is a newcomer,

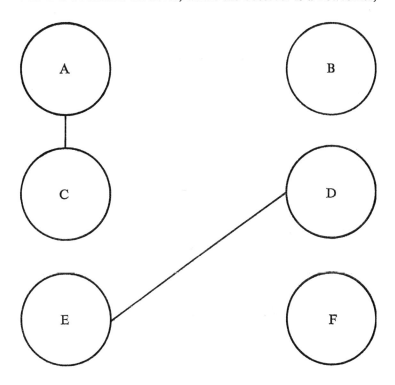

Atomized—pairs and isolates

where twenty or thirty households are involved, or where the question is whether the same kinds of clusters keep reappearing, only some sort of systematic recording and analysis will bring out the true state of affairs.

This general technique has many versions. It can neatly summarize what groups intermarry in a large city, what kinds of people form cliques in a high school, what individuals talk to each other most in an office.

It is a natural starting point for a study of the flow of communications within a neighbourhood. And when done at a scale larger than the pair of individuals, it helps us distinguish three vitally different social arrangements. The first might be the structure of a rooming-house district; the second, the structure of a Chinese neighbourhood; the third, a high-rise apartment area.

Sociometric observation can get very complicated. There are simpler and faster ways of getting a sense of social life in one section of a city or another. Very often, all an intelligent observer

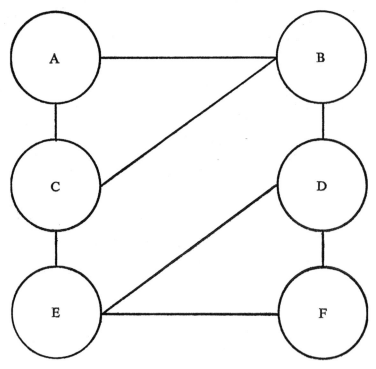

Tight-knit—overlapping sets

needs is a stroll through a neighbourhood to spot the main points of congregation of the local population – doorsteps, bars, stores, clubs, churches. If they are public enough, he can station himself there and take a small part in local life. Or he can deliberately create his own social situations. When Kevin Lynch, the city planner, was trying to find out what kinds of roads and buildings made strong impressions on people, one of his devices was to stop people on the street and ask them directions to other sections of the city, noting what they used as their points of reference.

Lynch also adopted a slightly more formal way of finding out how people visualized their cities. He asked them to draw maps. His instructions went like this: "We would like you to make a quick map of central Boston, inward or downtown from Massachusetts Avenue. Make it just as if you were making a rapid description of the city to a stranger, covering all the main features. We don't expect an accurate drawing – just a rough sketch."[2]

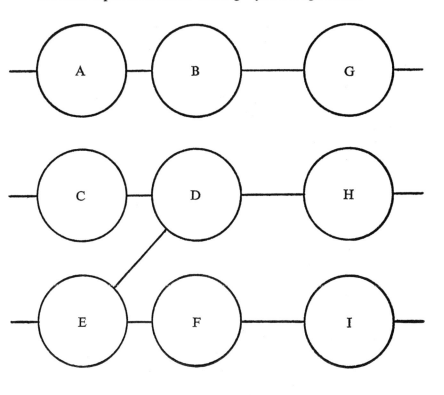

Specialized—extensive chains

And the interviewer was supposed to note the sequence in which the map was drawn. Everyone marked down Beacon Hill, the Common, the Charles River, and the Back Bay, but there were large areas of the central city which simply disappeared from these maps for lack of what Lynch calls "imageability."

With due allowance for skill in drawing and for visual imagination, we have a lot to learn about people's experience with the city from the maps they sketch. As an experiment, I asked my three eldest children to do maps of central Toronto. They are not elegant, but they are revealing. The seven-year-old's world is the path from home to school and its fringes, with her own block and the play areas she knows best blown up out of all proportion to their actual size. The nine-year-old has grasped the grid pattern of the streets and has had enough experience with the downtown portions of the subway to put some important thoroughfares into the central business district; the appearance of the rivers and of Highway 401 on the map, however, probably comes from book-learning in school. She still gives her own section of the city (from Bloor to Eglinton along Yonge) much more space than its due. The eleven-year-old is aware of too many details for a map on this scale; so many, that he gets some wrong and has trouble fitting others together. His map includes the lakefront, and shows places like the Royal Ontario Museum, the Exhibition Grounds, and the Airport, as well as streets and waterways. Each child's view of the city is selective, but the older children can roam mentally through more of its territory, and they select on different principles. It would be fascinating to see how children of the same ages in other parts of the city played this game.

Instead of starting with real cities, sociologist William Michelson of the University of Toronto asked different sorts of people to map out ideal environments. He did this because he happened to wonder what systematic connection there was between the things people wanted out of life in general and what kinds of communities they preferred, but his technique could be used for many other purposes.

The map-drawer began with his own dwelling, placed a number of facilities like schools, movies, shopping centres, and workplaces on the map, then drew a line around the area he would consider his neighbourhood. . . . [One] describes a house with a yard some 200 feet square, a neighbourhood including schools and a church within fifteen minute walk, and an area outside the neighbourhood containing shopping facilities, a restaurant, and a job. . . . [Another one] banishes everything but houses from the neighbourhood, puts a post-office and a store just across its boundary, places a well-defined street between the house and all other facilities, and then traces detailed separate paths to a wide variety of centres of activity. These are rather different pictures of what the residential parts of cities should be like.

To complement this picture of the ideal world, people can tell us a great deal about what they do with the actual space of the city by simply recounting where they go, what they do and with whom, during an average day. One version of this is the "yesterday interview," in which the interviewer asks the person to give a history of yesterday from 6:00 A.M. to midnight, including each activity lasting ten minutes or more. Another version is the diary kept under the same rules. Either one produces a valuable picture of how much time different kinds of people spend doing what, where, and with whom. If they compared their own "time-budgets" with their wives', many husbands would begin to understand why wives are often eager to talk, talk, talk when they get a chance – for so much of their time is spent alone or with no one but small children. The student of cities has other facts to learn from time-budgets, such as when and where in a city the most people are likely to be in sociable contact with others, how much of all the time available to city-dwellers goes into travelling, what activities most people do alone, what sections of the city are used in the daily rounds of old people, or rich people, or newcomers. How do the daily time-budgets of these individuals fit with the maps of the city they would draw?

Again we have gone from a simple notion to a complicated application. Some parts of these questions about the patterns of activity in the city can be broken off for a separate study. Just who is on the street, and when, is in itself an important fact about local life, and fairly easy to observe. Our students at the University of Toronto have found they can make an informative first contact with a section of the city by going to a local intersection and recording who goes by during scattered five-minute intervals. They set down not only how many people pass the corner, but also a rough judgement of age, sex, and whether they are alone or with others. They can do it by tallying within a grid:

These distributions vary sharply and informatively from place to place and from time to time.

If only the process of walking by could be slowed down enough for the observer to take copious notes, there would be many other things to jot down: the objects people are carrying, the way they are dressed, the languages they are speaking, how much they

ALONE

	MALE	FEMALE
Over 60	─╫╫─	
20-60	IIII	I
Under 20	I	I

IN GROUPS

	MALE	FEMALE
Over 60	IIII	╫╫ I
20-60	╫╫ IIII	╫╫ ╫╫ I
Under 20	II	II

dawdle or gawk. A camera can catch some of these things very effectively. . . .

Of course, it takes a little bit of nerve to tally passers-by or take pictures on the street. For observers with less *chutzpah,* the objects people leave around them also say something important about their lives.

Here are some ideas culled from different research projects: 1) count the proportion of door-buttons pushed down in automobiles on the street in different areas, in order to see how willing people are to leave their cars unlocked; 2) notice how many backyards in a neighbourhood contain grass, how many flower gardens, how many trash piles, and how many vegetable patches, to get an idea of the local style of life; 3) check the percentage of blinds which are drawn, to judge how much people are shutting themselves off from others on the street; 4) notice how many liquor bottles are thrown out on trash day, and what kind, to guess the home drinking patterns; 5) record how many houses have outside Christmas decorations, and how elaborate they are, to gauge how much it is an occasion for public display.

In fact, all of us make such observations, half-consciously, every day.

Considering how much a part of everyday life these various sorts of observation are, it might seem that "urban anthropology" is nothing but a dressed-up version of common sense. Is it? It does deal with things everyone knows something about. It should build on good, common sense. But also, it has more discipline and greater focus than casual observation does. When a woman steps into a roomful of other women, scans it quickly, then mentally ticks off the boutique-bought dresses, the hand-crafted shoes, and the genuine pearls, that takes both discipline and focus. It takes training and attention; almost any wife can (and, unfortunately, will) testify that her husband is an ignoramus on such matters.

The urban anthropologist's discipline shows up in his insistence on observing exactly how somebody says something or just how many people gather in a certain place, as well as his faithfulness in recording the observation for future reference. His focus is on social relations, especially on those which reveal something important about the way groups are organized in the city.

Many pressing questions about cities need this systematic first-hand treatment. What difference does it make to people's social lives whether they live in separate houses, chains of garden apartments, or tall buildings? Does the dislocation of urban renewal wound people irreparably? Under what conditions do people have strong attachments to their neighbourhoods? When are the dispossessed of the city likely to get together and protest their fate? What does it mean to become poor, to stay poor? How, and when, does assimilation work? Who, and where, are all the lonely people? Urban anthropology can produce at least some of the answers.

The satisfying thing about the anthropological approach to the city is that it brings theory, policy, action, and personal experience into contact with each other. Just as some city planners, uneasy at seeing almost all their colleagues working for governments and real-estate developers, have started to organize "advocate planners" to criticize official plans and offer alternative proposals on behalf of the people being planned for, so we need skilled and independent social researchers devoted to scrutinizing the facts and presumptions on which urban policies are based. Like Oscar Lewis, Herbert Gans, and Michael Harrington, they will have the chance to deal with vital theoretical issues along the way.

For the same reasons, urban anthropology has an important role to play in education. More so than learning about the history or the government of the city from books; it challenges the student to link his own fate and private experience to the life of the city as a whole. An inveterate city-walker myself, I often send my students out to walk a randomly-assigned section of a city and report back on what they have seen. Even the lifetime residents often find themselves in areas they have never really looked at before. Most of them learn something important about their city and about themselves.

One final virtue of the methods of urban anthropology is that they still leave room for the gifted amateur. I mean amateur in the exact sense of the word: someone who does something for the love of it. Survey research and much of the large scale quantitative analysis so important to the study of cities depend on teams of specialists and expensive equipment. A few of the techniques I have described here are also easier to use with computers and other machines at hand. But most of the procedures are feasible for a single person with a camera, a tape-recorder, a sketchpad, or just a quick eye and a ready notebook. Many of them consist of making observations most people make anyway, but doing so more systematically. There is nothing wrong with the back-to-nature yearnings of mushroom-hunters and bird-watchers. Why not get back to human nature by watching people?

2 The Lower Ward

W. E. Mann

What is life like in a slum area? Is there any organization to the attitudes, values, and behavioural patterns of its members? How do the slum society, its social institutions, and its values contribute to patterns of crime and delinquency? Taking a blighted area south of Queen Street and west of University Avenue as its focus, this article, written in the early '60's, tries to answer these and related questions in a sociological analysis which resulted from participant observation and interviews. While this section of Toronto is one of shrinking population, its social characteristics have changed little in the ensuing years.

Written by the editor of this book, W. E. Mann, a slightly longer version of this article first appeared in a volume edited by S. D. Clark, *Urbanism and the Changing Canadian Society.*

Speaking in the Ontario Legislature, April 14, 1951, J. B. Salzberg, the member for St. Andrew's riding, Toronto, claimed "my riding is the most colourful, most dynamic, most cosmopolitan, and most interesting of all ridings in the province." Continuing, he added, "there are slums in my riding. In the lower part, there are areas that should have been cleared years ago."[1]

Here is how one resident of Salzberg's Lower Ward describes the process of slum development:

> When a city grows, "they" put the cream where the money is, and the garbage where they figure the garbage is. . . . What they should do is reverse the process! I was born down there; I'm no bum, and a lot of guys born down there are not bums. Maybe I'm marked on account of being born

down there, but that is all wrong, especially in today's world.

Another conception of life "down there" is furnished by a local hotel manager:

> The people here go on day to day because they have never been shown anything else. Their education has been very limited; they know nothing about the arts. They come to a point where they just exist and go right on at that level. They have had no real personal contact with anything better, so they just follow along from day to day. They don't seem to want to break away. They don't say, "Well, damn it, I've had enough of this, I'm going to get out of this and get something better." . . . This doesn't come into the minds of the majority.
>
> They give and take, give and take, and whatever they can grab, they'll take; they don't live on any principles. Their moral standard is low. A lot of them never clean up properly. They know they are dirty, so they just say, "Well, to hell with it!" They live in a mood where improvement is something they just don't think about. In fact, they just don't think about anything too hard or too deep, but stay at a good safe level. What was alright last week will be alright this week.

In the value system of Toronto's city fathers, and of the Metropolitan Toronto Executive, the Lower Ward cuts little ice. Its population of about 8,000 persons counts for little politically; it has no influential citizens, and a small number turn out to vote. Although known to harbour many kinds of deviant activity, its crime is typically petty and not highly organized. While Jarvis Street in the East End and Dundas and Spadina, a mere quarter mile to the north, have been the subject of newspaper headlines demanding clean-ups, nobody has got very concerned about the bookmaking, prostitution, or juvenile delinquency in the Lower Ward.

Before beginning a recent "survey" of the dope and vice rings allegedly focussed at Dundas and Spadina, Metropolitan Chairman F. G. Gardiner dropped into a hotel in our area. One observer reports:

> He came down with four detectives. . . . He has the idea. . . . "I guess I'll drop in and see what those birds are doing." So he comes in and sits down like a lord muckeddy muck; he's the whole cheese, he's going to look things over. I could stand it if he said to himself, "Guess I've got to go down there, but I won't show how I feel," but he just sits up there, looking down on us. . . .

The alleged attitude of Mr. Gardiner only reflects the status which Toronto assigns to the Lower Ward. Actually, this "corner" below Queen Street and from University to Shaw is, apart from its obvious commercial and industrial importance, a hidden "no man's land" to most respectable Torontonians. Swarming with business people, factory workers, cars, and trucks in the daytime, its busy thoroughfares like King, Richmond, Spadina, and Bathurst are deserted at night. Then the occasional visitor may be easily frightened by the pervading bleakness and sense of desolation even on Queen Street, which is much more illuminated than streets further down toward the bay.

But the Lower Ward is not without significance to the city. Economically, it includes the substantial Jewish garment industry, the huge Loblaws merchandising complex, the internationally known Massey-Harris-Ferguson plant, Tip Top Tailors, Molson's Brewery, and the main Toronto National Employment Service office, colloquially known as "the Slave Market."[1b] Its population, too, provides a large pool of unskilled labour which nearby plants, both large and small, find convenient. Its many rooming houses provide accommodation for hundreds of single men, and its various hide-outs around truck depots and railway yards are used at night by many winos and transients who might otherwise spill over and cause embarrassment to more respectable areas. Also attractive to uptown people, some of whom work in the district, are certain night clubs which furnish "entertainment" and a certain night club flavour, not unaccompanied by "eager" female companions. Finally, the Lower Ward is well-known for its "Little Europe" of shops and stores, which weekly draw to it thousands of New Canadians intent on shopping for old country foods and similar items in their mother tongue.

Transitional zones are characterized by a great heterogeneity of population, and the Lower Ward is no exception. Table I gives a breakdown of the ethnic groups for 1961; since then, more Hungarians, Japanese, and Portugese have moved in, some Poles, Ukrainians, and Jews have left, but the gross heterogeneity has changed little. In one block of eleven houses in the centre of the area, there were, in 1959, Macedonians, Poles, Ukrainians, Jews, Germans, Chinese, and Greeks as well as a black and an English family. In 1960, a careful estimate indicated that the Anglo-Saxons or Old Canadians made up close to 40 per cent of the population, followed by Italians, Ukrainians, and Poles, in that order, along with a fair sprinkling of Germans and central Europeans and a small number of Jews, Japanese, French-Canadians, Negroes, and

TABLE I

ETHNIC GROUPS IN THE LOWER WARD
(CENSUS TRACTS 49 AND 63) 1961

ORIGIN	NUMBER	PERCENTAGE
British	2,632	36.0
French	579	8.0
Italian	511	7.0
German	276	6.0
Dutch	50	0.7
Polish	923	12.7
Russian	92	1.2
Scandinavian	39	0.5
Ukrainian	960	13.0
Other European	824	11.0
Asiatic	173	2.4
Other, including Negro, Indian	286	3.9
TOTALS	7,345	102.4*

*Certain percentages have been rounded off to nearest figures.

TABLE II

RELIGIOUS DENOMINATIONS IN THE LOWER WARD
(CENSUS TRACTS 49 AND 63) 1961

DENOMINATION	NUMBER	PERCENTAGE
Anglican	940	13.0
Baptist	258	3.5
Greek Orthodox	488	6.6
Jewish	68	0.9
Lutheran	195	2.7
Presbyterian	434	6.0
Roman Catholic	3,256	44.0
Ukrainian Catholic	569	7.7
United Church	811	11.0
Others	326	4.4
TOTALS	7,345	99.8*

*Certain percentages have been rounded off to nearest figures.

Indians. Population heterogeneity is reflected in a considerable religious differentiation, although sects are noticeably absent. Table II gives the religious affiliations for 1961; it appears that little change in the percentages of the population affiliated with the various denominations has occurred since 1951.

Various forces acting selectively have combined to change drastically the original ethnic and class character of the area. Although the area was almost entirely Anglo-Saxon and middle-class before World War I, successive waves of Ukrainians, Poles, and Italians have "pushed" out the socially respectable and economically secure. Home-owning Anglo-Saxons, many still present in 1945, had, by 1960, largely been replaced by home-owners of other ethnic groups or Old Canadian renters. Many of the early European settlers have also sold out since the last war, and most recently Italians are moving up to replace Ukrainians and Poles as the largest New Canadian bloc.

The Lower Ward's ecology is closely related to segregating forces operative in Toronto, as they are in every large city. Adjacent to the main railway tracks, heavily populated with truck depots, smoke-blackened industrial plants, and office buildings, and lying just west of the central business district, it is perhaps the least desirable residential section of Toronto. The air is heavily polluted, the side streets are littered or dirty, the roads are crammed all day with cars and lumbering trucks, most buildings, including churches and recreational facilities, are ugly or depressing, and the majority of the houses have deteriorated[2] or are sub-standard.

The economically transitional character of this area is a consequence of its ecological situation. Socio-economic forces are pulling large offices and plants to uptown or suburban locations, numerous offices and small factories are hard to rent, and practically no new commercial buildings have been built in fifteen years. Houses are being torn down at the rate of ten to twenty a year, principally to meet parking demands, and the population is steadily declining. The whole district, too, is zoned commercial-industrial, which means that no new housing whatsoever may be built – a Planning Department policy that dooms the Lower Ward to old, worn-out housing and eventual extinction as a residential area. Meantime, as some established firms move out, the district slowly fills up with those types of business concerns to which convenience and accessibility to the downtown streets are crucial.

Situational factors are decisive in selecting the population that is drawn to, and remains in, the Lower Ward. The area's low social status, bleak physical appearance, confused moral climate, and residential and social instability tend to attract persons and families sharing one or more of the following characteristics: weak intelligence, poor physical health, low social or economic status, disorganized or unstable personalities, or strong feelings of social protest. Among these, one finds the physically or mentally handicapped,[3] the psychologically ill,[4] the very poor, compulsive drinkers and alcoholics, deserted wives, common-law households and other moral non-conformists, bootleggers, thieves, and families of mixed racial heritage.

Specific institutions, both legitimate and illegitimate, also operate selectively to draw in certain types of residents. Flophouses and cheap rooming houses, most numerous just above Queen Street, are augmented by a dozen hotels with rooms to rent, besides hundreds of households that take in roomers or boarders to supplement the family income; according to the 1956 census, 750 out of 1,493 households take in lodgers. These facilities explain why the 1956 census recorded 1,553 unmarried males in the area. In 1961, there were 4,976 men as compared with 3,811 women in the area. Considerable rental housing, much of it owned by a few absentee landowners or handled by trust companies and available to families regardless of size for comparatively moderate rentals, tends also to concentrate in the Lower Ward a significant number of large families, owing in part to the scarcity of such accommodation in most other parts of Toronto. According to the 1956 census, there were 119 families with five children or more.

Another important characteristic is a high degree of anonymity. On certain streets as many as three families, together with several single individuals, will live in one three-storey house, and members of one family may not know the names of members of another. A similar anonymity is characteristic of certain streets where the houses are not close together, but separated by parking lots or commercial buildings. This situation allows individuals, and even families, to hide out or become "lost" to relatives, creditors, or enemies, and thus commends the area to certain types of people.

Economically and socially, the Lower Ward is an area of minimal competition; for many residents, it is a place of final retreat from socio-economic or personal failures. As one informant put it:

They're here because they can't make a go of it elsewhere, something like the Eskimos or other tribes living under very hard conditions. It's been found that rather than fight it out with people in other areas, it is easier to sort of retire to an inhospitable area . . . you've got the ground there to yourself. . . . I think it's a feeling of not quite being able to get along and hold one's own among other people.

In the Lower Ward, such people are relatively safe, that is, unthreatened. By the same token, those who attain a little higher degree of economic, moral, or organizational stability become uncomfortable and move to a more congenial district. (A few people of the European ethnic groups in their late fifties or sixties are exceptions to this, hanging onto their homes and fearful of change.) These are usually replaced by families from East End slums or from slum or low-status districts of towns in Ontario, the Maritimes, or, occasionally, the West.

Most of the mobility within the Lower Ward is within the area itself, a fact borne out by examination of moving patterns of school children. However, a sizable percentage move to East End slums, and something like 15 per cent of the movers in a given year shift to a higher status district. The rate of mobility is also characteristically high. In one school, the rate of pupil turnover was almost 100 per cent in a ten-month school year. Of this turnover, 75 per cent is attributable to only 25 per cent of the families, the "hard core" types who, through sheer economic pressure, may move three or even four times in a year. This group, especially, merely shifts residence a few blocks away within the neighbourhood.

Since the Depression, ecological forces have tended to concentrate two types of residents in this area: impecunious or low-status immigrants, and low-status Old Canadians. In this paper, attention will be focussed on the latter. Although members of this group may have some limited friendship ties with New Canadians, usually as neighbours or drinking friends at the neighbourhood pub, generally speaking Old Canadians refuse to mix with immigrants of other ethnic groups. Their expression is, "We don't bother with them." On many streets where New Canadians predominate, this practice of "minding one's own business" results in a considerable degree of social isolation for Old Canadians. When the immigrants begin to "take over" a particular street, the residual Old Canadians express their hostility at being pushed out in various ways, such as stigmatizing the immigrants as "D.P.'s" or "dirty foreigners" or refusing to patronize New Canadians' stores along the side street or on Queen. Occasionally, hostility erupts in violence. On one street, a ferocious physical conflict occurred in 1959; the police arrived after several hours of fighting, just in time to prevent the use of knives and guns.

Voluntarily segregated from European immigrants, the Old Canadians are also cut off socially from the larger Anglo-Saxon community of Toronto. Just living in the Lower Ward means they are stigmatized as slum dwellers. Thus one rather exceptional housewife of the district, who boards Children's Aid foster children and meets frequently with other such women from "up there," said she receives many curious questions, such as, "How could you ever live in a district like that?" A successful storekeeper from Queen Street reflected the attitude of the average Torontonian towards the Old Canadians when he called them "white trash" and then hastily changed the expression to "cheap English." It is widely believed that all the Old Canadians here must be shiftless, ignorant, dirty, unmannered, and given to foul language, sexual licence, and huge families.

Social distance between the slum and the non-slum in Toronto is reflected in the expressions "up there" and "down here." The usage "down here" reflects the residents' concept of their lowered status. Hositility to the population "up there" is indicated by the following statement of one resident:

> Up there a lot of people are trying for something – I don't know what. At least "down here" there's a sort of truth and basic reality. . . . There's no use putting on the old B.S. down here, because if you haven't got it, you ain't got it, and that's all there is to it.

In sum, the Old Canadians are segregated both from the surrounding residents of another ethnic culture and from the respectable working- or middle-class community of greater Toronto. They are an outcast group.

Within the total body, however, two distinct subgroups of Old Canadians may usefully be distinguished. The first and much smaller one is made up of Anglo-Saxons who, while identifying with the area, commonly through long residence, still maintain some connections with the larger Toronto community, usually through institutional allegiances. They tend to accept standards of responsibility, morality, or entertainment belonging to "up there"; they also usually possess as reference groups organizations or institutions such as a church whose roots and orientation are "up there." In most cases, these individuals are largely marginal to the slum society, sharing essentially upper working-class attitudes and values and living in considerable isolation from indigenous slum institutions and codes. While frequently exhibiting what might be considered leadership traits from a non-slum standpoint – for example, intelligence, organizing ability, or broad social insights – their marginal situation undermines any opportunity of their performing leadership functions with the main Old Canadian group.

The predominant group of Old Canadians may be considered as of the lower lower class, using Warner's classification,[5] provided it is clear that this does not signify any identifiable class consciousness as such. They are lower in the sense that they are in the lowest social rank and usually at "the point of no return." As one informant indicated, "The people here feel defeated . . . beat! Here they are, and they don't think they can get out – they've grown up in this kind of an area, and it's all they know." Educationally, they may have attained Grade Eight; occupationally, they are stuck in non-skilled trades or find themselves frequently unemployed; and, in income, although a few make $80 a week, the majority earn less than $3,000 a year. In health, in social intelligence, and in achievement, they also tend to fall into the very lowest bracket. Perhaps a more descriptive term than lower class is "socially residual," since it avoids misleading class overtones and suggests a highly generalized lower social status.

Just above Queen Street, the boundary of this area, the picture is significantly different. A local school principal with experience both north and south of Queen Street described this difference as follows:

> Above Queen, the population is more heterogeneous than here, more New Canadian and Negro. . . . Their New Canadians in the main tend to be more ambitious; they have a greater desire to learn and get ahead. Their area, too, is more residential. . . . A considerable number who transfer from the school there transfer to "better" districts. That's the chief reason for their student turnover, whereas here the reasons for turnover are different. Also we have two opportunity classes with less than 300 children; they have only one for 1,200 children.

In brief, the area below Queen seems to "trap" or "shelter" residual Old Canadians who not only are barred from upward movement by deficiencies of various types, but who are typically fearful of venturing out of their neighbourhood. One informant indicated, "The majority of the youngsters and adults down here tends to be rather a beaten down group."

Fundamental to their adjustment process and the resulting social system is the precarious economic situation of the Old Canadian group. Lacking salable skills or educational qualifications, this group enters the employment market heavily handicapped. The young boys, fresh out of Grade Eight or Nine, are forced to take any job, such as that of delivery boy, messenger, or unskilled labourer in a factory. To be "big enough" to earn money is very important to the teen-ager; the amount at the beginning is less significant. The young men typically change jobs frequently, quitting abruptly over hurt feelings, or being fired by "fed-up" bosses. In the process of job hunting, vague notions of qualifying for semi-skilled or apprenticeship-requiring jobs are gradually defeated and a significant percentage end up as truck drivers; an analysis of the 1958 provincial voters' list for this area indicated that about 15 per cent of the men, the largest proportion in any given occupation, were drivers.

Many factors urge this choice on the younger men. In the first place, since the area is dotted with truck depots, this work is convenient, an important factor in the Lower Ward; also, word of openings travels quickly along the grapevine, for instance, in the pubs. Although among the bigger companies the trend is towards careful screening of applicants and an emphasis upon stable, young married men, much hiring is still casual or somewhat haphazard. Secondly, for various reasons, this occupation has more prestige than factory employment: it is more masculine, is outside rather than inside, gives the individual more freedom and a greater sense of independence, involves more variety and excitement. Thirdly, it has advantages over comparable jobs in providing opportunities, for instance, for regular short stop-offs, commonly made at grills or beer parlours, for contacts with promiscuous females, and often for extra earnings through overtime.[6] Long-haul trucking in particular, which involves out-of-town driving, boasts all of the above "rewards" in addition to a generally high status in the truckers' world.

Thus truck driving tends to select men who claim they "can't stand indoor work," who want a sense of independence on the job, are mechanically inclined, and also value a sense of belonging. As an occupational group, truckers share a common work experience and a system of values and work codes that serves along with their union and its drinking club – in the East End slums of Toronto – to integrate them more than many lower status work groups. One pub manager spoke of the drivers who regularly gather in his pub: "They come in, and they laugh it up. They talk to one another over the tables, maybe three or four tables away; there seems a much closer association than among other groups. They seem to have more things to talk about." Those issued with distinctive uniforms by their companies, Loblaws' drivers for instance, give signs of a particularly strong sense of status and group unity.

Certain aspects of truck driving are functional to the value system of the young Anglo-Saxons in the Lower Ward – for example, the convenient location of the work itself. This fits in with the common emphasis placed on avoiding great effort and also facilitates identification with the neighbourhood and its small, insulated social world. Relative freedom on the job and lack of careful supervision also permit a casualness of attitude that accords well with the social temper of the Lower Ward and its norm of impulse gratification. The appeal of the excitement and danger involved in daring driving is not to be underrated and it clearly answers the conditioned need for excitement. In certain types of trucking, accidents are quite frequent. One long-haul driver told the writer, "Four of my chums have been killed in the last year. The last one was crushed while loading at the back of a truck." It is easy to see how truck driving would appeal to the youth of the Lower Ward, conditioned to a life of accidents, mobility, danger, and thrills in boyhood. In fact, the cultural complex surrounding the truck driver's work life – with its considerable group identification and pub-centred recreation, its expression of impulse, and its casual acceptance of illegal violence, not excluding wildcat strikes or the pitching of bricks through windshields – is fundamentally identical with much of the social climate of life in the Lower Ward.

In its impact upon the family and other social institutions, this occupation is also significant. Whereas its long and often erratic work hours undercut opportunities to play supportive roles in the family, its focus on the pub and drinking codes fosters identification with all-male groups and with the local pub as a second home. A male culture is accentuated as being separate from the female-housekeeper-mother culture. The truckers' way of life and erratic hours of work also militate strongly against participation in formal meetings and associations and favour the casual, primary group kinds of social participation characteristic of slum society.

Up to 50 per cent of employed Old Canadians not engaged in trucking have jobs that involve considerable overnight or shift work which likewise disrupts family life and formal social participation. Night watchmen, porters, janitors, foundrymen, and those in similar low-status jobs have to accept their turn on undesirable shifts. One housewife expressed a common female reaction. "When he's on the night shift, he's too beat to bother with the children; I have to do everything." This puts the responsibility on the wife-mother to hold the family together. A similar situation tends to prevail where, as is frequent in the Lower Ward, the father is disabled or unemployed or has deserted the wife. In 1959, some seventy families and ninety single individuals were receiving welfare, twenty to thirty families were on Mother's Allowance, forty to fifty individuals or heads of families were on old age or disabled pensions, and at least fifty individuals, mainly heads of families, were receiving unemployment insurance.[7] Altogether, between 125 and 150 families were dependent upon governmental assistance. Here again, family and associational relationships were probably severely disturbed.[8]

The economically marginal situation of the Old Canadians shapes the social system at various levels. It affects family stability through the widespread practice of subletting: most of the households of three to six children are squeezed into half of a six-room house, with the upstairs rented to another family or to single individuals. It stimulates borrowing and lending of food and household utensils between neighbours and the use of the neighbourhood grocery store, where credit is provided. While these latter practices help to focus socio-economic activity upon the small neighbourhood, they often lead to strained relationships rather than good neighbourhood integration. Low and uncertain incomes also encourage buying things on time in this area. A large percentage of families are harassed by debts which often run from $500 to $1,000 per family. Codes governing borrowing and lending between housewives have their counterpart in the neighbourhood pub, where the regulars, particularly work partners, make loans to one another. Here the code of repayment, usually on payday, is rigidly observed. Interestingly enough, credit unions which two churches organized in the 1950's failed to win substantial interest among the Old Canadians. The United Church Credit Union was popular, however, with congregations of other ethnic groups and helped them in social ascent. Credit unions are too formalized, too dependent upon secondary associational experience, too integrated with the world of "up there" to gain strong support from Old Canadians.

It is customary for Old Canadians to expect loans and even gifts of cash from local churches. Transients and families on welfare resort to clergy most frequently, but other Old Canadians are not adverse to buttonholing the clergymen for money or gifts of food and clothing. The churches of the area – Presbyterian, Salvation Army, Anglican, United, and Roman Catholic – are all heavily committed to such assistance. In fact, along with extensive children's recreational activities, economic assistance bulks largest in their weekly programs.[9] In addition to giving $30 worth of meal tickets a month to any Scotsman who is hard up, one Presbyterian church also hands out over $200 a year in cash and groceries, large amounts of clothing, and several hundred Christmas baskets. One Anglican church recorded over $2,000 in cash donations in 1957 in addition to large quantities of clothing. A Roman Catholic church averaged about ten requests a day from transients in 1958 and often gave $1.50 to each.

In addition, its St. Vincent de Paul Society gives considerable economic assistance to needy families and operates a second-hand clothing store on Queen Street where prices are characteristically low. The Salvation Army runs a large hostel for men in the area as well as a large clothing and furniture depot at bargain store prices. It is estimated that up to 1958 the churches altogether gave annually upwards of $5,000 in cash or meal tickets and another $5,000 in food and clothing. (Christmas funds and baskets would easily run to another $10,000). Protestant church rummage sales, their most popular social function and money-raising effort, must also be classified as an indirect form of assistance to those on the margin of subsistence.

Two missions almost entirely devoted to welfare work also give thousands of dollars of assistance annually. The Evangel Hall, a Presbyterian mission, feeds over 100 men, including transients, old-age pensioners, and alcoholics, every evening with free sandwiches, buns, and coffee, and gives away considerable clothing and food to families. The Scott Mission,[10] with a permanent staff of fifteen, located on Spadina half a mile north of Queen Street, feeds 200 men twice a day and averages twenty grocery and fifteen clothing donations daily, about one-quarter to one-third of which go to Lower Ward residents.

The attitude of many Old Canadians towards church hand-outs is, "Grab all you can." This code is illustrated by the way in which Sunday School Christmas parties and the Christmas basket operations consistently involve cheating on a wholesale basis. The operation of this norm tends to victimize the churches which liberally give away money, food, or clothing and confirms their marginal position in the local social system. The fact that residents have no conception of the actual source of hand-outs or the limitations on their volume strengthens the notion that clergy and churches are fair game.

One resident expressed a typical attitude towards the church when he said, "If I went inside your church, the walls would fall down." Another expressed a fairly common view when he said, "A lot of the guys look on the church as something for the birds; some have even got a great hatred for it." Some Old Canadians are too proud or hostile to ask churches for any help, but the majority will use them for economic assistance or recreation for children while refusing to support Sunday services or mid-week organizations. Interviews of a sample of residents and analysis of church attendance records indicate that less than 10 per cent of the Old Canadians and less than 5 per cent of their menfolk attend church regularly. Thus, the local United Church – with two large, well-equipped buildings, a staff of four, and a $24,000 budget – counted less than ten men from the area as regular church supporters. Also, lay leadership, even in Roman Catholic organizations, tends to be given by ex-residents of the area who come down on Sundays from "up there." Those who attend are usually the more ambitious ones, who will soon leave the area, or the quieter, more organized, and more respectable types. On the other hand, except for the Italians, the local New Canadians have a fair church attendance record.

The economic aid rendered by social agencies and the local public schools likewise fails to gain these institutions full acceptance from the local population. In spite of systematic donations of shoes and clothing for needy children, usually obtained from uptown schools, and generous Christmas party gifts, parents accorded local schools little co-operation. In fact, by both children and parents is the school generally regarded as the spokesman for an alien ideology and culture. This is reflected in such things as the comparatively high rate of absenteeism (9 per cent at one school, compared with a city-wide rate of 4 per cent), the infrequency of parental calls at the school, and the impossibility of organizing Home and School associations.

Social agencies and their workers, in spite of frequent hand-outs, are also the objects of distrust or exploitation. By unspoken agreement, the city welfare department, Mother's Allowance, and other such welfare agencies are generally exploited to the limit. Behind this practice lies the belief that these institutions are fair game since they represent an alien or hostile social system. Frequency of cheating leads some welfare workers to snoop – occasionally dropping in at unreasonable hours – in the hope of securing decisive evidence. Such manoeuvres, or the enforcement of what appear as unreasonable regulations, increase the resentment of welfare recipients. The following statement by Mrs. B., the landlady of welfare recipient Mrs. L., who rented upstairs rooms from her and who, at the time of the interview, was sitting in the room, records this reaction:

> We resent the way the welfare workers snoop around and also the regulations that you can't even work part-time and still get relief. Mrs. L's worker is against her helping me and is always asking what I pay her. Early one morning the worker came to the house without even knocking; she simply opened the door and said, "Anybody home?" and began walking upstairs to Mrs. L's rooms. My husband got up from bed in a hurry, very mad, and said, "You know it's not right to come in without knocking." The worker went upstairs anyway and found Mrs. L. in the bed in my son's room. He's married you know, but his wife left him some years ago for a coloured man. She said to Mrs. L., "What's the idea, why aren't you in the room with your children?" Mrs. L. said the children had measles and that my son had given her permission to sleep in his room to avoid catching the germs as he was out of town for a while.

Support for social agencies or the schools is similarly limited even in the Roman Catholic separate school with 980 pupils. To quote one assistant priest, "A parent-teacher organization is out of the question. The parents wouldn't show up. They are not interested in their kids' education." This statement does not apply to all immigrant groups, and the judgement, of course, stems from an ethnocentric middle-class outlook, in which education is *ipso facto* given a high value; in the Lower Ward value system, schooling is not ranked highly and therefore many parents take little interest in their children's educational advance. Similarly, public school pupils tend to resent schools, evade homework consistently, and fail frequently; many are still in Grade Eight at the age of fifteen. One informant, not yet thirty, recalling his school days, said, "Often when I go by Niagara Street School I'd like to put a bomb under it. It was like a sadistic hole."

Hostility towards educational and other institutions such as churches and social agencies is not untypical of slum areas. Thus Myers and Roberts, writing in *Family and Class Dynamics in Mental Illness* of lower-class (category v) patients, note that "most display a deep-seated distrust of institutions and persons of authority."[11] Other American studies of slum residents and neighbourhoods support this conclusion and confirm the existence of a value system at cross purposes with that of the dominant middle-class community.

In general, the operation and structure of schools, churches, and social agencies[12] in the Lower Ward insistently identify them with "up there." They represent to the Old Canadians the clean, law-abiding, educated, organized, and successful society of the "haves" from which they are excluded. In practice, they operate as institutions of social control, aiming at the conformity of residents with the goals and codes of the larger community. The functionaries charged with operating these institutions together constitute a loosely interwoven group fundamentally alien to the values and social system of the residents of the Lower Ward. The police – considered by local teen-agers and many adults as their natural enemies – are regarded by most such officials as colleagues on the job. Also, such functionaries inevitably consult back and forth about mutual interests and problems and tend to defend one other against criticisms from local residents. Practically all of the teachers, doctors, clergymen, and social workers live outside the Lower Ward, travel "down" to it each day, accept the codes and pecuniary advancement goals of the larger community, and possess a self-image of themselves as professional or semi-professional workers, an occupational "cut" far above that of Lower Ward residents. They also share a somewhat common work situation, in which feelings of discouragement resulting from an incapacity to understand local norms and behaviour patterns and their social distance from residents are often mingled with feelings of inadequate social or personal recognition, and of hostility towards certain goals or doctrines of headquarters. Moreover, these functionaries tend to act consistently as members of bureaucratic organizations, whose universalistic norms, impersonal forms of control, rules of procedure, and allegiance to secondary types of associations cut across the values and ways of life of the local social system and culture. In fact, the very emphasis put by these powerful institutions upon formal, secondary, and largely impersonal relationships may indeed accentuate the primary group, informal, particularistic bases of the Old Canadian Lower Ward social system.

In a sense, these institutions and functionaries may be likened to an "occupying force" in a conquered territory, operating under orders, both explicit and implicit, from army headquarters in the home country. Here, specific directives are, of course, issued from separate bureaucratic centres (church, police, and social agency headquarters) not commonly under one explicit directorate, but consultations on policy and problems are not uncommon. Here, also, functionaries have their base in buildings neither built nor financially maintained by Lower Ward residents, are paid salaries by outside, largely alien bureaucratic institutions,[13] and generally regard their work in the Lower Ward as both different from and much more demanding than that in most other areas of Toronto. In addition, they usually identify themselves with uptown and regard their stint or activity in the area variously as "difficult," "trying," "disciplinary," or as a necessary step in the process of professional advancement. Occasionally, a few may see it is "fascinating" or adventurous.

In handling the welfare problems that often bring together teachers, clergymen, social workers, policemen, and even civic officials, these functionaries understand and accept the rules and norms of bureaucratic investigation and decision. This rationalized structure, readily accepted if occasionally criticized by the functionary, constitutes a completely dark and forbidding world to Old and New Canadian residents alike. When the residents criticize this world, the functionary, even if constrained to sympathize, feels he must try to interpret it constructively, and in so doing implies his identification with it. Such interpretations frequently deepen the gulf between functionary and slum resident, rather than clarifying it.

The task of an occupying force is seldom free from strain, and, in the process of meeting the situation, adjustments are usually made with respect to orders and directives from headquarters and their implementation. In coming to terms with the Lower Ward's culture, institutional workers typically modify the goals and standards they are supposed to support and also attempt to get "headquarters" to adopt more realistic policies. Occasionally, this accommodation involves a process of partial acceptance of certain codes and goals well-entrenched in the indigenous social system. This adjustment and partial identification makes functionaries critical of certain rigidities within their bureaucratic apparatus and may lead to serious strains and stresses, hidden or overt. The social distance of headquarters personnel from the actual situation and people of the Lower Ward, whether it be civic departmental heads, church headquarters officials, or school administrators, is at the root of those inappropriate goals and standards which sustain tension between functionaries in the "occupying force" and their superiors in the bureaucracy.

Such tensions are most obvious among the clergy, faced with great discouragements in securing support and making converts. While Roman Catholic priests are most critical of headquarters' policy with regard to the ethnic Catholic churches of the area – which refuse to die gracefully at the second generation stage – non-Roman Catholic clergy tend to attack the central authorities because of niggardly financial grants, inadequacies of staff, or indifference to the need for new policies. One young minister expressed a common complaint:

> If you could only get through to "them." Any request [for a change] has to go through various levels of authority. We don't have direct contact with the real persons with the power. A minister I know said he left the ministry – for social work – because he couldn't get enough support. . . . A policy of thrift still dominates the thinking of our leaders, and they are too little daring.

Similar tensions, although usually less acute, afflict local workers in schools, the welfare department, the city-run recreational centre, and the police force. For instance, whereas the district Mother's Allowance supervisor may be vigorously orientated to keeping down welfare payments and may have his own tricks to catch and disqualify unwary applicants, field workers sympathize with many welfare recipients and often wink at the heavy drinkers who should be reported and penalized. Complaints made to the writer by local recreational workers and police officials indicate a similar lack of agreement with headquarters policy.

Thus the adjustment of the alien institutions to social realities in the Lower Ward is seriously handicapped by the bureaucratic process and the social distance of high-level functionaries, trapped and sheltered in a highly rational middle-class bureaucratic world, distant from the peculiar needs of the "occupied" territory.

In 1959, two institutions with uptown affiliations, by cutting themselves off to a great degree from "headquarters," succeeded in meeting significant local needs and, in so doing, threw light upon the indigenous social system. One was a free medical clinic run at St. John's Anglican Church in the south-central part of the area, operated in loose affiliation with both that church and the nearby Western Hospital. Begun in 1923, the clinic gave attention for four half-days a week to a variety of simple medical needs, including pre-natal care, infants' diseases, immunization, eye glasses for children and adults, and minor illnesses and accidents.

It served eighty to 100 patients a week and accepted anyone. Faced with a threat of closure from hospital authorities in 1958, study revealed that its local appeal lay in being a neighbourhood institution, convenient, simple, unpolished, and informal in appearance, and in providing more personalized and efficient attention, with a minimum of red tape and a much smaller fee than the public clinic at the nearby Western Hospital.[14] The fact that both the church and the clinic had severed practically all ties with the diocese years before kept the clinic free from denominational and bureaucratic controls; the presence on its reception staff of persons born and raised in the area increased its acceptability and identification with residents of the Lower Ward.

The Stanley Park (Civic) Recreation Centre, in the south-west corner of the district, was, until 1959, the focus for a tremendous amount of recreation for youngsters up to sixteen living west of Bathurst Street. When the Massey-Harris-Ferguson Company decided to buy the property for additional parking space in 1960, local residents raised a storm of protest. Nothing in the previous fifteen years so mobilized local opinion as this threat to the residents of the loss of "their" recreational centre. The city's argument that a new, polished, million-dollar social centre was nearing completion on Trinity Park grounds, just north of Queen Street, did not satisfy them. Stanley Park was a neighbourhood centre housed in an appropriately ugly, old red-brick building, formerly a bank, with a program including boxing, tumbling, hockey, baseball, swimming, ping-pong, and basketball, which kept hundreds of children active after school hours. It had a staff, headed by an Irishman raised in a working-class area in the East End of Toronto, which identified with the people, drank beer with the men in the local pubs, and protected their secrets (for instance, the location of bootleg dealers and gatherings of winos). Many old boys from Stanley Park had sent their sons back to play hockey or baseball on the Stanley Park teams – and their victories reflected glory on the district. The new institution on Queen Street was just out of the neighbourhood, too polished and bright to be "their" centre; it would inevitably belong, for some time at least, to the alien world of "up there." So the struggle for the old Stanley Park Centre was a fight for personal neighbourhood, particularistic values against the impersonal, alien bureaucratic world of "up there." However, protests in the press were all in vain; the Centre is now demolished.

The social system of the Old Canadians of the Lower Ward may be regarded at this point as an ambivalent structure hostile to but dependent upon the middle-class culture predominant in Toronto. The encircling community possesses the great preponderance of power and impresses its main values, goals, and codes upon all members. Certain ecological factors, however, tend to weaken the impact of such values, goals, and codes upon the Lower Ward. Here there is a cultural derogation of the educational system, a widespread indifference to reading, including the daily newspaper[15] and popular magazines – except perhaps for love and murder stories – and an intense concentration of interest and activity upon the local neighbourhood. The significant social world of Lower Ward residents is an area perhaps four to five blocks square; beyond this is largely foreign territory. Indifference to secondary associations, which encourage mobility and diffusion of interests, and insulation within certain local institutions like the pub, further strengthen the isolation of these residents from middle-class influences.

Nonetheless, to an important degree, Old Canadian residents of the Lower Ward are still exposed to the principal goals of the larger community while being denied access to means of pecuniary and social ascent. This dissociation between goals and available means leads generally to the following types of reaction: 1) feelings of frustration producing a general proclivity towards verbal or physical violence, evidenced most frequently in beer parlour fights, and towards escape patterns, notably heavy drinking and sexual promiscuity; 2) a withdrawal from social and political responsibilities, evidenced by profound indifference to current events, non-reading of newspapers, and excessive electoral apathy, along with a lack of interest in voluntary associations aimed at community improvement; 3) an orientation towards minimal economic security rather than the culturally prescribed goal of socio-economic ascent (in seeking mere subsistence, many middle-class codes may be partially jettisoned; for example, legal codes against bookmaking or bootlegging, cheating of welfare workers, or sharing limited housing accommodation with strangers) ; 4) an ideology of living for the moment, elevating whim and impulse above middle-class norms of budgeting, thrift, and care for the future; and 5) a concentration of social participation upon small informal groups, such as the family, the gang, the work or the pub group, which are functional to adequate social adjustment within the Lower Ward situation.

One focal point of the local social system, the family and "extended" kin group, emerges as a significant institution. Among Lower Ward Old Canadians the family is characteristically weak

in authority, more matriarchal than patriarchal, loosely integrated, and the scene of a great deal of open conflict. Romance
is not intensive before marriage and soon disappears altogether,
giving place to a sexual dichotomy in which men and women
build up and live in separate, almost water-tight cultures. Family
codes have little in common with those of middle-class families.
Children learn to swear profusely at four or five years of age, pick
up the "facts of life" before ten, usually have their first sexual
experience by twelve or thirteen, may leave home temporarily or
permanently at sixteen, and consider marriage seriously at sixteen
for girls and eighteen for boys. Illegitimate children are not uncommon – although low in numbers in view of early sexual
activity – and are often raised in the grandparental household.
Parents show little interest in or control over their children's play
and friendship behaviour and are usually content to let them
wander the streets or, where possible, attend church or school
clubs. Up to one-third of the couples in certain streets live in
common-law relationships. Broken homes are fairly common, as
is supervision by Children's Aid societies.[16] After a few years of
marriage, periodic sexual promiscuity, often with neighbours,
beer parlour acquaintances, or pick-ups, becomes a frequent
pattern and meets few informal punitive sanctions.

Such a loose family system is largely an accommodation to
socio-economic imperatives. Crowded living quarters leave no
room for children to bring in friends, with the result that the
streets or the recreational club become the real home. Precocious
sex experiences and early marriage quickly rub off the romantic
element in sex relationships and emphasize physical and social
compatibility. The many frustrations of low-status existence put
a premium on liquor and sex as releases. Dissociation from middle-
class success goals leaves families with no strong orientation towards intensive child care or training or the repression of aggressive impulses. The financial impossibility of securing a divorce
fosters common-law alliances.

Closely associated with the nuclear family, and particularly
with the mother, are usually several kin[17] who live in, or close to,
the Lower Ward. Weekly or more frequent visits of the mother-
in-law or other such members of this "extended" kin group are
common, and one or more of such relations sometimes live with
the family. Participation in this larger kin group and support from
it in times of emergency are important characteristics of the
Lower Ward social system. Interviews with a representative
sample of residents indicated that this pattern is true for some 70

per cent of the families; in the majority of these, one or more relatives lived within a mile or two of the nuclear family. In such interviews, the following was a typical answer to the question, "Do you have close relatives living close by?" "Yes, we have relatives nearby; one in the East End, and one near the Western Hospital. One drops in three times a week. Several others who live farther away come once or twice a month." The great majority of such kin alignments are from the mother's family; apparently, a major function of such relationships is to support her in the absence of close integration with the husband, whose strongest bonds are often with males at his place of work or at the local pub.

What the extended kin group does in support of the family and specifically the mother, the teen-age gang does for the adolescent boy or girl. Like the typical family, this primary group also appears highly disorganized and unstable to an outsider. The rapidity with which gang members come and go and the loose connections which bind the often numerous peripheral hangers-on to the tiny nuclear group are largely an accommodation to the local social situation and not an indication of a collapsing institution. High mobility rates, frequency of imprisonment, intense competition for rank, and impaired capacity for sustained personal relationships, related to defective family integration, lie behind this loosely structured type of organization. The fact is that practically every boy and most girls twelve years of age or older strive to gain gang membership. These groups possess a clear-cut structure, with a value system, an inner core of three to four members and an outer circle of from four to eight floaters, a hangout, a strong neighbourhood identification, flexible rules of meeting, and their own codes of morality. Moreover, they play a basic role in initiating youngsters into the neighbourhood culture, including early sexual experience, drinking, stealing, passing "hot" goods, and learning how to "live it up" on good days without being dismayed at the thought of what tomorrow may bring. Lower Ward gangs assist members in learning codes governing loyalty, self-respect, competition, and the rules for acceptance of ethnic groups, besides conveying some sense of belonging to a group and to a neighbourhood. They also teach adolescents how to participate simultaneously and with ease in both the legitimate larger society and the delinquent world of the slum. Such acculturation to a dichotomous culture is essential to later adult adjustment to life in the Lower Ward.

The teen-age gang is an integral part of the Lower Ward Old Canadian social system. Its popularity and appeal are closely related to a situation of congested living and weak family controls and to parental absenteeism or harshness which fosters a sharp break between teen-agers and their parents. Early leaving of school and the need for status in a pre-adult world and for support in breaking with parental restrictions and controls foster gang development. In the Lower Ward, gangs are strongly neighbourhood-focussed. They tend to draw their members from a small area, "hang out" in local Queen Street restaurants, and "pull" their jobs within the district. However, through trips to cheap dance halls and settlement houses outside the area, they meet other teen-agers from fairly distant areas and partnerships become established which introduce Lower Ward adolescents to an enlarged community but one still dominated by low-status codes and standards.

Among housewives, the formation of close relationships with one or two neighbours constitutes another type of primary group association. Residential mobility is a constant threat to such relationships, although many are strong enough to survive moves to lower-class districts in the East End. In the representative sample interviewed, 60 per cent admitted to at least one close neighbourhood friendship. Frequently, this was with a next-door neighbour or the housewife in the other half of the subdivided house. On some streets, a friendship group numbering three or four housewives meets daily for coffee. Other housewife friendships are built around meetings at the local beer parlour, usually between 2:00 and 4:00 P.M. Not infrequently, these neighbourhood friendship relationships are strained by serious quarrels, and regroupings, temporary or permanent, occur. As one school principal observed, "Living in small *cul-de-sacs*, or cut off by factories or parking lots, it is natural that their relationships will be intense and demonstrate a constant on-again, off-again pattern."

This neighbourhood pattern is associated with a considerable amount of gossip and knowledge of each other's business. Personal relationships become all-important, especially in the dead-end or broken streets where the population of the immediate neighbourhood may total only twelve families. Long-established families – and every street has a few which have lived in the same house for ten to twenty years – often act as a focus for this neighbourhood "knowing." Here, too, neighbourhood stores, which dot the Lower Ward practically one to every block, facilitate the regular meeting of close neighbours and strengthen their identification with the locality by providing a convenient centre for gossip and socializing. This is inevitably more characteristic of social life in the more easterly parts of the area, where grocery shops tend to be managed by Anglo-Saxons, than in the western sections, where New Canadians dominate the corner-store business, but even here a great deal of "social" shopping goes on, helping to strengthen identification of New Canadians with the Lower Ward district.

Women's friendship ties also tend to be related to certain church groups, such as the mothers' meeting or mothers' club, and to Roman Catholic-sponsored bingo games. Most of the non-Roman Catholic churches have one or two such groups for local Old Canadians whose program is almost entirely social and where old friendships are maintained and occasionally broadened. (These clubs are only nominally formal organizations; their strength lies not in the church connection or the formal structure, which is usually very loose, but in the ease with which they accommodate the primary group friendship interests of their membership.) Again, a sizable percentage of the housewives, especially those without husbands or married to quiet, unsociable men, commonly attended bingoes in or near the Lower Ward every week. Since 1958, however, Roman Catholic churches have discontinued bingoes in the vicinity of the Lower Ward, and this occasion for renewing friendship ties in an exciting atmosphere no longer exists.

Relationships arising out of work or pub associations, rather than out of physical proximity on the street, dominate the men's social world. Primary group ties predominate here too. Very few men actively participate in churches or unions, although some, usually the older ones, belong to veterans' clubs, two of which are located in the area. These last, however, like church mothers' clubs, can hardly be classified as formal associations, since they make their appeal principally on the basis of offering cheaper beer and better facilities for playing cards than the pub.

It is the beer parlour, commonly called the pub, that dominates the social life of the Lower Ward Old Canadian men. This is almost equally true of the older New Canadians in this area. Of the seventeen drinking establishments in the area, fourteen (three along King and eleven along Queen Street) are centres for neighbourhood social activity. Four of these are modern and attractive in design, having cocktail bars, dining rooms, and beverage rooms seating 200 to 300 persons. Almost all the others are plain to run-down in appearance and small in size, accommodating from forty to seventy persons apiece in the men's and ladies' rooms. The total capacity of all seventeen establishments is approximately

1,800. All but two of the fourteen have ladies-and-escorts rooms. Open from noon to 6:00 P.M. and from 8:00 P.M. to midnight (although those with cocktail bars stay open later), these pubs daily serve a changing clientele of "regulars" plus casual visitors. The first group of "regulars," crowding in just after noon, consists largely of nearby office and factory workers and truckers, some of whom bring a sandwich while others buy a light lunch. The four pubs equipped with dining rooms and cocktail bars serve a popular businessmen's luncheon. Around 1:30 P.M., a new group enters, principally "old-timers," including pensioners, unemployables, and men retired or on workmen's compensation. These non-workers usually sit towards the rear and gossip idly for hours over a few beers. At 3:00 o'clock, housewives will begin to fill up the ladies' room, staying till 4:30 or 5:00 P.M. Between 4:00 and 4:30, office and factory workers, truckers, and other workers flood in for the after-work beer and chat. Most chairs will be taken. In the evening, another group of largely local residents – except in the four establishments with cocktail bars – pours in. Thursdays to Saturdays, all fourteen beverage rooms will be well filled between 9:30 and 11:00 P.M.[18] After 11:00 some leave, while the after-show group will fill up the bigger places; a small group will remain till midnight, and move to the cocktail bar or dining room, staying until the last possible moment. This general pattern is not confined to Toronto's Lower Ward.[19]

With the partial exception of the four selling cocktails, all fourteen pubs in the Lower Ward draw largely from the immediate neighbourhood. Thus, one attracts its customers from a radius of about three blocks to east, west, south, and north; another from one block east, four west, and three south. Certain ones draw heavily from one or two ethnic groups; for example, one caters to Finns, one to Central Europeans, others to Old Canadians. Specialization also occurs to some extent in terms of gambling "facilities" or social levels; a few have restrictive standards of acceptability, while several have almost no standards at all. Interviews of our population sample and other evidence suggest that 70 to 80 per cent of the men have one or two favourite pubs and patronize these at least twice a week.

In spite of certain distinctions, all fourteen pubs seemed to possess a common culture, atmosphere, and web of social functions. The culture is characterized by lower-class standards of furnishings, dress, manners, and language, directness of personal interaction, a strong interest in sports (especially boxing and wrestling), sex, and drinking, and a concentration on informal, primary group, particularistic relationships. A noisy, permissive atmosphere, bordering occasionally on licence and simulating the freedom of the working man's living room, is also characteristic. A man may read, sleep with head on table, stare at the wall, swear noisily, get into a fight, talk with a stranger, begin and cease conversation at will. A fundamental norm is open acceptance of idiosyncrasies of behaviour and moral outlook and different social types and races. Thus, the handicapped, the man with no roof in his mouth, the half-breed, the Negro, the wino and transient, the prostitute, either pretty or emaciated, the homosexual, pimp, or gambler are all accepted without stares or other forms of social ostracism. However, most managers try to enforce a code against excessive drinking or fighting, according to their respective standards.

In social function, the pubs act as working men's social clubs, with slight variations in atmosphere and rules but with a common orientation. Here is how one observant resident of the area puts it:

> I believe the pubs have real social functions; they are the poor man's club, the equivalent of the rich man's Granite Club. They're treated well there. Going there may help solve problems, domestic or job difficulties. Also they get a sense of importance there, perhaps in ordering the beer, or showing off in talk with the guys. They do band together to meet emergencies, for instance sickness. . . . The poor have to find people on their level; this is so, in the pub. . . . The pub keeper has high status. . . . He is well-fixed financially, but it takes a lot of work. He treats the clientele with kindness; they have to learn how to treat their people well, and some are difficult to handle.

In the normal functioning of the working man's club, certain needs of the whole male population and of specific groups within it are met. In the absence of any neighbourhood recreational or cultural centre for Old Canadians, the pub serves as the neighbourhood or community centre. Here one meets practically the whole neighbourhood group, especially on Fridays and Saturdays, learns the latest gossip, and identifies with the neighbourhood. This is also the place where the two worlds of legitimate society and underworld come together, in an acceptable, convenient form. Here one can dispose of or buy "hot" goods, either openly through a waiter or in the washroom, place a bet,[20] "pick up" a woman, or get the particulars on a "blind pig." On the other hand, one can participate freely in the legitimate male world, talk about sports, sex, work, unions, or even politics.[21] In the absence of other facilities for male recreation, it provides a recreational service, in permitting animated conversation, watching of television, and participation in gambling through bookies. Socially, it is "the place to go," and, within its nexus of primary group relationships, the individual finds his locus and social standing. He sits with his buddies, demonstrates his degree of technical knowledge (for example, of truck driving) and of social information, exchanges jokes with waiters and old-timers, and, in these and similar subtle ways, validates his belonging to and status within the neighbourhood group. Thus, in the almost complete absence of effective participation in formal associations, the pub community secures a sense of integration and conveys a sense of status to its regulars. Certain pub groups, particularly those gathering at regular hours almost every day, tend to resemble the extended family in the freedom, depth, and intimacy of their interrelations. Moreover, for people of the Lower Ward, as one informant put it, "the pub gives them a release from pressures, restrictions, crowdedness, and drabness, and some kind of real lift."

Within the pub, the publican or manager tends to play the role of head of the household, endeavouring to maintain the harmony and integration of the group and the goodwill of all patrons. Although a strong pecuniary interest is not absent, a number of these men become deeply involved in the individual personalities and problems of their "regulars." An extended family-like structure seems to emerge, where the beverage room appears to function as an enlarged "living room" and the pub society in effect compensates for the weakness of family and kin relationships among the male group. In sharp contrast with cramped, smelly living quarters at home, the ladies' beverage room offers both husband and wife a pleasant setting removed from the incessant demands of young children.

Whereas housewives tend to gain social support from particular kin members, such as mothers, sisters, or brothers, many men become dependent upon their pub buddies. Pub regulars support their drinking buddies in various ways. They may offer free drinks when a man is broke, loans of money until next pay-day, rough and ready advice on marital or occupational problems as well as companionship in hours of anger, trouble, or perplexity. In addition, they may organize collections to help with financial emergencies or to send flowers to a buddy confined in a hospital. Aggressive urges resulting in verbal battles or fist fights may also find release within such an accepting group which functions, in co-operation with the publican, to shield the offending party from the police. As one pub keeper pointed out:

> We have one or two fights a week. . . . We try to avoid calling in the police. For one thing, it has complications. A report goes from the police to the Liquor Commission; an inspector comes around to ask questions and fills out a form. Too many fights, and we may be asked to close up for a week or two.

The publican, who is called by his first name or "Pop" and often acts as a father surrogate, plays many roles: he gives advice on legal or medical problems, provides aid in finding a job or offers a job recommendation, helps fill out legal documents such as income tax forms, cashes cheques, large or small, makes loans of money (in one pub, for instance, they have a floating fund of $100 for such loans to regulars), sends flowers to patrons ill in the hospital, helps with their hospital or funeral expenses, and even serves as a pall-bearer. In addition, he provides information on deviant activities, gambling, bookmaking, bootlegging, prostitution, and such, and in general gives the impression that, like the father of a family, he stands ready to help with any reasonable – and many unreasonable – requests.

The pub plays a crucial supporting role for certain specific groups. Perhaps the most important of these are the single men, particularly those who rent accommodation in rooms above the beer parlour. Almost all of the ten smaller establishments have ten to twenty such rooms to rent and let out about 50 per cent of these to "regulars." For these men, the beer parlour is precisely their living room and the publican their "grand-daddy." Thus, one of the more responsible pub keepers observed:

> We look after our roomers if they get sick. . . . Some of them have been here twenty years, and quite a few ten years. Especially on Sunday morning, a beer before breakfast goes very good, and so we let them have one. The law says you can't serve beer in the rooms, but that's one law I don't observe.

These hotel residents, besides hundreds of other single men trapped in tiny single rooms in the area, often without a radio, find in the beer parlour an informal, home-like atmosphere, friendship, and entertainment in the television set – much of which is unavailable elsewhere.[22] Some virtually live in the beer parlour, stretching out a beer for an hour or picking up free drinks from a stream of friends.

The pub also functions as a sort of home for the winos; it is conservatively estimated that there are upwards of 200 in the area. These alcoholics scheme incessantly to secure the price of a glass of beer or a quarter towards a bottle of cheap wine,[23] and customarily hang around certain pubs looking for treats or handouts. The pub is also the most convenient place where such drunks may get cleaned up or, in cold weather, find temporary shelter and warmth. Although practically all pub keepers try to keep out the worst winos, these unfortunates constantly think up new ways to get in and work their "angles." The fact is that not only will no other place have them – the church missions usually feed them and then force them outside – but the pub is the only society in which they can feel at home. So, for this group, the beer parlour functions as home and also as base of operations. Professional deviants, such as bookmakers, bootleggers, and prostitutes, likewise use the pub as a convenient base, and, of course, the latter meet their assignations "upstairs"; some hotels have special rates for one or two hours, to accommodate the prostitute trade. One publican intimated, "I know eight bootleggers personally . . . they don't hide it. They come here frequently."

Specific functions are also performed for old age pensioners, the unemployed, nearby workers, newcomers to the area, and the lonely. Pensioners and the unemployed, with so little to do around the house or in the area, pass away the time and gain acceptance within a group of their fellows at the pub. Nearby factory and office workers who flood in at noon or after work find the beer parlour a congenial restaurant, whose facilities are often superior in relaxation, entertainment, and conversation to those of most nearby grills. Newcomers to the area and those who are afflicted by pangs of loneliness find conversations are easy to strike up and drinking friends easy to make. In an area where mobility and social isolation rates are high, this function is not unimportant.

The Lower Ward's hotel-pubs thus function to meet many community and subgroup needs. They also facilitate the simultaneous participation of residents in both the illegitimate and the conventional value system. Certain drinking establishments located at strategic corners, particularly the corner of Bathurst and Queen streets, equipped with dining rooms and cocktail bars, provide opportunities for participation in a wide range of conventional and illegitimate activities. The presence of a nearby complex of institutions, including a wine store, a brewer's outlet, several all-night grills, a movie house, a steam bath – where homosexuals congregate – a brothel, and several smoke shops and drug stores, enriches the variety of both deviant and legitimate services and makes this corner the focus for recreation, entertainment, companionship, and deviant services for much of the area west of Spadina. It is also an acceptable meeting ground between the Lower Ward and the surrounding urban community. In particular, seekers of deviant services from working- and middleclass areas invade the Lower Ward in great numbers at this busy intersection and help perpetuate its Toronto-wide notoriety. Among deviant activities, gambling, bookmaking, prostitution, promiscuity, homosexuality, fencing, bootlegging, thievery, and plotting of crime are all prominent around the corner. As one resident commented, "There are a thousand ways around here to get your mind off things." This is not to minimize these activities throughout the whole Lower Ward – for instance, bootlegging is carried on in one or more houses in nearly every residential block of the area – but simply to note their point of concentration.

The extensiveness of institutionalized and spasmodic illegitimate activity is associated with basic economic, social, and characterological tendencies in the area of the Lower Ward. Certain illegitimate businesses, bookmaking or bootlegging, for instance, may be started by "amateurs" simply as means of increasing an unsatisfactory income. While many bootleggers and some bookies carry on in a part-time, amateur fashion, others quickly shift into full-time operation. The local demand for bootlegging, given the popularity of drinking, the large number of compulsory drinkers, and Liquor Commission closing regulations at night and on Sundays (Sunday is the big day for local bootleggers) is high. The appeal of gambling to both Old and New Canadians and the formidable difficulties of getting to the racetrack make for a steady demand. One elderly, knowledgeable informant[24] claimed that bookmaking is the biggest business in Toronto. A high police official stated there are probably 200 "back rooms" in the city, many of which would be in the Lower Ward. The protest character of this activity and its promise of financial gain inevitably make it popular. Likewise, fencing is a natural concomitant of the local pattern of petty thievery, the low income of most residents with the consequent interest in "bargain" prices, and the lack of condemnation of such an activity in the local mores. Its characteristic informal, unorganized form and concentration in the beer parlours simply indicate an adjustment to the larger social system of the area.

The Mertonian thesis that deviant activities are related to dissociation of cultural goals and institutional means is generally illuminating for our area. While participation in illegitimate activities often represents an attempt to compensate for exclusion from middle-class goal achievement, in other cases it also represents a means to acquire a livelihood (as prostitute or bookie) or to augment what is earned in more legitimate channels – the janitor at one large local church operated as a bookie on the side. Another type of reaction to goals-means dissociation is that of listless apathy, represented in this area by numerous individuals for whom television is the only source of recreation and entertainment. This is common among isolated women and some men, especially those with no pub or neighbourhood connections.

In accounting for deviant behaviour, Cloward has pointed out the significance of opportunities to acquire the illegitimate skills and values and to discharge and practise them. While opportunities to learn petty thievery, gambling, bootlegging, and bookmaking are not lacking in the Lower Ward, apparently few organized criminal gangs exist to train young men in big crimes, as there are in some large American cities. Apart from one or two criminal "mobs" who move their headquarters from place to place along Queen Street, especially vicious or highly organized criminals are not attached to the Lower Ward. Something of this type of crime seems to be found perhaps a half mile to the north, where big gambling clubs function along with "dope rings"[26] and more highly organized prostitution. Thus, a lack of the requisite institutions of an organized adult mob which trains men in big crime, along with the general bent of the Lower Ward's social system, which emphasizes small primary group activity, militate against the emergence of powerful criminal mobs or machines.

Illegal and immoral practices are, however, thoroughly meshed with the legitimate and conventional social patterns in the Lower Ward. While the police usually wink at bootlegging[27] and make only spasmodic efforts to stamp out such habits as gambling, prostitution, and fencing, school, church, and social work functionaries eschew any systematic efforts to investigate or expose such practices and businessmen along Queen Street maintain, in general, a discreet silence. Each important element in the indigenous social system – family, neighbourhood group, teen-age gang, and pub community – is tied in directly, or by a conspiracy of silence, with the deviant social structure. This is inevitable, for what the authorities "up there" label as delinquent or immoral or illegitimate is frequently an adjustment to the peculiar socioeconomic conditions of the district and meets important needs of the community or subgroups within it.

3 Skid Row

Keith Whitney

Every big city attracts to it a number of homeless, transient men and also seems to generate forces within itself which push some of its own men into this rootless kind of existence. Toronto is no exception; in fact, it appears to have one of the largest skid rows in North America. The following article sketches the physical aspects of this depressing phenomenon and introduces us to the kind of men who inhabit our skid-row institutions.

The author, the Rev. Keith Whitney, is an associate minister of the Metropolitan United Church, located on the edge of Toronto's skid row. He has both a sociological grasp of the problem and intimate, day-to-day experience with the men involved. He is also a graduate of a course in the urban ministry offered by the Canadian Urban Training School, an inter-denominational educational institution headed by Dr. Edgar File; part of the course involves a plunge into the skid-row area, where the student has to make out for two days on a total allowance of $5. This article appears for the first time in this book.

To the great majority of Torontonians or visitors to the city, skid row is an unknown land, a geographic limbo occupying a certain small section of the downtown area and considered a necessary evil. The average person considers it the home of the derelict, the alcoholic, and the bum, the group that occupies the lowest rung on the social ladder. It was there before the Depression, but its situation worsened in that period, and what remains today is usually considered but a vestigial remnant of that era.

The fact is that the city's skid row, though occupying much

the same piece of territory now as in the Depression, is steadily increasing in size, at a rate of about 5 per cent per year; Toronto's skid row has now become one of the biggest on the continent. Among those who work with the men, estimates range continent. Among those who work with the men, estimates range from 4,000 to 14,000; the most common and reliable figure puts the population of skid row between 8,000 and 10,000. A complex variety of institutions cater to the needs of these men; in fact, the services available in Toronto are of such a calibre that they tend to draw men to the city from afar, and this helps to account for the annual increase in numbers.

The main focus for skid-row operations in Toronto is the area bounded by Yonge Street on the west, River Street on the east, Carleton Street on the north, and King Street on the south. Here the majority of hostels, flops, soup kitchens, bars, pawn shops, and other supporting "services" are located. The men tend to move in a circular fashion within this section, although they will travel outside it for a few blocks for certain objectives. This section of town is one of the oldest districts. For one reason or another, the homes are not adequately maintained. Row housing predominates and reminds one of the barracks of another era. The side streets are poorly lit and usually in need of the services of city cleaners. As you walk along such streets as Dundas, east between Church and Parliament, and let your eyes move up beyond the first floor of the many small stores and businesses, you will get a glimpse of the dingy living facilities on the second and third floors. Many people are packed into the flats above the first-floor stores, people whose lives are unknown to the average Toronto citizen. More often than not, there are few or no curtains on the windows. Children and elderly people can be seen peering out the windows, watching the world go by. If you look up, the maze of wires gives the feeling of being hemmed in. Inside the apartments, there are gaping holes where the plaster has come loose, most of the walls are in need of paint, laundry is hanging in the kitchen, unshaded light bulbs hang from a drop cord in the centre of the ceiling, stove pipes run from room to room. Access is normally by a doorway opening onto the street, down a long, poorly lit hall, and up a rickety set of stairs that disappears into the blackness at the end of the corridor.

The stores themselves are quite a contrast to the exclusive shops just a few blocks away on Yonge Street. For one thing, there is not nearly the same amount of available floor space. There are fewer varieties of goods to choose from on the shelves, and there is a heavy concentration of starch commodities. The majority of the city's pawn shops are located on Church street between Shuter and Adelaide. The many public houses that give a certain character to the area operate close to capacity most evenings of the week. They are often equipped with various forms of recreation, including such pastimes as shuffle-board; it is the lower-class equivalent of golf. Conspicuous by their absence are the large chain stores such as Dominion, with the result that food generally costs a good deal more.

Most of the men on Toronto's skid row come from the Maritimes or Newfoundland, from high unemployment and low-income areas of Ontario and Quebec, or from the Indian reservations of the province. They have travelled across the country, often from coast to coast, in a sporadic search for work; they settle in Toronto for a spell before moving on to try their luck elsewhere. When they get together in a hostel, they talk about the days they went west for the harvest, the time of the "big bump" in the coal mines of Springhill, Nova Scotia, the miserly wages paid for picking tobacco on Western Ontario farms, or the way in which labourers are exploited in the nickel belt of Northern Ontario. They have been around, and they share their "tough breaks."

While the bulk of the men, perhaps 50 per cent, are over fifty years of age, a great many being pensioners of one sort or another, up to 20 per cent are under twenty-five. Many of these have come from the Maritimes.

The general assumption that all men on skid row are members of the drinking fraternity, that almost all of them are alcoholics, is quite erroneous. Recent research done in Toronto as well as in other major urban centres in Canada and the United States has shown that only about one-third of the men have a problem with alcohol; of these, only a fairly small percentage can accurately be described as chronic alcoholics. Approximately another one-third can be classified as moderate drinkers; some of these wind up in the Don Jail and become part of the "revolving door" system, while others work themselves out of the skid-row environment into a more stable situation. Finally, there is another third which drinks little or not at all. A large proportion of these are older men on some sort of medical or veterans' pension. This last category and many of the second category do not make a habit of frequenting the hostels of the area. They usually live in a single room or share accommodations with others, often moving from rooming house to rooming house. (The over-fifty group on skid row tends to be labelled by Manpower counsellors as "competitively unemployable"; there is almost no chance of them getting and holding a steady job.)

One of the distinctive things about the skid-row man is the way he dresses. At first glance, it may not appear that his clothing is too down-at-the-heel, but a closer inspection usually reveals another story. Most of it has been secured from missions or welfare agencies or from rummaging through garbage pails located in the network of back allies. While perhaps providing some warmth and protection, it uniformly looks seedy or out-sized. Among the older men, some form of headgear is worn, varying from hand-me-down felt fedoras to toques. The overcoat seldom fits. Likely as not, it came from another decade as far as style is concerned, and it often is two sizes too large. The pockets bulge, as it is a custom to stuff personal belongings in large pockets; they serve as luggage. For instance, they may contain a safety razor, handkerchiefs, and some cutlery, especially a knife; personal identification papers will also be shoved into one of the pockets. Few men wear ties, and their shirts do not often accommodate the wearing of neckwear – sport shirts and pullover sweaters are the order of the day. Trousers are rather naturally quite baggy and may well come from the same decade as the overcoat. Permanent-crease materials have yet to filter down to the skid-row population, so the pants characteristically show no signs of having been pressed. Socks are for the most part of the heavy wool variety; more often than not, they need darning desperately. Footwear varies from running shoes to heavy work boots, and, again, shoes are typically acquired at clothing depots. Few shoes are of the right size. Usually, the soles are half off, and the uppers are ripped and scuffed from hard usage. String usually takes the place of laces. Few men manage to acquire rubbers or overshoes. In general, the men are grateful for something to wear, but they are quite aware that their clothing is cast-off, not good enough for anyone else but them. Their clothing types them, and the number of men wearing such articles tends to type the whole of skid row.

What is not known to most Torontonians is that a sizable segment of the city's skid-row population is made up of people who have some money but who live in the area either because they have known it for years and feel at home there or because of the services it provides. There are the flop-houses which offer cheap accommodation (usually for $1 a night) plus some companionship; there are the places where one can get clothing cheaply or for nothing from church clothing depots; the area offers coffee and conversation for nothing, and some girls are available for cheap sex. In addition, one can turn a quick dollar by walking a few blocks to a car wash, by shovelling snow in the winter, by working at a church for a cash handout.

By and large, in addition to the older men and the pensioners, the skid-row area seems to attract the undereducated, the under-skilled, and those who have been pushed downward socially, either by circumstances or their own failures. An example of the first type might be a young Scottish immigrant to Canada whom we can call Ian. He had found work in a small town not far from Toronto, and it looked as if he and his wife were reasonably well-settled in the country. But he came to Toronto looking for a better-paying job, and one night the police picked him up sleeping in his own car on Temperance Street, a small street running west of Yonge just below Queen. He was booked on a charge of drunken driving and remanded for two weeks; when brought before the judge, his case was dismissed. But in the meantime, the police had im-pounded his car; with payments not paid, he lost it. Back at home, his wife, impatient and disgusted by the turn of events, suddenly returned to Scotland, leaving him to fend for himself in Toronto. Initially, he slept outside, later resorting to flop-houses, which he found to be cheaper than the hostels; later, he got welfare and went to the hostels. Then he simply disappeared.

A different kind of story and situation is revealed in the case of Bill, a single Maritimer in his late forties. He used to be a good travelling salesman, having worked for over fifteen years for the same grocery chain. He is intelligent and articulate, tall, dark-haired, and dignified in bearing when not drunk. It was heavy drinking that lost him his job and brought him to Toronto. Here he went through the revolving door process at the Don Jail. As he went downhill, his appearance became pathetic: his clothes became unkempt, and he would sneak around late at night to secure help from downtown clergy. One of them used to let him sleep in the church boiler room when he had no money for a room. Like others, he tended to use the churches and was caught stealing things – first a picture, then a clock. On one occasion, a minister spied him in a basement area with the clock under his big old coat – its cord was still fastened to the wall. Asked where he was going, he said, "To the pawn shop." Slowly, he put the clock back in its place.

From a sociological standpoint, the concentration of transient men in the skid-row area is closely related to the variety of in-stitutions located there which make it possible for them to get by. The high rate of pedestrian traffic makes it possible to panhandle easily; the available pawn shops facilitate picking up cash from one's own possessions or from the things one steals; the many alleys between the streets not only furnish garbage to be picked over for usable articles or items of clothing, but they offer some protection from police when one drinks a bottle of cheap wine. The many pubs offer entertainment and drink, when one can afford it, the wine stores make cheap Cattawba or Old Sailor available at about $1 a bottle, and the parks and extensive church lawns around Metropolitan or St. James Anglican Church offer a place to rest, to sneak a drink, or to gamble. For sights and a change of scenery, the men can move over to Kensington Market to the west, or go to the docks south of Front Street to watch the boats, or rest on the public benches of the Union Station at Bay and Front, or view the flowers at the conservatory in Allan Gardens at Gerrard and Sherbourne. Public washrooms are a problem; the nearest one is at Broadview and Queen, a mile to the east. If men cannot afford the cost of a room in a flop-house or hostel, they can seek overnight shelter in doorways of rooming houses, in vacated buildings scheduled for demolition, in freight cars, or beneath the underpasses and bridges of the Gardiner Expressway.

Since the biggest problems of the skid-row existence are food and overnight shelter, it is necessary to describe in detail the extensive facilities offered the skid-row residents in this connection. There are four main hostels carrying out these functions, three run by religious groups and one, Seaton House, by the city. One of the oldest and best known of the church institutions is Fred Victor Mission, run by the United Church, at the corner of Jarvis and Queen Streets. The big building includes a home for the aged, a 125-bed hostel, a clothing depot, and a sanctuary for the existing congregation. Men in need of lodging can come in the evening and apply for a bed at a regular price of seventy-five cents. Occasionally, they will be let in for fifty cents, but if they can only produce a quarter, they will not be turned away. For their money they get something to eat and drink, and the chance to spend a leisurely evening, followed by sleep in a clean bed. They are awakened here, as elsewhere, at about 7:00 A.M., provided a lunch if it seems essential, and asked to vacate the premises. All the hostels are run on the basis of an early morning rising, which is supposed to get the men out in time to pick up a casual labour job, which may start at around 8:00 A.M. During the day, the men in this hostel have the opportunity to see one of three counsellors who attempt to help them with their problems.

The Good Shepherd Refuge is set up to handle emergency situations regarding food, lodging, and clothing. Located on the corner of Tracey and Queen Streets in the designated urban renewal area, it is run by the brothers of the Roman Catholic Church. Basically, they attempt to give shelter to the many new persons coming into Toronto weekly from other parts of Canada looking for employment. The Refuge has a dormitory of sixty beds, and guests of the brothers are allowed to stay for as many as five days while they are seeking work and other living accommodations. If they have a need for clothing, it can be secured from the clothing depot on the premises. One of the major efforts of the Refuge is to alleviate the hunger of many hundreds of persons daily. At 4:30 P.M. each day, a hot meal is served to an average crowd of about 650.

The Salvation Army Hostel for Men is located on Sherbourne Street just north of Queen. The hostel, along with the Salvation Army welfare services, the Harbour Light Treatment Centre for alcoholics, and the annex for older men, provides meals, clothing, and lodging. Like the Fred Victor Mission, the Hostel charges a nominal fee of $1 for a bed, of which there are 295 available each night. The annex's 125-bed compound is always full, and there is a waiting list. The procedure is the same as elsewhere – a time for lights-out and then an early rising in order to have time to look for work. All three of the religious operations are funded through their parent organizations.

The last major hostel operation is Seaton House on George Street between Dundas and Gerrard, operated by the Toronto welfare department. It too is a dual operation. There is a semipermanent residence which houses 340 men who are medically unfit for work, who are supplied lodging and meals. Then from late November to late April, the men's hostel, which accommodates 240 nightly, is in operation. This is primarily geared for those who are seasonally employed and are working elsewhere during the spring, summer, and fall. The operation is similar to the others: food, shower, bed, and early rising. The clientele of all these hostels are mostly transients, many of whom spend their whole lives making the rounds.

Another hostel that is related to the four mentioned but different in its operation is The Harbour Light, run by the Salvation Army. It is located on the corner of Shuter and Jarvis Streets. Its primary function is to help alcoholics deal with their problem – drinking. It has sixty-five beds, and the average stay of each resident is about fifty days. The men pay as much as they can afford towards the total cost of their room and board, and government welfare contributes a set amount for patients who cannot afford to pay.

If a man is over fifty, he can become a member of the Good Neighbour's Club, Jarvis and Shuter, right across from Harbour Light. Here he can meet men his own age, relax over coffee, watch TV, play games, from morning to night, every day. Both older and younger men can move on up the street to Gerrard to the back of the old Avonmore Hotel, where Holy Trinity Anglican Church and Saint Luke's United, along with other sponsors, have a Friendship Centre. It is a place where everyone is welcome. Coffee is served by a group of volunteers, and the men can watch TV, play cards, or sing along with the old piano. It is open ten months of the year each afternoon and evening.

If a man lives west of Yonge Street, he can find accommodation much closer. Evangel Hall, on Queen Street near Portland, is a Presbyterian operation that is open daily and serves sandwiches and coffee each evening. While on a limited budget, they do attempt to help out men who are in need of a place to sleep (they supply them with tickets to Fred Victor Mission or the Salvation Army) or some clothes. In addition to the hostels, men get free meals at several places. At College and Spadina, St. George the Martyr Anglican Church runs a drop-in centre four afternoons a week in the building of the Scott Mission. University Settlement, just south of the art gallery, is open one afternoon a week to senior men who seldom get outside. The other major place to acquire a free meal in Toronto is Scott Mission, at Spadina and College. Each day at about 10:30 A.M., the doors are opened, and two sittings of approximately 350 persons (average for one year) are fed. This institution is basically a family operation begun by Dr. Morris Zeidman, and secures its fundings from donations. It is heavily involved in community and family work as well.

Skid-row men not only become dependent for food and accommodation on these various institutions, but they also come to despise them and to use them. Skills in conning churches and social agencies for hand-outs are developed, and the skid-row regular often steals small items that can be easily stuffed into his pockets. His hand-to-mouth existence, the loneliness and hopelessness of his life tend to make many men alienated from middle-class norms. They often view the hostels as places to be used or avoided; the long line-ups for food and lodging, the mechanical methods of processing, the lack of personal interest, the tendency of some places to manipulate the men to secure financial aid from the welfare department–all this lies behind a considerable resentment towards the bigger hostels. Many men prefer the flop-houses that dot George, Shuter, Sherbourne, lower Jarvis Street, and Dundas east of Church. Here, enterprising owners have turned ordinary houses into "flops," making the front part of their homes into miniature hostels. There will be several beds in each room, sometimes as many as eight, each with a mattress of some sort. The men lie on them with their clothing on, often passing a bottle of wine around before dropping off to sleep. The atmosphere is freer than that in the hostels, and the air will be much more ripe. In general, the profane talk and wine-guzzling of the flop-house is preferred to the patronization and depersonalization of the regular hostels, and the cost is about the same.

No one knows the number of men who make it out of Toronto's skid row, but the experts suggest that the figure is very small. By and large, these individuals are caught in a self-perpetuating system that includes the pawn-shop owners, the jails, the wine shops, the flop-house operators, the small rooming houses, the social workers, the churches, and the police department. While it is true that most of these men seem to have opted out of society, the present system tends to confirm their outcast character and their dependency. Stuck in this institutional system, the average man is unable to make basic decisions about his own life; others require him to eat here, sleep there, bum for money, and so on. Undertrained, socially retarded, competitively unemployable in many cases, he is in desperate need of a supportive community and a sense of new direction. In a way, he gets the first from his fellows in skid row, but, in the present structure, he does not receive the second.

The solution to Toronto's skid row does not lie in the addition of new or better services of the type presently available, no matter how easily it can be shown that the present facilities are inadequate. Nor does it lie in making the present operations more efficient or better co-ordinated. All such moves would simply make the present arrangements, facilitating dependency, more successful. What seems to be needed is a team approach focussing on rehabilitation efforts and not sheer physical maintenance. Halfway houses or governmental institutions providing living-in retraining for marketable skills seem to be part of the answer. At present, between the churches involved and the city welfare department, some millions of dollars are being spent annually just to maintain the dependency structure. A portion of that money expended on well-planned rehabilitation procedures and facilities might make a big difference in a few years.

4 Life in the Heights

W. R. Delegran

City planners have traditionally pinned their hopes for improving the lot of the poor on placing them in public housing and, where possible, locating such units close to middle-class districts. The first such venture in Toronto was the Lawrence Heights public housing development, near Lawrence Avenue and Bathurst, an established, middle-income area. In this article, W. R. Delegran examines the social problems and strains this scheme brought to those in public housing, how it affected their attitudes, and to what extent it changed their lives.

The study's findings were the result of Mr. Delegran's intimate association with the residents as a social worker and of analysis of data collected from a lengthy questionnaire. The questionnaire was administered to 20 per cent of the householders on a random basis; less than 5 per cent refused to answer it. Mr. Delegran is presently teaching sociology at Seneca Community College in North York; his article appears for the first time in this anthology.

INTRODUCTION

Ecological Factors

Lawrence Heights was created in 1957 as a discretely concealed, 101-acre public housing enclave in Metropolitan Toronto. It has only limited accesses from the north, east, and south. The eastern approach passes through a well-established, middle-income area and is sealed off to road traffic at the border between public and private homes. There is nothing here that is calculated to arouse the interest of anyone travelling the main traffic arteries.

In contrast to the shoddy physical environment so often associated with low-income housing, the development in Lawrence Heights is arranged with more imagination and concern for the occupants than the usual suburban tract. Houses and courts are interspersed with open space, and the roads are wider than average.

The public school occupies a central location in Lawrence Heights and serves the project exclusively. Since it has contact with more households through the children than any other local institution, it plays a vital role. The junior high school, which has a 40 per cent student population from the project, and Bathurst Heights Collegiate, which has 10 per cent coming from this area, occupy peripheral locations in the west and south-east respectively.

Adjacent to the public school is a small plaza which includes the offices of the Ontario Housing Corporation and the North York and Weston Family Services. The Community Centre controlled by the Department of Parks and Recreation has offices and nursery space for the Department of Welfare's Social Services. It is about 200 yards directly south of the public school. The whole project is bisected by an expressway and linked again with a concrete bridge.

The local businesses and institutions outside the project that are most often patronized by the people of Lawrence Heights include two major shopping areas – the one in the north-west is Canada's largest indoor shopping complex and represents a serious attempt to bring downtown facilities to the suburbs; the other, in the south-west, is patterned along more traditional lines – and both are within walking distance. There are some service industries, distributors, and warehouses in the vicinity, but there is no heavy industry.

The apartment buildings have been restricted to four floors, partly to regulate population density but also to reduce the hazards of low-flying aircraft stationed at the R.C.A.F. base two miles to the north. Most denominations have churches not too far away from the development, and two evangelical groups bring their message to the Community Centre each Sunday. There are no local hospitals or treatment clinics, and many forms of entertainment are far from the neighbourhood.

Although the physical planning of Lawrence Heights *per se* has much to recommend it, the high, sturdy fences and hedges that clearly delineate and maintain the boundaries between tenants and owners are not likely taken from the architect's blueprint. Their very existence would indicate that the creation of good accommodation for the low-income population has encouraged others to put up their own "wall" and to adopt a policy of containment designed to protect a middle-income life-style.

It is apparent from the comparative population statistics in Table I that Lawrence Heights is a female-dominated, child-

TABLE I

1. CHILD POPULATION (0-14)

Lawrence Heights	North York	Metro Toronto
2,526	89,829	452,026
or	or	or
50% of the total population	33% of the total population	28% of the total population

2. ADULT-CHILD POPULATION

Lawrence Heights	North York	Metro Toronto
44% (A)	61% (A)	61% (A)
56% (C)	39% (C)	39% (C)

3. AVERAGE NUMBER OF CHILDREN PER FAMILY

Lawrence Heights	North York	Metro Toronto
2.6	1.5	1.4

4. AVERAGE NUMBER OF ADULTS PER FAMILY

Lawrence Heights	North York	Metro Toronto
2.3†	2.0	1.9

*The figures for North York and Metro Toronto were obtained from 1961 Census. Lawrence Heights does not correspond to a ward for census purposes, so that some approximation had to be made. Ontario Housing also provided their 1965 population count and breakdown.

†Senior citizens make this figure abnormally large and disguise the number of one-parent households.

Population Characteristics of Survey Sample

No. of one-parent families 44
No. of two-parent families 156
No. of children .... 631 = 3.1 per family
Average age of female adults............ 40
Average age of male adults............ 41

5. AVERAGE NUMBER OF PEOPLE PER FAMILY

Lawrence Heights	North York	Metro Toronto
4.9	3.5	3.3

6. POPULATION ACCORDING TO SEX (ADULT)

Lawrence Heights	North York	Metro Toronto
749 (M)	134,475 (M)	798,709 (M)
887 (F)	135,484 (F)	820,078 (F)

Ratio male to female in Lawrence Heights — 7.5:9

7. RELIGION

Lawrence Heights	North York	Metro Toronto
44% (P)	58% (P)	59% (P)
23% (RC)	19% (RC)	28% (RC)
28% (J) *	17% (J)	5% (J)
5% (other)	6% (other)	8% (other)

8. NATIONALITY (ETHNIC ORIGIN)

Lawrence Heights	North York	Metro Toronto
63% (British)	58% (British)	59% (British)
14% (Jewish) *	11% (Jewish)	3% (Jewish)
5% (French)	3% (French)	3% (French)
3% (German)	4% (German)	4% (German)
15% (other)	24% (other)	31% (other)

---

*These different percentages under Religion and Nationality are probably explained by the fact that all would say they are Jewish when asked their religion but not necessarily when asked their nationality.

---

oriented community with more children to care for and fewer adults to do the caring than is common in the rest of North York and Metropolitan Toronto. The average number of adults per family for Lawrence Heights is deceptive (i.e., 2.3) and is explained by the large number of senior citizens in the project who have no children living with them. The 44 per cent figure listed in (2) provides a more accurate picture and reinforces the fact that 270 of the 1081 households are being supervised by one parent. The ratio of men to women in Lawrence Heights is 7.5:9 compared with 1:1 in North York.

This is an atypical population in its concentration of children, imbalance of the sexes, and large but incomplete families. It is also atypical in terms of car ownership, with only 60 per cent of the households having vehicles. The average income of $65.00–$70.00 a week is well below average both for the township and the city as a whole.

The amount of formal education which the respondent and spouse received is shown below:

None	1%
Some grade school	20%
Finished Grade Eight	22%
Finished Grade Nine	14%
Finished Grade Ten	20%
Finished Grade Eleven	6%
Finished Grade Twelve	8%
Finished Grade Thirteen	5%
Some college	3%
College graduate	1%

Educational achievement does not vary too much in relation to sex. While males tend to be the least and the most educated, the females show a clear and decided majority in the middle range with far more completing Grades Eight and Ten.

The following lists occupation according to sex:

	MALE	FEMALE
Homemakers	—	120
Labourers	74	19
Semi-Skilled	33	6
Skilled	6	—
Pensioners	22	13
Clerical	7	14
Supervisory	6	—
Professional	2	—
Students	3	—
Unemployed	8	—

The number of women working outside the home compared with the number of men is 1:4, and most of them are doing some kind of labouring, clerical, or semi-skilled job. More than 20 per cent of the homemakers are receiving government assistance.

Many of the respondents' parents had different jobs in their day than the respondents have now, for a much higher number were doing supervisory or semi-skilled work. The actual supervisory positions do not seem to differ that much, but the semi-skilled trades include many crafts that technological advances have now made obsolete.

The number and nature of labouring occupations are not too different between the generations, although jobs differ. Because significantly fewer occupy this semi-skilled category today, it would appear that many of the respondents have undergone an occupational downgrading which has removed the workmanship or craft quality from their jobs.

It could be argued that many of the positions listed as semi-skilled are really skilled, but this does not drastically alter the basic picture because the balance of skilled workers in the older generation would be much higher than for the present one.

Although the residents tend to arrive here from the city proper, their jobs do not move with them, so they are confronted with an expensive commuting problem. From 113 households where one member is steadily employed, 64 per cent work in Toronto, 29 per cent work in their own township, North York, and 7 per cent travel to an adjacent suburb.

RESULTS OF THE SURVEY OF THE TENANTS' VIEWPOINT
Images Of and Feelings Toward "The Heights"

What is the inhabitant's conception of "Lawrence Heights"? To the social scientist, this housing project is a suburban appendage which does not blend with the general character of the area. To this sociologically distinct physical unit, the respondents, when asked where they live, sometimes attach the name "Lawrence Heights" or "The Heights," but they are just as likely to give the name of their street or of the main intersection nearby.

Where did they live before they came here? Although located in the largest suburb of Metropolitan Toronto, the project was not built to meet a local need. Before arriving at the project, 75 per cent of the respondents lived in the city, and 50 per cent of these came from the West End.

Do they prefer living here? About 75 per cent of the respondents who "migrated" like it better than where they lived before, mainly because of the superior accommodation. Twenty-five per cent of them feel they have upgraded themselves in terms of neighbourhood as well, and they comment favourably on the clean air, convenient location, and open space for children's play. But an equal number feel that the quality of living does not extend beyond the house or living accommodation into the neighbourhood and that it would be ideal if their present quarters could be moved to a more suitable environment. By this they mean many different things. Some desire to live a quieter and less public life than is permitted here; others see the area predominantly populated by social misfits. For some, the move has meant separation from friends and relatives and an isloation from facilities they have grown to accept as part of a community. It has made others aware of being set apart from those who live on an ordinary street. Encounters with these "outsiders" often confirm their fear of living in a "camp" or "jungle" inhabited by an inferior breed of person.

How many call Lawrence Heights "home"? The transient character of Lawrence Heights is emphasized by the residents' responses to the question about whether they consider this their real home – where they really belong – or just a place where they happen to be living. Of the 194 respondents who replied to the question, 102 consider it just a place where they happened to be living, while eighty-nine call it home.

How much do they like it here? Although not many consider Lawrence Heights an excellent place to live, 83 per cent say it is good or average. Most of them were thinking of the actual accommodation when replying to the question, but space for children to play without having to worry about them was an important consideration as well. The schools, project location, fresh air, quiet, and privacy are listed next in importance. The general maintenance is also given as a reason for liking the prospect. To sum up, the things the tenants like about "The Heights" are essentially physical – the things they dislike are essentially social.

Neighbourhood Problems and Solutions

Most of the things that tenants dislike about Lawrence Heights relate to the general social milieu. They view it as a swearing, drinking, fighting, noisy, destructive population with few controls (particularly over children); therefore, control must be imposed from outside by the Housing Authority, police, social agencies, etc. This action is frequently initiated by neighbours, but not always for the right reasons. Sometimes they report certain behaviour because it is offensive; on other occasions, it is used as a means of revenge. The good maintenance work in the project is partially offset by the lack of maintenance in other ways; that is, broken glass in the roads, clutter in apartment corridors and courts, and inadequate repairs. Rent scale is rated third among their dislikes; they say it is impossible to save, as each increase in income, including overtime, is absorbed in rent. Poor transportation, lack of privacy, gossip, restriction of freedom, overcrowding, recreation needs, stigma, fear of disturbing neighbours, lack of community spirit, and the mixing of young families with senior citizens are other problems connected with living here.

Many respondents express the difficulty of dealing with salesmen. For every three people who have no problems with door-to-door salesmen, there are about four who do. They are frequently aggressive types selling inferior products at high prices.

Because the local plaza accommodates a barbershop, grocery, druggist, clothing, and fish and chip stores, the respondents were asked for their comments about the services being offered by these business people. Ninety-three per cent indicate dissatisfaction with the grocer, who has a reputation for being mean to the children (frequently short-changing them) and behaving in an ignorant and discriminating way. The grocer would no doubt argue that the children "steal him blind" and that, when they spend the change from a purchase, they go home and tell their parents he cheated them.

At least 60 per cent of the respondents discuss the things they dislike about Lawrence Heights with neighbours, a fact which suggests that no repressive measures are practised by the Housing Authority.

The respondents feel they are given adequate police protection and shopping facilities, but they reserve their most positive response for the school (and here they are referring most specifically to Flemington Road Public School). This is clearly considered the least of their problems.

In order to make a final assessment of the social character of Lawrence Heights, the respondents were asked the following question: "Can you say that living in Lawrence Heights has had any effect on you or any member of your family which probably would not have occurred had you lived elsewhere?" Thirty-five percent claim that living here made no difference, 22 per cent feel it has had a good effect, but 42 per cent claim that living here has had an adverse effect on one or more members of the family, generally the children. More than four times as many claim it to be a bad experience rather than a good one for their children, partly because the brutal exposure to a harsh social environment limits opportunities for growing up "nice."

The neighbourhood also makes its impact on the adults. Here are some of the more recurrent themes. They sometimes find the grounds and hallways (in apartments) messy, which is embarrassing when friends from outside come to call, and people fight each other rather than co-operate. The public exposure of the poverty and misfortunes of others repulses some, who retreat from the community in the hope of preserving their own standards and values.

The stigma attached to project living is also acute with some. To hear it referred to by outsiders as "the jungle," "the camp," "poverty village," or simply "Oh, there!" hurts personal pride, makes them feel inferior, and produces the depressing, hopeless feelings that are the common attributes of alienation.

What is the tenants' approach to social problems? Local social action groups are likely to be most effective in the area that the respondents feel needs the least improvement – the schools. They are less certain about doing anything about juvenile delinquency or improving race relations and quite pessimistic about the larger and more abstract problem of cutting graft in government. At the same time, many of them do not feel that there is very much delinquency here. A great many others feel that race relations need no improvement within the project and that the various peoples get along well together – an attitude that could very well be true, but hard to confirm.

The vehicle most often suggested for improving the schools is a Parent-Teachers Association, but it is not thought advisable to follow the traditional form so familiar to most public school systems. What these parents are looking for is an opportunity for coming together in an informal setting.

The respondents seem to feel that the answer to a great deal of juvenile delinquency lies in the home. They also recognize that counselling services, improving and increasing local social activities, and taking trips outside the project can be useful in curbing delinquency.

Although acknowledging the problem of graft in government, they have no clue about how to begin solving it; there is certainly no confidence in the capacity of any local group to do anything about it.

As the survey progressed, these problems did not seem as significant to the respondents as those involving transportation, schools, police protection, teen-age behaviour, shopping facilities, small children, and the housing management, and an attempt was made to determine the strength of local groups as they relate to these issues. Not more than 10 per cent were questioned, but the results were not encouraging. The overwhelming feeling is one of non-involvement and the need for caretaking by outside bodies. Some acknowledge that problems could be solved by local groups, but too much apathy prevails within the neighbourhood and too close an identification exists within the various families, particularly with the children, for the respondents to possess enough group solidarity to withstand much pressure. Right or wrong, they tend to defend their children's behaviour, and this often creates bad feeling.

An overwhelming majority emphatically state that the solution to community problems must be found within a legally and socially acceptable framework.

About 55 per cent would also be willing to seek a solution by contacting a public official either as an individual or as part of a group. There is no obvious tendency here to favour group activity.

Any action that appears non-conformist in any way – and this includes aggressive behaviour – is taboo.

Does anyone do anything about community problems? When the respondents were asked if they knew of any organizations or local groups that were doing something about community problems, 73 per cent were not aware of any at all. Those organizations mentioned most frequently have the Community Centre as the focus of their activity, but very few of the respondents are connected in any way with such groups.

When asked to name some of the things they feel are particularly difficult to deal with, the respondents mention money problems, sickness, and high rents as the immediate, concrete realities. Alcoholism, unemployment, too little education, and too many children are not mentioned. These opinions make it abundantly clear that the tenants and the various agencies serving them define the problems differently or at least examine them from a different viewpoint. It would also appear that public housing is failing to serve its basic function, that is, to provide *economical* shelter.

Attitudes and Values

A series of agree-disagree items provided a method of exploring some attitudes and values for the first time while confirming others.

Education

Practically all respondents believe that a good education is essential to getting ahead and that school authorities do not discriminate among the children on the basis of parents' income, race, or religion. There is strong support for the view that the teachers are genuinely interested in the children and are just as capable as any in the Metropolitan school system.

The general response to schools and staff is highly favourable (particularly to Flemington Road Public School), but the respondents feel that effectiveness could be improved still further if the teachers knew more about the kind of children who come from this neighbourhood. About 50 per cent also feel that over-crowding at Flemington Road Public School reduces the institution's effectiveness.

The respondents show considerable optimism about the educational chances of the children living in Lawrence Heights, as nearly 50 per cent feel that their children will graduate from high school, meaning either Grade Twelve or Grade Thirteen.

They also recognize that the minimum education for any young man who wants to get along in the world is Grade Thirteen. Nearly 25 per cent of the respondents consider a university education essential, with almost an equal number choosing Grade Thirteen. Another 28 per cent feel that a young man should have as much as he can handle. Only a few consider it desirable to leave school before graduation.

About 60 per cent see no barriers for their children getting as much education as they need; the other 40 per cent say that insufficient funds will terminate education prematurely.

In the respondents' eyes, an optimum time to start school seems to be around four-and-a-half years, and practically all of the parents say that nursery school experience is a good preliminary to this, although they do not necessarily prescribe it for their own children. There is an equal committment to the idea of day-care centres, an attitude which is strongly supported by the fact that 25 per cent of the families are incomplete and being cared for by the mother. When the mother works, it is hard to find a responsible person to look after the children at a price their mother can afford to pay.

The respondents equated the "good life" for their children with the means for attaining it and stressed education as an ultimate goal far above anything else for both boys and girls. To hold a good job, be a respectable citizen, marry, own a home, and have time to enjoy oneself are further attributes of the "good life," but they are more a consequence of education than something attained directly. There appears to be little stress on material things, hough it could be argued that such would certainly be an vious by-product of education.

Barriers to Success

Although the school has a homogenizing effect on the children by providing equal treatment and opportunity for all, the parents feel this undiscriminatory approach to life does not extend far beyond its walls. About one-third of them feel that poverty, race, and/or religion will hamper their children's progress as they approach adulthood, as had been their own experience. Religion is thought likely to be the least important of the three factors in this regard.

Work

What are their goals for their children? When asked what occupations they wish their children to follow, one-third say it will be the child's choice. Another third name professional occupations, and the remainder include trades, white-collar jobs, and marriage. However, attitudes differ when the comments are subdivided according to the child's sex. Professional jobs still claim a third of the parents' votes in both cases, but they are not prepared to give their daughters the same freedom of choice that they give their sons. In the third category, girls are favoured for white-collar jobs (23 per cent) while boys are directed to the trades (16 per cent). Marriage is also considered an occupation for girls, and 11 per cent of the respondents hope their daughters will pursue this career.

What are their children's chances of success? The chances of their children advancing in a selected job or profession are considered just as good as those of anyone else by most of the respondents.

Should he move to improve his position? The respondents would not hesitate to recommend that a young man move away from family and neighbourhood for a job that offered a new way of life and respectability, although it paid the same as his present position. They would offer the same advice if the young man happened to be their own son.

What is important when selecting a job? Interest and enjoyment rather than money are the most important objectives for a young man to consider when he is deciding on the kind of work he wants to do. The young man (and this could mean the respondents' own son) is not expected to follow adults' direction in this respect, but to decide for himself as earlier he was encouraged to decide his own occupation. Sixty-six per cent of the parents endorse this view; another 13 per cent stress the importance of advancement and some kind of future, while 17 per cent point out that education is the most important single factor in job selection. Money and fringe benefits as criteria for choosing a job are given only token recognition.

What makes a person successful? If a person should succeed, most of the respondents recognize it as a reward for hard work and application of native ability rather than pull, influence, or just plain luck.

Is economic security paramount? As far as the respondents are personally concerned, economic security and need for a predictable income are reflected in their response to the kind of job they would select if they had a choice. Seventy per cent would take the secure, poor-paying job, 21 per cent would take the good-paying job with a 50/50 chance of losing it, and only 4 per cent would take a highly paid job with a great risk of losing it.

How do they rate occupations? The respondents consider a job excellent if it requires a degree of skill which can be attained only after considerable effort and education. Such an occupation would allow them to make a necessary and valuable contribution to society in return for financial reward, security, prestige, and personal satisfaction.

Who actually is "getting ahead" around here? When the problem of advancement or getting ahead is applied to the "respondents' world," much of the earlier optimism shown toward the children is lost.

They feel that 50 per cent of the people in the neighbourhood are trying to get ahead but finding it difficult; only about 10 per cent are actually making some progress, while 30 per cent are contented as they are. The remaining 10 per cent are undecided about this.

As far as the respondents themselves are concerned, 75 per cent identify with the larger segment of the neighbourhood which is trying to get ahead but finding it difficult. Another 22 per cent claim some advancement, but a significantly small number (3 per cent) classify themselves with those who are contented in their present situation.

A much higher percentage of the respondents' relatives and friends are getting ahead (62 per cent) than of the respondents themselves. Another 32 per cent are part of that segment that is trying to get ahead but finding it difficult. Only 6 per cent are contented with their present circumstances.

The respondents are part of a majority population which appears clearly committed to following an upwardly mobile course by modelling themselves after their more successful relatives and friends outside the project, while rejecting those who are contented to remain.

Where are they going? What are some of the components of this "success image"? That is, what does getting ahead mean to these respondents? It means having their bills paid, having a reasonable amount of money to spend, and, for some, having their own home. Education is only about a third as important as these other factors – this is really their children's vehicle for getting ahead, not their own. Furthermore, they are not concerned with abstractions such as status or utopian ideas such as living in a more co-operative society. They do not harbour any grandiose schemes for acquiring more material things than they need.

Ideal Value System

Their ideal value system encourages them to say that most people can be trusted, that you can succeed if you try hard enough, and that there are still basic principles and rules that should be followed in your daily life. Seventy-five per cent express the belief that there is still some morality in business practice. In addition, they firmly believe children should receive more discipline from their parents.

Politics, Religion, and Government

On matters relating to politics, religion, and government, the respondents were more marginal in their answers. Although about two-thirds of them feel that voting serves some purpose other than giving a politician a job, they are divided about the genuineness of these public officials' attempts to meet the needs of the average man in the street. Two-thirds of them feel that the country would be improved if politicians were replaced by a few strong leaders. About half of them doubt if the clergyman really serves anyone's interest but his own. In fact, they would say this about more than 50 per cent of the entire population.

Juvenile Delinquency

It is the general feeling of the respondents that juvenile delinquency is not prevalent in Lawrence Heights. Most of them guess it to be only 10 to 20 per cent, with the average around 18 per cent. Some idea about what delinquency means to them can be obtained from the rating they give the following activities: taking narcotics, stealing, and drinking are rated very serious by practically all the respondents. "Teen-agers who pick on little children or hang around in gangs" are considered very serious by two-thirds of them, and one-half consider late hours and cursing by teenagers as very serious. Smoking and sloppy dress are considered serious by only about a quarter of the respondents.

Welfare Recipients

About 40 per cent of the sample treats welfare recipients the same as everyone else – it practices no discrimination and exhibits no hostility. The remainder is more severe in its attitude, classifying the recipients as either deserving or undeserving poor.

Social Relationships and Activities

Membership in Formal Organizations

About 60 per cent of those interviewed belong to formal organizations outside the development, such as churches and unions; political and social clubs receive only token recognition, and 11 per cent who claimed membership in a union attended meetings irregularly. A small group, 6 per cent, had leadership positions in Girl Guides and Boy Scouts. The church group was the largest and most involved, with ninety-two respondents claiming some affiliation, but, in a significant number of cases, it would be the children rather than the parents who went to church or Sunday School. All of this would tend to confirm most of the literature on the subject, which claims that membership of low-income families in formal organizations lacks depth and range and is alien to their way of life.

Interaction with Neighbours and Friends

About half of the people in the project are neighbourly in so far as they talk to one another at least once a day. Only 7 per cent never bother chatting with anyone. It is reasonable to assume that most of these contacts are short, casual exchanges, but many of them are fairly lengthy and sometimes involve intimate conversations. The interactions been adult males are more likely to be terse and formalistic than those among their female counterparts.

Nearly 75 per cent of the people get together just to talk, play cards, watch TV, or engage in some activity of this kind.

Most of the people they get together with are friends (47 per cent) rather than relatives (21 per cent), neighbours (21 per cent), or friends and neighbours (11 per cent). The friends of about 60 per cent of the respondents live outside Lawrence Heights.

Relatives

Although interaction with friends and neighbours is more common than with kin, the latter interactions are more intense. Relatives are more important than neighbours for 78 per cent of the respondents. The closest kin ties are with the sisters and brothers of the respondents. Parental and in-law connections are next in importance. Extended kin relations – that is, aunts, uncles, cousins – are seldom mentioned in the usual sense, although separated women sometimes refer to close female and male friends as aunts and uncles, for the children's sake.

Many of these relatives are scattered throughout Metropolitan Toronto, with the greatest concentration in the city itself. Friends are also more likely to live outside Lawrence Heights, but in the metropolitan area.

When a parent is ill, it is usually the spouse or children who do the homemaking. This would explain a significant amount of absenteeism from school, as almost 25 per cent of the parents would keep their children home from school for this reason.

The children are again high on the list for looking after their brothers and sisters if the parent has to go out, but neighbours and friends also help out in these circumstances. Some say they seldom leave the house, but, when they do, they take the children with them.

The fact that the spouse is not often found caring for the children in these circumstances suggests that he or she is either unavailable or also going out. At other times, however, he is expected to help out in over 60 per cent of the households.

Social Activities

Of the 131 respondents who were asked if they felt their life was too confined to home, 38 per cent answered in the affirmative. This circumscribed living is reflected in their weekend social activities; about the only three things that take them out of the project in significant numbers are work, shopping, and visiting relatives and friends. Many of them stay home and relax – do housework, wash cars, watch TV, or entertain with a card party or hockey game on TV, although some belong to bowling and veterans' clubs and others enjoy a beer at the local hotel. Only a few obtain glimpses of the sparkling and costly downtown entertainment.

Recreation

About half of the families interviewed participate in Community Centre programs in some way. Calculations on the involvement of eleven households would indicate that approximately 13 per cent of the project population is involved in the Centre's activities.

Twenty-five per cent of these people participate in some kind of club activity, either after school or in the evening. These include athletic and craft programs for children, a drop-in centre and charm school for teen-agers, home management courses and sewing and garden clubs for adults. Card groups (bingo, euchre, and cribbage) are next in popularity. Participation in sports programs is rated third in importance. Nursery school and senior citizens' activities were also mentioned. It must be remembered that some of these programs here were not available two years ago, so that the Community Centre is carrying out an expanding program.

Attempts to determine the tenants' attitudes toward the Community Centre and its staff produced the following responses: they feel the Centre treats everyone equally and is trying very hard to make Lawrence Heights a better place to live. Most of the staff succeed in getting people to relax and enjoy themselves and provide assistance for those in trouble as well.

The teachers' lack of background knowledge on the children in the school also applies to the Community Centre staff, although there is a greater chance that the staff members will be more knowledgeable in this respect.

The respondents generally admit that the staff knows a great deal about what happens in the project, and 17 per cent of them feel that they pry too much for this information. Fifty per cent disagree with this; 33 per cent are undecided. Nearly 50 per cent agree that the staff tries to make people do things their way, but the conflict has not reached the point of complete dissatisfaction with the staff.

To sum up, the people feel the Community Centre and its staff have a positive effect, if perhaps too imposing a presence.

The respondents' image of a community centre as a place that serves all age groups is clearly confirmed by this research. What the respondents feel should take place here and what is actually occurring coincide to some extent. Activities such as euchre, bingo, and some sports activities are already taking place, but there is plenty of room for expansion. Competitive team sports are given a high rating for future consideration. Games like bowling, baseball, hockey, darts, tennis, volleyball, horseshoes, and ping pong are among those listed. A drop-in centre for teen-agers is also mentioned, although this is now a reality.

Dances would appear to be reasonably popular, along with concerts, drama, talent shows, and open houses. There is also some demand for arts and crafts, presently linked with the very young and very old. One of the problems with dances in the past has been the prohibition rule which does not permit the serving or drinking of alcoholic beverages in the Centre.

Discussion and lecture groups are not likely to bring in large numbers unless centred on pertinent problems.

The current state of affairs suggests a need for more adult, teen-age, and child activities. Unfortunately, the size of the Community Centre makes it difficult to provide programs to meet the needs of all these age groups, so that transferral of some activities to another area (such as the public school) may be necessary. This transfer should be relatively smooth in the light of current attitudes toward the school.

When the respondents were asked what should happen in a housing project, sports again were given prominent importance. Since this refers more to the outdoors, however, emphasis is placed on playgrounds, swimming, rinks (artificial), benches, picnic tables, swings (with plenty of supervision to ensure safety), and constructive activity.

A need for some kind of Social Services and Tenants' Organization was also indicated, the former to be located in the Community Centre, the latter to be composed of residents and specialists and not necessarily restricted to matters of recreation.

ANALYSIS

Any abnormalities in a population are reflected in its living pattern. Lawrence Heights is no exception to this rule, for the disproportionate number of incomplete families and the large number of children determine many of its essential features. When the husband and father is present to complete the household, his limited earning capacity frequently casts him in a subordinate role. Both personal and social problems emerge from this situation.

The respondents' personal problems clearly derive from insufficient funds. Bills, high rents, sickness (prescriptions), and transportation (two fare zone) are basically financial problems, and the tenants' solution is quite logical – more money.

A cursory examination of their "belief system" suggests that the solution to these problems rests with themselves, for they say that almost anything can be accomplished through hard work and a reasonable amount of ability. Nevertheless, it is difficult to accept these as the *real* values of people struggling for the necessities of life. The Canadian dream – whatever it may be: a university degree, wealth, the presidency of a corporation, the executive suite and all its attendant pleasures – is totally irrelevant to life as they are living it. Although there is no room for them in this "success pattern," neither is there any apparent striving to be part of it. It may be said they "idealize" the middle class, but don't really wish to be like them. Why then do they subscribe to this Protestant Ethic? Simply because giving lip service to middle-class goals permits some kind of adjustment or accommodation to "respectable" society. Why is this necessary? Because they are dependent on this segment of society. They rely heavily on "the establishment," as the Housing Authority, welfare, and police departments are quick to confirm. One is left to conclude that their declaration of these values is a kind of arid formalism calculated to insure their survival in a middle-class world. They are *linguistic tools* that have been fashioned, not necessarily consciously, to satisfy the *expectations* of middle-class investigators with whom they must try to cope; the expression of these beliefs is not an attempt to open the doors to the affluent society. At the same time, it would be wrong to assume that this unassimilated work ethic is the only guideline for living. It is granted that the middle-class values to which they ostensibly subscribe serve a purpose in their *relations* with authority, but they have another set which reflects their need for the basic things in life. Plagued by *insecurity*, there is *no* pursuit of material ends beyond that required to obtain some control over their livelihood – to have sufficient food, to be able to pay the rent, to obtain treatment for a medical problem without going into debt. As problems, they are very concrete and have a sense of immediacy about them. In their world, counselling in any sophisticated sense is considered irrelevant, although, here again, they are prepared to "play the game" and submit to the clinician's psychological probes if this is the price that must be paid for the help they need.

The neighbourhood problems have an essentially social rather physical character about them and are related to a population mix which features uncontrolled children and a fairly high level of alienation among the adults. This does not mean that the composition of the population is the *cause* of these social problems, but that a *correlation* exists between them. The causes rest in the *precariousness* of the tenants' subsistance, in fact; it is for this reason they do not accept protest movements for initiating change. Joined with the fear of not having needs satisfied is the anxiety attending a violation of such matters as housing or welfare regulations. This fear of being "reported on" by neighbours encourages many tenants "to keep to themselves." Such a philosophy undermines the building of a community in the same way that low income prevents healthy individual development and causes discord in the family. But here again, the problem does not rest with the people doing the reporting or those being reported on, but with *regulations* which circumscribe the respondents' lives to a far greater extent than if they lived outside the project's boundaries. At the same time, it would be wrong to assume that all of the establishment is militantly antagonistic – the outstanding exception is the public school, which has made serious attempts to "disestablish" itself and become a viable institution within the subcultural setting by stripping away some of the demands of the larger system and expanding opportunities as a result of interpreting education in its broadest sense. It is a "village pump" for some adults and teen-agers as well as children. The neighbourhood is the other area which holds the promise of a developing community spirit. Social life is not exclusively regulated by the housing development's boundaries, but the daily routine of the dominant members, that is, the women, is confined to the point of highlighting the importance of locality. The few scattered coffee groups could take the initiative in this approach and provide the foundations for the *rules* they should be living by in the project, that is, *their own*.

There is something ironic in the fact that the solidarity so essential to the tenants' well-being is present only among the more economically secure Canadians who use that solidarity to promote the myth of Lawrence Heights as a welfare community maintained at their expense.

5 Family and Kinship in Riverdale

Stewart Crysdale

This article is a careful examination of family life, its style and characteristics, in an old and established, but little known, working-class district of Toronto. The area is just east of the Don River and south of Gerrard Street. The article was prepared as part of the author's doctoral dissertation for the Department of Sociology at the University of Toronto in 1968.

Now teaching sociology at Atkinson College, York University, where he is chairman of the sociology program, Professor Crysdale's career includes a fascinating number of experiences. After securing a Bachelor of Commerce degree and working in the publishing field, Dr. Crysdale enrolled in Emmanuel College, Toronto, where he acquired a Bachelor of Divinity degree. He then served numerous pastorates in the United Church and later became assistant secretary under the Reverend Ray Hord in the United Church Department of Evangelism and Social Service. During these years, he wrote many articles and three books, perhaps the best known of which is *The Changing Church in Canada.* This article previously appeared in *Canada: A Sociological Profile,* compiled by W. E. Mann.

Like other predominantly working-class communities, Riverdale is characterized by networks of highly interactive, primary, informal, social structures in addition to the conjugal family.[1] Sixty-two per cent of members of the entire sample reported that they visited back and forth informally with others at least once a week, and another 23 per cent about once a month. This com-

95

pared with 33 per cent who said they attended church once a month or oftener, 17 per cent who went to union or other occupational group meetings at least once a month, 23 per cent who took part in some social or recreational activity this often, and 12 per cent who attended fraternal, civic, or educational groups about once a month. There was a good deal of overlapping in attendance at different types of organizations, but it may be estimated that one-half the respondents were reasonably active in one type of formal group or another.

Studies elsewhere have stressed a dichotomy between the working and middle classes in the greater involvement of the former in primary groups and the greater participation of the latter in secondary organizations.[2] The distinctions in this respect between members of these classes living in Riverdale were not sharp. It is true that upper white-collar workers in the sample were slightly less active in primary group relations than other workers, but lower white-collar workers were slightly more active than blue-collar workers, and the differences in any case were not great. Further, blue-collar workers were in fact a little more active in secondary associations than their white-collar neighbours, if participation in religious and occupational organizations is included. At the same time, people in the highest income brackets were considerably less active in primary groups than those with moderate incomes, but it is not clear whether this was because of choice or because many of them put in a good deal of overtime.

An additional complication in the Riverdale case is that respondents who were members of one or more organizations were much more active in primary relations outside the conjugal family than those who did not belong to any organization. In the absence of comparative studies in other parts of Toronto and elsewhere, it is not possible to say positively whether Riverdale is a deviant case in this regard or whether the patterns of involvement in primary and secondary relations in a transitional working-class community downtown in a metropolis are more complex than those in more stable and homogeneous working-class communities. There are good reasons, theoretically and empirically, to think that the latter is the case.

The main point for consideration in this chapter, however, is not whether primary groups are more salient for the interests and adaptation of blue-collar workers in Riverdale than of white-collar workers living there. This question is no doubt important. For instance, it has been noted by other researchers that middle-class patterns of participation in secondary organizations and of family behaviour are nowhere more clearly demonstrated than among upwardly mobile working-class families.[3] Anticipatory socialization – the internalization of the values, norms, and behaviour of groups towards which one aspires and is gravitating – is an important indicator of potential upward mobility. The relatively high rate of participation in secondary associations in Riverdale may be partly an indication of anticipatory socialization.

But the main point to be stressed in this chapter is the functional significance of primary group relations in helping or hindering people of various backgrounds and in different positions in a working-class community to adapt to the pressures of the larger urban-industrial society and, in particular, to its demand for flexibility and mobility.

PRIMARY GROUP FUNCTIONS

Small, face-to-face, primary groups such as the family, kinship circle, and peer group function as bridges between the individual and the larger structures of society: school, church, industry or business, city, regional, or national government. It is difficult to conceive of a viable or human life for man in a society of huge, complex structures apart from the mediating and ameliorative activities of small, intimate groups.

In these activities primary groups perform two principal sets of functions. One of these is to socialize individuals, both children and adults, so that they may become effective members of the larger structures and society as a whole. This is done by transmitting to individuals the basic values, norms, practices, and skills of society in whole and in its major parts. In the process of transmission, small groups establish priorities, interpret the roles of various members, and teach the symbolic meanings that are appropriate for social facts.

Frequently, for example, Riverdale parents were observed to emphasize to adolescent children, particularly those in Grades Seven and Eight, the importance of continuing into secondary school. Several times the interviewer's visit was explicitly used by parents as an occasion to reinforce the value of securing a "good" education. A hydro lineman was getting after his Grade Eight son for not "doing his homework." He said, "Here's a man from the university. He can tell you what it means to go on in school." But the impression was subtly conveyed that it would have been even better if the interviewer had been an engineer instead of a social scientist.

The other principal set of functions performed by the primary group is to protect its members from excessive pressures and intrusions from large and powerful social structures. The peer group of adolescents serves this function for its members, shielding them from parents, teachers, police, and adult society in general. When the performances of adult groups fail to accord with their formal protestations, or when they become intolerably threatening to adolescents, gangs offer alternative sets of meaning, interpretation, and social cohesion.[4] Informal cliques and peer groups at places of work afford similar refuge from the strains imposed by management on workers for conformance with rules and expectations and for higher productivity. The working-class family probably offers the greatest protection against the strains of the external world, not only for infants and young children but for young people and adults as well. In this function, the conjugal family of parents and children is supported by modified kinship systems in which the wife's parents often play a central role.[5]

A most impressive aspect of family life in the Riverdale study was the capacity of stable, accepting familial circles to help workers withstand the shocks of long- and short-run change in the urban-industrial system. When a young man strove to improve his position relative to his father or his own previous jobs, his home often acted as a buffer against the strains of learning new technical and social skills. One young married man, with two small children, had spent two years as a motor mechanic apprentice, working at low wages in a garage and taking courses at night school. He had another two or three years to go. His wife gave him every encouragement, taking on part-time jobs, and her mother let them have the house at very low rent. The mother and a sister also baby-sat to let the wife work occasionally or get away with her husband for an evening.

Similarly, if a man skidded downward in the job scale, usually the easy-going climate of home kept him from blaming himself too severely. A man in his fifties who had been manager of a warehouse was demoted when a large American company took over the firm. But he found it possible to accept a demeaning job as a helper in the same plant largely because, he said, his wife "didn't want him to go out looking for work at this stage in life." She liked her job as a clerk, and their house was paid for. Besides, their two sons were both married and had good jobs, and they got together in the old home every weekend. One lived in Scarborough, and the other lived further east, near Coxwell.

If a worker remained at the same level while others around

him got further ahead, he could take comfort from his status and prestige in the family circle and project unfulfilled dreams into hopes for greater accomplishments by the children.

The interviewer spent a Friday evening with a semi-skilled set-up man who had worked at the same job level in one factory for nearly twenty years. He had no hope of promotion because of limited education and his age. But he was a warden in the church nearby and had a long and prestigious reputation as a scoutmaster and district commissioner. One son was also a "scouter," and the wife and daughter were guide leaders. He and his wife had just returned from the weekend shopping trip. "We eat well," he remarked, and he took pride in the fact that the house was comfortably furnished. His nineteen-year-old daughter joined in the interview, along with his wife, and both strongly supported and illustrated the worker's criticism of Canada's selective and restrictive educational system. In the course of the evening, a married son and his wife dropped in and took part in the discussion, also verifying and elaborating the points made by the father. It was an enjoyable, reinforcing experience for the family. Before the evening was over, another young man, a former neighbour, joined the group with his wife, and, after a relaxed visit, they went bowling with the son and his wife. Later, the father's brother and his wife called and entered easily into the discussion. Family solidarity again was strongly demonstrated in talking about a variety of topics. The interviewer was told that this was a typical Friday evening.

Although the process of accommodation worked both ways in resolving conflict between work careers and family life, the general impression was that the family came first in the vast majority of cases. When shift work interfered with regular home routines, the husband was under continual pressure to change shifts or find a new job. Overtime was welcome because of the added income it brought, but among low-skilled workers there were usually limits to how much pressure the family would take, particularly if the worker had a choice. One ironworker told the interviewer he was taking a week's holiday after three months of overtime, to "see the family and get caught up on my drinking." His wife and older children were obviously pleased that he was home for a while.

At the same time, the families of the minority of workers who were taking retraining or other courses to improve their positions absorbed a considerable degree of inconvenience and often loss of income in order to help the trainee achieve long-range benefits. In most cases where there was a family to support, the wife was the key to the situation, usually working full- or part-time as well as doing most of the housework and caring for the children.

CHANGES IN FAMILY ROLES

Under the stress of occupational changes and in response to broad liberalizing tendencies, the roles of husband and wife were changing in Riverdale. It was now common for wives to work full-time, a thing that "was not done" among self-respecting families a generation ago. "The war changed all that," according to several middle-aged respondents.

But differences in how families adapted to new conditions were apparent as between blue- and white-collar, middle-aged workers in Riverdale, and between younger and older blue-collar families. Traditional divisions of labour and obligations around the house between men and women were more noticeable among blue-collar people generally, although they were giving way in younger families. Even when wives of older blue-collar workers held down steady jobs, they usually continued to do the cooking, washing, and housecleaning. But where both husband and wife worked in older white-collar families, the man usually helped in the kitchen, drying the dishes at least, and often he would take a hand in cleaning floors and carrying out the garbage.

Household roles were more fluid among younger men and women in both blue- and white-collar families. Young fathers in both classes often felt little embarrassment about changing the baby or warming its bottle if the wife were working or out visiting with her family or friends. Older men in blue-collar circles did not, as a rule, approve of this behaviour. They expressed their disapproval in humour and sarcasm rather than in reasoned argument.

Wives of older blue-collar workers deferred to their husbands more than white-collar wives. In the few cases where the wife of an older blue-collar worker entered the discussion with the interviewer, sometimes to correct or interrupt the man, the climate became tense and resentful. In this event, the man felt obliged to prove his spouse wrong or apologize for her in word or gesture. But among white-collar and younger blue-collar couples, it was usually taken for granted that the wife should take part in the discussion on equal terms with her husband.[6]

Differences were also noticeable in customs having to do with entertaining and drinking. When older blue-collar workers got together in their homes, the women usually congregated in the kitchen while the men occupied the front room, watching television and talking. When beer, liquor, or coffee was served, the sexes drank separately. Particularly was this so when strangers were present. For women to drink in the presence of strange men was a mark of lower-class, not working-class, behaviour. Decent women did not do this. On Friday or Saturday nights, however, when close relatives usually got together, there was freer mixing of the sexes. Inconsistently perhaps, in white-collar or middle-class circles, women were more apt to join the men in more or less equal association even when strangers were present.

These differences in sex roles were at least partly a reflection of changes in the work roles of women in this generation. Thirty-one per cent of all the wives of Riverdale's chief wage-earners were in the labour force. Whereas many wives of blue-collar workers had part-time jobs or were working in such low-status positions as waitresses, factory operatives, or store clerks, the wives of white-collar workers were apt to hold more prestigious jobs as office clerks, stenographers, or secretaries. It was largely a question of how much education they had. But when the wife's education and work role were comparable with those of her husband, a radical revision of the traditional roles of husband and wife in household duties and in sociability followed. Pressure towards the reduction of role conflicts and inconsistencies among women in the work force was clearly evident.[7] As women in working-class society tend increasingly to assume roles that bear a status approaching or surpassing that of their husbands, their influence may be expected to increase in determining the aspirations, educational attainment, and starting points in the careers of their children. Their influence, as a number of studies have shown, is already in the direction of upward mobility.[8]

PRIMARY RELATIONS OF MAJOR GROUPS COMPARED

Workers raised in Toronto were somewhat more active in informal, primary group relations than those raised elsewhere, as might be expected. They were more likely to have relatives and old friends within easy reach. There were few variations between the three other groups comprising the sample. Seventy per cent of native Torontonians visited others informally at least once a week, as against 59 per cent of both migrant groups from Ontario-Quebec and the East Coast, and 58 per cent of non-British immigrants. Within each of the in-coming groups there was a small tendency for people raised in urban centres to be more active in primary interaction than those raised in the country. Rural migrants who had come to Riverdale within the past five years and who were heads of families of children were less active in primary relations than others.

Occupational class did not make much difference in the frequency of visiting back and forth, but there was less primary group interaction among those who attained higher levels of education. Whereas 70 per cent of those with some high school visited at least once a week, only 44 per cent of those who completed Grade Thirteen or went on into university did. However, workers who had not gone beyond Grade Eight were less active in informal group relations than those with some high school, 59 per cent of the former visiting others once a week or more. This may have been a reflection of the fact that rurally-raised people had less education and were not as active in social relations as those with more urban experience.

Sharper distinctions occurred between occupational classes concerning *who* comprised primary groups. Table I shows that white-collar workers were more inclined than blue-collar to mix with a wide variety of people. Sixty-four per cent of them named a broad variety of groups with whom they associated informally most regularly, compared with 49 per cent of blue-collar workers. One-half of the latter chose their close associates from among one of the following: relatives, neighbours, or friends from back home or from work. This compared with one-third of white collar workers.

Differences in the composition of primary groups were greater between occupational classes than between regions of upbringing. Among the latter, non-British immigrants were somewhat more inclined to choose their close associates from a variety of people than the other major groups in the sample. That is, their primary groups were a little more heterogeneous and opened to them a wider range of interests. This is in accord with the finding that heterogeneity of primary group composition was strongly associated with higher levels of education. Immigrants included a higher proportion of well-educated, urban-bred persons.[9]

For the entire sample, 72 per cent of those with Grade Thirteen or some university chose their closest associates from among a variety of people and not chiefly from one group, whether relatives, neighbours, or friends from back home or from work.

TABLE I

CLOSEST INFORMAL ASSOCIATES OF CHIEF WAGE-EARNERS
BY OCCUPATIONAL CLASS
(Percentages)

	WHITE COLLAR	BLUE COLLAR	TOTAL SAMPLE
Variety of people	64%	49%	52%
Relatives	29%	35%	34%
Friends from back home		6%	5%
Neighbours	2%	5%	4%
Friends from work	2%	4%	3%
Church or club friends	3%	1%	2%
Totals	100%	100%	100%
Numbers	(58)	(239)	(297)

Among workers with some high school, 63 per cent chose a variety of close associates, and, among those who did not go past Grade Eight, 41 per cent associated most closely with a variety of people. The preferences of workers with different educational attainment for close associates are presented in Table II.

Among the factors examined, then, educational attainment was most strongly associated with both the rate of primary group interaction and with the type of people with whom respondents visited most often. Workers who had completed Grade Thirteen or entered university were less active in primary relations, and, when they did visit, they were not so likely as others to choose one group or another such as relatives, neighbours, or friends from back home or from work. Their higher education, job status, and income put them in touch with a wider variety of people. In turn, their broad contacts led to further opportunities for advancement. Once entrance was secured to social groups and situations favouring upward mobility, the social milieu continued to lead upward in a spiral. This pattern did not vary systematically among the four major groups in the Riverdale sample according to region of upbringing, but it occurred to a greater extent among non-British immigrants than among native Canadians who were raised in Toronto or who migrated from central Canada or from the East Coast.

TABLE II

CLOSEST INFORMAL ASSOCIATES OF CHIEF WAGE-EARNERS BY EDUCATIONAL ATTAINMENT

(Percentages)

	Up to Grade 8	Some High School	Grade 13 or some University
Variety of people	41%	63%	72%
Relatives	41%	28%	12%
Friends from back home	6%	4%	4%
Neighbours	5%	2%	8%
Friends from work	4%	2%	4%
Church or club friends	2%	2%	
Totals	99%*	101%*	100%
Numbers	(164)	(107)	(25)

*Figures are rounded to nearest percentage.

The inference that less frequency and broader diversity in primary relations accompanied more "positive" adaptation to change in urban-industrial society is supported by the findings of Marc Fried in his study, "Transitional Functions of Working-Class Communities: Implications for Forced Relocation."

> The more flexible and optional affiliation with close-knit networks . . . is more clearly and cleanly associated with post-relocation adjustment-adaptation. This finding shows that 22 per cent of those with extensive close-knit network ties, 31 per cent of all those with moderate close-knit ties, and 52 per cent of those with minimal close-knit ties were successfully adjusted to the post-relocation situation.[10]

Again, Fried found that,

> . . . among those people whose interpersonal relations were primarily local before relocation, 22 per cent were satisfactorily adjusted after relocation, but among those whose interpersonal contacts were predominantly non-local, 54 per cent were in the well-adjusted group.[11]

STRUCTURAL AND CULTURAL FACTORS IN FAMILY ORIENTATION TO MOBILITY

It is evident from the foregoing observations that the interrelations between structural-ecological and cultural factors and the adaptation and mobility of workers in the Riverdale sample are extremely complex, and broad generalizations cannot be drawn from the study of this community for wide application. Nevertheless, it is clear that the cultural backgrounds per se of the four groups in the sample do not strongly predict rates of mobility or patterns of adaptation. At the same time, the level of educational attainment does predict both the rate of upward mobility and the broad pattern of adaptation to change.

Perhaps even more significant for an understanding of the functions of primary and secondary associations in a working-class community in the processes of adaptation and mobility is the absence of strong distinctions between blue- and white-collar patterns in participation in secondary associations and the attenuation of distinctions in primary relations. Fried pointed out that transition to a higher occupational and social status is less attractive for the working class because it implies less involvement with the solidarity and comprehensive networks of close ties that are typical of working-class community life and social organization.[12] And Eisenstadt among others noted that assimilation of immigrants was accompanied by a reduction in the importance of close-knit networks and by the gradual development of individualism and of a stronger orientation to formal structures.[13] While the Riverdale data were generally consonant with these findings, the loosening of close-knit, homogeneous ties and the development of more positive orientation towards striving for upward mobility were more strongly associated with educational attainment than with occupational class.

For example, the respondent who was most active in political circles was a blue-collar worker. He had been a skilled pattern-maker but had had to take a poorer paying job as a shipper-receiver for reasons of health. He was secretary of the local Progressive Conservative Club and served on several regional political committees. He was also an active member of the Presbyterian Church. His style of family life was working-class, but his pattern of primary-secondary associations, according to the stereotype, was middle-class. The strategic difference between him and his neighbours and relatives was that he had completed several years of high school. Had it not been for financial stringency in youth and ill-health later on, this man might have risen into a middle-class occupation. It might be said that he was not typical of the working-class. But there were many like him in Riverdale, so that the picture of the working-class drawn in much of the literature as deeply involved in close-knit, homogeneous ties and inactive in secondary associations of all sorts, a social enclave relatively untouched by the main-stream of technopolitan society, does not fit our population of chief wage-earners well.

It does fit lower-class residents in Riverdale more closely – those whose pattern and style of life differ markedly from typical blue-collar workers in that they do not follow or aspire after orderly work careers and do not generally accept the value system of the urban-industrial, predominantly middle-class society.[14] It has been stated that this study is not concerned with lower-class people in Riverdale, and again the question may be appropriately raised as to whether the populations examined in some well-known studies, purportedly of the working-class, were indeed working- or lower-class. Herbert Gans made the distinction in his study of Italians in Boston's West End, whose life he likened to "urban villagers."[15] Gans also stressed the "person-orientation" of non-mobile circles as against the "object-orientation" of the upwardly mobile.[16] Again, however, it is questionable whether his population of relatively homogeneous, second-generation immigrants, whose life centred around close-knit family ties, is comparable with a heterogeneous population of workers in a transitional, metropolitan, downtown community such as Riverdale.

There is little doubt that as a worker moves up or down the occupational ladder his pattern of primary and secondary association is apt to change. The relation is reciprocal. His pattern of associations – that is, his concept of community and commitment to it – affects his motivation and orientation towards the larger society, with its stress on striving and achievement. And his shift in positions affects his choice of social circles, both primary and secondary. Fried appropriately observed:

> Coming to terms with the disjunctive influences from assimilation and mobility aspirations, on the one hand, and from the commitments to and collective meaning of community life, on the other, is the major adaptational problem associated with social mobility.[17]

It must be concluded from the Riverdale data that in this case the patterns of primary, close-knit ties were generally just as apt to be functional for the positive orientation and adaptation of the worker to upward mobility as they were apt to be dysfunctional. The most important single factor which determined the way it would be was the level of education the worker had attained. To the extent, then, that access routes to continued education and training are kept open for the worker, other things being equal, primary associations such as are found in Riverdale are not likely to deter increased flexibility and mobility.

Some may say that the above reasoning begs the question posed by other research, that the cultural value systems of working-class family life typically comprise the quest for more schooling and the drive for achievement in work careers that characterize middle-class families. Albert K. Cohen built a convincing case for a general theory of subcultures on the basis of a dual explanation of differences between working- and middle-class orientations towards mobility.[18] One set of explanations was situational, in that middle-class families were better able to provide for their children the education and access to secondary associations which favoured upward mobility. This set of factors corresponds to what has been called the "ecological opportunity syndrome" in the present study. But Cohen also stressed another set of explanations which he called the family frame of reference, or the psychogenic factor. He made it clear that distinctions between middle- and working-class family behaviour were based on the concept of "ideal types," which grow out of empirical evidence and yet do not necessarily exist in every situation.[19]

According to this theory, child-rearing in working-class families is apt to be easy-going and accepting, permitting non-conformance within fairly wide limits and exercising discipline through corporal punishment but not through the withdrawal of love. Middle-class parents, however, are said to contrive the child's environment and time deliberately to facilitate socialization into middle-class values and ways. He is surrounded with books, educational toys, good music, and the right friends. Moreover, middle-class parents extend to their children "conditional love," something to be won by effort, achievement, and conformance with the parents' wishes. When love is contingent and precarious, an adaptive, socialized anxiety is thought to be generated which is allayed only by constant striving and the avoidance of disapproved behaviour. In contrast, the children of working-class parents not only find ready acceptance at home but also in close kinship circles and other, neighbourhood peer groups. The pressures towards achievement are conditional. The result is greater internalization of middle-class values by children raised in that stratum and higher performance in school and in conventional tests of intelligence.[20] By the time children are in Grade Eight, the residual effect of situational factors predetermines the disproportionate numbers of middle-class students who are directed into the academic stream and find their way to university and superior social and occupational opportunities. So the cycle repeats itself.

The importance of psychogenic factors in affecting children's values and choices in schooling and occupation is not questioned in this study. But, as mentioned, the clear distinctions between working- and middle-class family behaviour and orientation, which might have been expected in view of the literature, did not come to light. Several recent studies suggest that modifications should be made in "ideal type" constructs of child-rearing behaviour and value orientations of families in different occupational and social strata today.[21]

Enquiry along these lines was beyond the scope of the present study. But there are strong indications that cross-pressures – structural and environmental as well as cultural-valuational – are at work in the downtown, metropolitan, working-class community to produce complex patterns of primary-secondary association that are unlike the ideal types developed in the literature of the past twenty years. It is suggested that one of the functions of the downtown working-class community is to provide just such an ambivalent environment for a variety of workers and their families who are at different stages and heading in different directions in the adaptive-mobility process.

Yorkville Subculture

Reginald G. Smart and David Jackson

As the home ground of the revolution of the young, no volume on Toronto would be complete without an article on the Yorkville district. Yorkville is to Toronto what the Village is to New York and Chelsea is to London. It is a magnet for the young, freedom-loving set, famous across Canada and well-known in most hippie circles in the United States. In a few square blocks north of Bloor Street congregate the youthful swingers and would-be swingers, drugtakers and pushers, teeny-boppers, bikers, and greasers. Police surveillance, overt and covert, is incessant. In the early years of Yorkville's history, 1965-7, Toronto's city officials were daily announcing their concern over the area, and confrontations between the officials and the Yorkvillers were frequent and dramatic. The officials' concern has lessened now, and many of the "regulars" of the scene have either moved a few blocks west or dispersed across Metro.

This article focusses on the subculture of Yorkville during the period 1967-8. It resulted from participant observations by Gopala Alampur, who lived in the area for some six months. This version of the article is excerpted from a more lengthy sociological study published by the Ontario Addiction Research Foundation. Certain case study items and details on methodology and hippie ideology have been deleted.

The senior author, Dr. R. G. Smart, a Toronto psychologist, has been a frequent contributor to the Addiction Research Foundation's journal, *Addictions*, and other scholarly publications. He is widely known for his 1968 report on the use of marijuana in Toronto's high schools.

109

Conceptualization

Various ways of conceptualizing Yorkville can be suggested. Yorkville is, of course, a geographic area, a busy part of a large city with streets, roads, pedestrians, traffic, etc. However, "Yorkville," like "Hollywood," creates an image of particular, eccentric styles of life. It could be seen as a kind of non-alcoholic skid row for young people – where youthful social drop-outs congregate for shared drug experiences. One could focus on the drug marketing aspect of Yorkville or on its place as a forum for non-political social rebellion. Still further efforts could be made to see Yorkville as an example of social pathology – a manifestation of sickness in the larger society or in certain aspects of our present family structure. One might, too, define Yorkville as a place for psychologically disturbed youngsters.

The conceptualization of this particular study depends on none of the above positions. In fact, an effort was made to minimize conceptual presuppositions and free the study of any special position. Broadly speaking, this study had an ethnographic framework. That is, Yorkville was studied as a viable subculture or as a set of symbolic and material arrangements made by a society embedded in a larger society. As Howells has said, "Culture consists of everything that has ever been accepted as a way of doing or thinking, and so taught by one person to another."[1] We attempted to describe the ways of doing and thinking which are accepted in Yorkville.

The general aim was to describe the culture through the words and perceptions of its members, with a minimum of interpretation. The position taken is mainly a phenomenological one – that is, that the culture is as its members describe it, although contradictions among certain attitudes or between attitudes and behaviours are pointed out.

Method

In this study, traditional ethnographic methods were employed. These were chiefly participant observations and interviews with informants. On October 27, 1967, an anthropologist with ethnographic experience (Gopala Alampur) went to live as a hippie in the village. He grew a beard, wore typical Yorkville clothes and beads, and took part in the life of the "village" until May 1, 1968. This was essentially participant observation, although informants were used later. During the six months of field work, his room

became so popular that the landlord insisted he leave, a cc
experience for residents of Yorkville.

To those who asked, he said that he was wandering arouno
world studying various religions and cultures. Because he h
studied hill tribes in India and was acquainted with cultural anthrc
pology, this explanation was accepted. He received no obvious
police protection so that his special status was not obvious. He
told those who were interested that he planned to write a book
about his experiences in Yorkville.

Physical Setting and the Festive Appearance

Surprisingly, few shops and restaurants in Yorkville cater to the
needs of the "villagers." A few restaurants allow hippies to sit
until the restaurant becomes crowded, but those who are not prepared to order and pay for food are put out. Since many villagers
have no permanent address, one or two shops allow their addresses
to be used, and incoming letters for various people are pinned on
a notice board.

According to the time of day, week, and year, the population
changes in growth and substance, to create sharp contrasts between
the setting and the inhabitants. At times, the inhabitants and the
setting accentuate one another, and at other times they clash. It is
not unusual to see people in various wild modes of dress sitting on
curbs or wherever they can find a place, watching other people in
equally different dress strolling by.

From Friday afternoons to Sunday afternoons a festival atmosphere prevails. Visitors outnumber the natives; teen-agers wander
aimlessly up and down the street. People appear in garish, colourful costumes. It is not unusual to see some wearing shorts and
going barefoot in mid-winter. Most are in a lively holiday mood,
some carrying lighted incense, some with designs painted on their
bodies. Popcorn salesmen find a ready market for their wares, and
the coffee houses are full. Some of the girls make paper flowers
which they carry as they walk around; they may give the flowers
to their boy-friends or try to sell them. Artists are often seen
drawing portraits on the streets. One can find people roaming the
streets of Yorkville at almost any hour of the day or night. Villagers living on Yorkville Avenue also enjoy peering through their
windows at the large crowd of weekenders on the weekend
nights. . . .

THE FOUR MAJOR GROUPS

Very few people in Yorkville like the labels usually applied to
them. During the interviews for this study, no one was willing to

say that he was a hippie. Even those considered hippies by others in the village answered the question, "Are you a hippie?" with, "I am I" or "I am a person." However, people we interviewed were less reluctant to apply labels to other groups. But it is essential to divide the major groups into some "ideal types" if we are to describe the people in the village and the ways in which they relate to each other.

The Hippies

"Hippies" are typically between the ages of sixteen and twenty-four years with an average of about nineteen or twenty. About 60 per cent are males.

One of the most distinctive features of the hippie in Yorkville is his appearance. There is no uniform, but there is a costume – a style characterized by comfort, freedom, and eccentricity. Hippies are set apart by their shabbiness; torn and dirty clothes, worn shoes. During the winter, some wrap rags around their shoes to keep their feet warm; in the summer, many pad along the pavements barefoot.

The costume aspect in the hippie dress is designed to reflect individuality; hippies may look alike in characteristics such as long hair, dirty clothes, and beads, but each is dressed to portray a unity. To add to the element of self-expression, some hippies decorate their bodies, especially the face and hands, with paintings of flowers and other designs. They also write inscriptions, such as "love," "flower power," or "LSD," on their clothes. Badges with inscriptions are commonly worn.

There are child-like, carefree features to their dress, expressed in beads, bells, and the flowers which some carry in their hands. The poncho is a popular costume, often worn with high boots to which bells are attached. There are no limits to the number of necklaces and beads that are worn.

In many instances, hair is worn long and usually uncombed, yet there is a certain charm and style in its appearance. Beards of every dimension bristle, flow, and sprout from the young men's chins. The general impression is that, "I am unique, I am relaxed and having fun, and I don't care what the conventional world thinks of it."

Hippies generally do not work. Actually, the hippies resent work because they see it as forcing conformity to an oppressive system. They resent giving up eight hours of their day to a boss. Their goal is to simplify the complex systems of society, and this leads them to decry bureaucracy, the search for status, and the power games which are so evident in most organizations. Thus, they repudiate the Protestant Ethic and do as little work as possible. Most hippies are not conventionally acquisitive, and they totally reject materialistic goals. In discussing their attitude towards work, there is an element of asceticism; they strive for freedom from the oppression created by possessions. Thus, the shabby dress and lack of permanent quarters make sense in ethical terms.

With this asceticism is a curious mixture of hedonism. One hippie explained his philosophy in these words, "To hell with it. I don't care. I want to live life the easiest, fastest way." If hippies do want to work, their appearance bars them from most jobs. Generally, they work at menial tasks like dishwashing. Because they have little money, they often are without a place to live. "Crashing," or staying with someone else who has a room, is common. In the summer, they often sleep outside. Some, in desperation, sleep in garages or hallways of apartments, but they usually stay within a twenty-block radius of the village. The most common ways of obtaining money are begging and bumming, selling drugs, working part-time (at such jobs as selling the local village newspaper), and committing petty crimes such as theft or prostitution.

"Doing your own thing" is the term the Yorkville hippies use to express their desire for independence. This implies that one should act independently of the opinion of others and submit to no group control. Whether this is a conscious wish on their part or a result of "abnormal" personalities is open to question. The hippies have no chosen leaders, and they form no governing structures. Perhaps it is the resistance to conformity to any norms – even those described as typical of hippies – which sets them apart from society and from other Yorkville groups.

Their disregard for convention extends into such basic concepts as time. Hippies, as well as other groups in Yorkville, usually stay up most of the night and sleep until the afternoon. Their time sense is present-oriented. Plans for tomorrow or for life in the future are either vague or grossly unrealistic.

Crucial to the definition of a Yorkville hippie is his use of drugs. Again, this is not exclusive to the hippie in the village. As one villager put it, "Hippies won't accept anyone who dresses well or doesn't take drugs." This drug-taking is a necessary but not sufficient requirement for being a hippie. Drug-taking is an extremely important part of the hippie's life.

Among hippies, knowledge of philosophy, religion, and psychology carries prestige. They are particularly attracted to Oriental and Indian religions as well as to mysticism and spiritualism. In Ruth Benedict's terms, they put greater value on activities which allow them to escape from reality than those which allow them to deal with reality.[2] Yet their knowledge of these subjects is superficial. Religious and philosophical terms are used more to make a good impression than to communicate substantial meaning. Philosophical books are carried but infrequently read; religions such as Zen Buddhism are often talked of but rarely understood.

Hippies are the most intelligent and intellectual of the groups in Yorkville. They enjoy parties and music – especially rhythmic, hypnotic types. Their commitment to peaceful pursuits is paralleled by passive behaviour on the streets. It is *not* normal for a hippie to be beaten up by more aggressive members of the village. With this non-violent image goes a reputation for being quiet.

Accepting and amicable relationships with others is a part of the hippie life style which has diffused throughout the entire Yorkville community. All groups recognize this as a valuable feature of the village. For the hippie, communal living is appealing; he may subscribe to an unstructured socialism which could be simply characterized as "helping others." Relationships with others – or, to use their term, "to love or groove on others" – are important to the hippies. Perhaps this is so because they have had difficulty relating to others in a satisfying way. Many describe themselves as having been shy and lonely before coming to the village. When they discuss their pasts or their plans for the future, there is a strong interest in dealing with people.

To this concern with human relationships has been grafted the concept of free love. Relationships, while important, are generally transitory. Sexual relations are seen as an aspect of human relationships, and hippies enter into them freely, without the concern for lasting fidelity of people in the "straight" world. If you like the person, a relationship is formed, and sexual relations follow naturally. The important factor is that a binding relationship need not exist before sexual relations can occur. In the jargon of the street, there are many "one-night stands." Sometimes couples live together for several months. The rituals of courting and institutions of legal marriage are merely another restriction of the hated "system." For this reason, children are not desired by couples. Conception is usually seen as an unfortunate mistake which the girl must deal with alone.

Most Yorkville hippies come from middle-class homes; their fathers are salesmen, clerks, executives, and professionals. It is notable that the hippie and the weekender seem to be uninvolved in status struggles, common topics among greasers and motorcycle gang members. In the words of one hippie, "Status is not our hang-up."

Hippies have made at least a temporary break with their families. In most cases, the family is remembered as an unhappy environment from which the hippie felt he must escape. Some hippies are products of broken marriages, while others describe a family where children did not fit in. Whatever the cause, the hippie recalls he wanted out.

Thus, the emphasis on "freedom" heard so often in Yorkville in part reflects the hippie's escape from an unsatisfying family life.

The Weekenders

"Weekenders" range from twelve to twenty years with an average age around seventeen. About 60 per cent are males, as in the hippies' group.

Weekenders are substantially different from hippies. They have various social and ethnic backgrounds. They do not come to Yorkville only to look at the residents, as do the "tourists," but to participate in the village life for the weekend. Consciously or unconsciously, they identify with the different groups in the village and take pride in building associations with the natives according to their group identifications.

The "teeny-boppers" are the youngest segment of the group. They are shunned by the residents because association with them could lead to arrest on charges of contributing to juvenile delinquency. Some of these are "runaways," children who have impulsively left home and now look for refuge in Yorkville.

Most weekenders are students in high school or university, but some are permanently employed. Some are fond of the party atmosphere of Yorkville, while others are searching for drugs or sex.

An employed weekender will occasionally live in Yorkville, but usually he lives with his parents or in an apartment in another part of Toronto. Many weekenders travel to Yorkville regularly from communities within 100 miles of the city.

Weekenders bring charm, colour, and money to Yorkville. They wear more expensive and more colourful clothing than the other groups. Bell-bottom pants, brightly coloured shirts, and psychedelic miniskirts are common. Unlike hippies, they are clean and well-groomed. Whether the costume is designed to resemble that of the motorcycle gang, the hippie, or the greaser, it is always more expensive and more conservative than is typical of those groups.

The weekenders' visits are not always restricted to the weekends. On a sunny day in early spring the village is peopled mostly by weekenders who are truant from school. Some can be seen sitting on the sidewalk trying to do their homework.

When the weekenders come, they bring money. They can frequent the shops and coffee houses, and they can buy drugs. A weekender generally buys drugs from a friend who is a hippie, who in turn buys from a pusher. A weekender is part of both worlds, he enjoys "pot" parties and other activities at the village, and he often carries "stuff" back for parties at home or at a friend's house. Some are pushers in their own schools or offices.

People from Toronto who enter the village as permanent residents generally begin as weekenders. As one hippie describes it, "They start off listening to the Beatles and hearing their friends talk about Yorkville." He attributes their entrance into village life to the realization that, "What is happening is not a social renaissance. People are smoking pot."

The weekenders – or "plastic hippies," as many of the village residents call them – are not committed to a group in Yorkville. They are in a state of transition; eventually they will either become committed to a village group or they will leave, having satisfied their curiosity.

Motorcycle Gangs

The weekenders may be faint carbon copies of the other groups in Yorkville, but the motorcycle gangs stand distinctly apart in dress, values, and behaviour. They are the oldest of the groups, ranging in age from eighteen to twenty-eight years. All official motorcyclists are males, but women are associated with them in roles carrying lesser status.

There are several gangs – Hell's Angels, Paradise Riders, Satan's Choice, Vagabonds, and Thunderbolts. These all-male organizations are composed of sixteen- to twenty-five-year-olds who are generally bigger and more sturdily built than the other inhabitants of Yorkville. The gangs are distinguished from hippies and from other gangs by their distinctive uniforms. They wear leather or levi jackets with the sleeves cut out, with jeans and cowboy boots. On their backs they wear their "colours" – mass produced emblems giving the name of their club. They wear long hair and beards. They seem to take pride in being dirty, but their chrome-plated motorcycles are always polished to gleaming perfection. The swastika and iron cross are commonly worn in military fashion on the chest or around the neck.

Each motorcycle gang has a formal organizational structure with a president, secretary-treasurer, lieutenant-at-arms, road captain, and assistant road captains. Each has specific duties, responsibilities, and privileges. Meetings are held weekly; while attendance is not compulsory, long periods of absence without an adequate excuse are frowned upon. At these meetings members are asked what they have done for the club that week. Also, grievances between members can be aired and suggestions for changes or for new activities can be made at meetings. Girls are not allowed to attend these meetings.

It can be seen that, in contrast to the hippies, the motorcycle gangs are well-organized along military lines. Members pay $10 for their colours and a dollar a week for dues which are used as bail money and to finance club parties. This banding together creates the important advantages of protection and prestige for members.

In the ethos of the motorcycle gangs, powerful elements of the romanticized cowboy are combined with aspects of the street gang. "Bike boys" generally prefer western movies. They talk of fights between motorcycle gangs as "range wars." One gang member described his activities in terms which could have come from a cowboy picture sound track. "We'd rather ride than fight. When there is a range war, you don't have to wear your colours." In other respects, the motorcycle gangs seem to be nothing more than street gangs with wheels. The members are quick to point out that the street gangs of Toronto are younger and poorer. But iron discipline, the wish to identify, and the emphasis on masculine bravery are predominant in both types of gangs.

The aggressiveness of the motorcycle gangs, together with their distinctive dress, gives them prominence when they enter the village. Some villagers see the bike boys as protectors, but most fear them and stay out of their way. The gang members often see themselves as defenders of the village, but they are always the enemies of the police. This is primarily due to their occasional criminal activities. Petty theft and vandalism are not uncommon among the motorcyclists. While members have been involved in some criminal activities at one time or another, it would be incorrect to imply that their major interest is delinquent activity.

The gang members' emphasis on sexual gratification and their relationships with women are direct and unambiguous. Females are property, but males are not. A motorcycle gang member may be married or go steady with his "old lady," but she is completely dependent on him for her status and protection. As his old lady, she will not be molested by other members of his gang or other gangs. The girls are conscious of their lower status and conscious that it gives them less autonomy than in either Yorkville or regular Canadian society.

The motorcycle girl is vulnerable if she is abandoned by her "old man"; she then faces the prospect of ending her association with the gang or possibly being "gang-splashed." There are kudos associated with unusual sexual practices such as oral-genital stimulation and intercourse in groups of three to fifteen people.

Most motorcycle gang members come from working-class families. Generally, their early experiences include violent or delinquent behaviour on the part of their parents. Unlike hippies, most live at home or with their wives outside of Yorkville. While a large number work regularly as drivers or mechanics, another subgroup works only sporadically to maintain themselves and their bikes. Some of the members of the gang have no obvious means of support, and one can only suspect that they get money from their families, other gang members, or illegal activities. Most members have done poorly in school, read few books, and appear to be primarily interested in machinery, sex, and alcohol.

Non-alcoholic drugs are not so important to this group as to the others in the village. They prefer alcohol, which is used at parties in much the same way as it is used by straight adolescents. However, motorcyclists drink far more heavily. Marijuana has been used by many gang members recently, but it is still not the preferred drug. A small number of motorcycle gang members push drugs for profit in the village, but the majority prefer to get their kicks from "booze, broads, and bikes," as one member put it.

Yorkville is one of the places most frequently visited by the bike boys. Like weekenders, they live most of their lives in other parts of the city. Yorkville is attractive to the gangs because of its tolerance for all types of people and because of the girls who can be picked up there.

The Greasers

"Greasers" are between sixteen and twenty-five years of age, and about 70 per cent are males. The term "greaser" is used because, "They put grease on their hair and grease in their food," to use the words of one villager. This statement implies that many come from eastern and southeastern European backgrounds. Greasers also have a large representation of people from countries such as the United States and the West Indies, although there are many Canadian-born members of the group. Greasers are more aggressive and more delinquent than the other groups. Usually they do not live in the village, but they go there frequently. With the greasers, there are basically two subgroups – the young criminal on his way to becoming a "rounder" and the drug addict whose habit has caused him to be completely alienated from straight society.

In terms of dress, they reflect the two extremes of the Yorkville spectrum. Those involved in drugs are attired in a dirty, unkempt way, much like the hippie. For greasers, this appearance is dictated by necessity rather than philosophical principle. The young professional criminal may be arrayed in a leather jacket and jeans or stovepipe pants, with ear-rings, chains around the neck, and other accoutrements which make him look hard-boiled. At other times, he may appear in continental suits, double-breasted jackets, and fancy shirts. The latter type of greaser generally wears short, well-manicured hair with the "grease" which gives him his name. In general, the greasers' group is fastidious in dress.

The greasers are distinguished from the motorcycle gang members by their lack of close group attachments. They do not have an organization. In fact, they are called the "paranoid people" because they fear that intimate relations may cause them to divulge evidence of criminal activity to informers.

Because of their suspiciousness, greasers rarely work with a partner. There are many more male greasers than females. Many of the girls are lesbians who work with a male greaser as a prostitute but have no sexual interest in men. The male greasers are very interested in "hustling broads" from the hippie and weekender groups. When a greaser forms a permanent liaison with a greaser girl, their attitudes are similar to that of the motorcycle gangs – women are property and are afraid to be unfaithful. They are only allowed to choose other men after they have been given up by their boy-friends. To the male greaser who is not a junkie, sex is more important than drugs.

Most greasers are highly motivated to achieve in material and economic terms. Often they take legitimate jobs as a cover against police surveillance. Their economic aspirations are middle-class, but their methods come from the underworld. A motorcycle gang member who looks down on greasers said they were "gonna" people: they are always going to do big things. As this description implies, their plans are often unrealistic. Many are entrepreneurs who become involved in the drug trade because of the lucrative profits it offers. As they talk about their criminal activities, it becomes apparent that they take craftsman-like pride in such activities as stealing or peddling. They rise early, by Yorkville standards, and this adds to the image of the energetic greaser businessman. Greaser girls take short taxi rides and hand out cigarettes to impress their village associates with their wealth. The general topics of discussion among the greasers are their recent exploits, fights they have had, and success or failure with women.

Among the village residents, the greasers have a reputation for starting trouble. For example, a hippie said that, "They want to take everyone on."

Greasers find the more passive hippies easy prey. Not only do they steal from them and cheat them in drug sales, but they sometimes force hippies to steal for them, through fear of physical punishment. Sadism is sometimes mixed with aggression.

Greasers generally appear less intelligent than hippies and weekenders. They tend to be grandiose and loud when in Yorkville and to dominate the discussion with their tales of exploitation and big schemes. For these reasons, it is not difficult to see why they are often feared and despised in the village. Motorcycle gangs enjoy the opportunity to beat them up because other villagers condone this activity as justified.

Usually the greaser lives outside the village, at home, with relatives, or in an apartment. They come to Yorkville for the same reasons the motorcycle gangs do – "To get some action."

Most greasers come from lower-class families and many have suffered severe deprivation in semi-criminal environments. This deprivation has caused them to seek relief in drugs or to fight aggressively for material symbols of the sort of life denied them. They resent the hippies as drop-outs and lazy ne'er-do-wells. As one greaser said, "Rich people can afford to be bums. Poor people have no choice."

Greasers display various patterns of drug use. Some indulge in very frequent, indiscriminate drug-taking. The term "speed freak," which is applied to some greasers, denotes the distaste with which the average villager views greasers addicted to amphetamines. Other greasers have a pattern of heavy alcohol and light marijuana usage more typical of the motorcycle gang member. In general, greasers are not devoted to the psychedelic drugs in the true hippie manner.

YORKVILLE AND THE LARGER SOCIETY

Some hard things have been said about the meaning of Yorkville. It should be pointed out that Yorkville could not have developed or continue to develop without the open or tacit acceptance of the larger society. All adolescent rebellions point to difficulties in the larger society, and it is interesting to speculate about what these difficulties could be.

In the past, the period of adolescence was short, but our society gives youth an extended period of adolescence. It is hoped that during this extended period a greater education can be obtained which will help the young adult to cope with the demands of our changing technology. The paradox of the extended adolescence is that there is a greater demand on educational institutions to keep pace with technological change. When these institutions do not keep up, the youth is made to feel that what he is learning is not relevant to the demands on him. He is made to feel that he has no real skills to help him in the working world. His feeling of inadequacy leaves him with no occupational identity. He may feel that it is necessary to rebel in some way against his situation and against the existing educational institutions.

In itself, the failure of the educational institutions has not created the dilemmas which cause migration to Yorkville. The church has also failed to maintain relevance in its dealings with some young people. Adult society has shown an increasing disillusionment with the religious institutions, and adolescents have also turned elsewhere for a spiritual identity. While many of the Yorkville inhabitants claim to be atheists, they try to find a spiritual identity in less institutionalized religions, such as the eastern paths to "liberation." There is a pressing concern for the development of a life philosophy in the village and for spiritual identity.

Many villagers emphasize poor communication with parents as a reason for going to Yorkville. The family is supposed to help the adolescent to find his personal identity as an autonomous individual. The pressures of the family have increased in a technological society which exhibits a large degree of de-personalization. Yet the increased educational standards of the youth have widened the intellectual gulf between parent and child. Much of what the parent has to say is not relevant to the broader interests of today's youth. Lack of communication in the home, referred to time and time again by the villagers, left the adolescent with no one with whom to identify. We saw that the Yorkville cult exhibited tendencies which verged on hero-worship. Villagers often decorate their apartments with posters of personalities, most of whom are from a time long past. The regression to the fantasies and hero-worship of childhood may be seen as a futile attempt to find the identity models which were lacking in the home life. The existing institutions, family, church, and schools, have failed to communicate with the adolescent in a way which he finds meaningful or relevant.

While many in the adult world look at the Yorkville experiment with despair, they still do not try to put an end to it. Perhaps Yorkville is allowed to exist because, to the majority of straight people, the hippie movement offers no real threat to society. The passive nature of this movement and its emphasis on love and peace stand as a direct contrast to the militancy of the racial violence, minority dissent, and student protests in North American society. The very introspection and passivity of the hippie movement may be seen as a welcome change from the violence of social movements which threaten the stability of the community.

It could be surmised that the Yorkville experiment is encouraged because the hippie ethos has a special appeal for the straight world. The adult society may be changing slightly because of its association with a viable alternative to the present way of life. The concept of work in the Protestant Ethic is being challenged as leisure time becomes more important. The straight world, while not accepting a doctrine of non-work, is redefining the position of work in the technological age. Also, the highly idealistic religious view of the hippies may appeal to an adult world disillusioned by the present lack of faith in institutionalized religion. The humanistic approach in the hippie philosophy may help the straight person to re-define his position in the system. Also, the use of psychoactive and mood-modifying drugs is increasing in the larger society, and many may feel that their drug use does not fully differentiate them from Yorkville inhabitants.

7 Digger House

June Callwood

As in other North American cities, the day-to-day scene and the participants of the hippie community in Toronto have tended to change every six months or so. Whether one talks of Greenwich Village or Yorkville, there is an incessant coming and going, a constant process of change; as a result, the norms, folkways, and leaders of one year are gone a year later. Thus, as everyone knows, the hippie scene of Haight-Ashbury in 1967 is now, in 1970, totally changed. Similarly with Yorkville: what Messers. Smart and Jackson witnessed and reported in 1967-8 was largely *passé* by the summer of 1969. Organized to cater to the more needy residents of Yorkville in the winter of 1967, Digger House has seen its clientele change markedly over the years. Through a description of Digger House, its environs, and the people it serves, Miss Callwood provides us with a kaleidoscopic view of Yorkville society last summer.

June Callwood, a well-known writer and TV personality, is highly qualified to describe the Yorkville scene: she has been close to its residents as a friend and, as well, has been a leading supporter of Digger House itself. Justly famous for her book, *Love, Hate, Fear, Anger and the Other Lively Emotions,* and her interest and identification with youth and Toronto, Miss Callwood, in the fall of 1969, was completing a series of articles for *Maclean's* on youth in Canada. The piece which follows appears for the first time in this anthology.

The Toronto street sign that reads *Yorkville* marks the tomb of

123

the hippie movement, which died of success after flowering for only a year or two.

The Movement represented, however, the implacable force of a good idea whose time had come – humanism without humbug – and it helped to change the world. The 1966 hippies were the gentlest and earliest embodiments of what Marcuse has called "the great refusal," the beginning of *Hell No, We Won't Go!* which retired God, Doris Day movies, – – – –, basic black, final examinations, brassieres, and charity.

The hippies came out of the middle class because no source but affluence and liberalism could have produced them. The bound beyond abundance is scarcely possible for those unfamiliar with it, and few can live for extended periods in a state of risk without having safety in their bones.

Because they were at first so few, and needed the confirmation of mutuality, the hippies clumped together in a downtown commune with a geographical hub: Yorkville. There they jubilantly and conspicuously proclaimed that they were in the brotherhood business: acceptance, sharing, peace, love, freedom, *happiness!* They fretted about inter-personal truth and talked until dawn; they discarded their last names as unnecessary luggage – some of them had famous fathers; they experimented with pot and acid, with sex based on camaraderie, and with costume clothing superimposed on practical, durable jeans. But the most reckless adventure of all was poverty; they found they could learn from it.

Fortunately, they had health to squander. Their childhood legacy of warm beds, orange juice, pediatricians, regular dental checkups, and summers at the lake paid off in adult durability as they thumbed rides beside frozen highways, slept in the rain, went without food for a day, two days, three.

They were deliberate bums, a breed not rare in human history but always significant. It has included founders of religions, philosophers, poets, explorers, inventors, revolutionaries. The hippies of the mid-'60's were gifting the Industrial Age's declining years with a new life-style, the first alternative in a hundred years to the work-or-school choices offered youth. Their donation earned them the usual welcome which society accords divergence: they were feared by most because they represented tempting anarchy – and, as always, fear fled from knowledge and emerged as anger; they were adored and romanticized by a few.

In the spring of 1967, their destruction began. Camera crews were making movies of them; love-ins made front pages; clergymen, sociology professors, and writers were weaving garlands for their brows; policemen were vigorously filling jails with them; parents and high-school principals were stamping on the most visible and vulnerable symptom of the movement: long hair.

It was a superlative aid to recruitment. The hippies found themselves smothered with tourists who glared at them, tourists of their own age who imitated their dress, motorcycle gangsters who plundered their girls, toughs fresh from training schools who stole their possessions, narcotics police who infiltrated them. One of the latter was a beautiful Oriental girl who worked as a coffee shop waitress and was singularly successful at identifying hippies who had smoked marijuana in her presence.

The population who came to Yorkville to stay was even more disturbing. A few were hippies, but the newcomers were much younger than their predecessors; the seasoned hippies, university drop-outs themselves, were slightly shocked to find their community invaded by high-school drop-outs. But hundreds upon hundreds of the new migration were not hippies at all, though their rags made them indistinguishable from the others. These were young people the hippies had never imagined: the broken-hearted and nearly destroyed victims of multiple foster homes, parents who were drunks, or insane, or hotly hostile, homes that were bleak and dangerous because of bitter, angry poverty. They were not school drop-outs, but school throw-outs. They had come to Yorkville in search of love.

For a heroic long while, the Yorkville hippies struggled to make good their promise of brotherhood and shared bread. They housed, fed, and nursed the desolate newcomers through suicidal nights and were aghast at their guests' greed for dope – any dope at all, but preferably the chemicals with destruction in them. Eventually, resources and human warmth were exhausted, and the hippies, imperceptibly at first, began to move away from Yorkville.

By the autumn of 1967, only a dogged band remained, hanging on in the hope of opening a hostel which would provide emergency food and shelter and a referral service for desperately-needed medical attention. It was shatteringly obvious that the newcomers, the products of malnutrition and neglected teeth and illnesses undiagnosed and untreated, crumbled readily under exposure and hunger. They had no money for medicine and, with the exception of Dr. Anne Keyl and Women's College Hospital, doctors and hospitals turned them away.

The remnants of the hippie movement who remained called themselves Yorkville Diggers Inc. Their tenacity almost cost them their sanity; by the end of 1967, they resembled men in shock.

The Yorkville Digger House opened in January, 1968, after a year's delay spent in trying to find a landlord who would rent for such a purpose. Very reluctantly, Metro Toronto made an old house available for $250 a month. It was supposed to accommodate no more than twenty residents at a time; a week after Digger House unlocked the front door, someone counted 115 young people sleeping there. There were appeals for food, to which the poor responded most generously: "they understand hunger," a resident explained. But many times there was no food at all in the Digger House, and one week the entire diet was rice. Another time, the residents dined exclusively on artichokes from a slightly spoiled bushel basket thrown out by St. Lawrence market.

A curious Board of Advisors was born, comprised of representatives from most of the community's social agencies, from the police, from the religious denominations who had donated the initial rent money, from elegant women's organizations. Three patrician ladies split the cost of putting twenty beds in the House, plus mattresses, pillows, blankets, and sheets.

There were miracles. One day a woman, a stranger, put $500 in the mail for Digger House. Holy Blossom Temple all but adopted the project, and the Jewish Family and Child Service sent staff help. One afternoon, when more than twenty young people were facing a day without food, Dr. Ernest Howse of the United Church sent a cheque for $100. Another time, when there was no money left for the rent, the Presbyterian Congress of Concern donated the required $250.

The Digger House staggered along, and gave social workers, employment services, doctors, and educators an opportunity to adjust themselves to a problem they had never faced: the waste products of the baby boom of the 1950's, cast aside mindlessly because the hurdles had been too high, accident victims of a collision between increased education requirements and decreased job opportunities for youth. The agencies and scientists were appalled at the extent and depth of the damage. A doctor who made a house call to Digger House every Thursday afternoon, free of charge, said he had never seen people so sick; a psychologist said that the diagnosis "agitated depression" would cover every resident; a social worker reported on their lack of "self-image," a school principal on their history of early school failure; Manpower noted that only a small percentage was employable.

Home-damaged and school-damaged, they had become a part of what the Durants term "unmoored youth"; they belong no-where, no one knows them, they have nowhere to go.

Some of the professionals who visited Digger House found the kids infuriating – they were too apathetic and unsure to keep appointments or follow instructions; others, who sat among them and listened, came to love them for their decency and candour and dignity.

Eventually, the gaps began to be filled. The Jewish Family and Child Service established the crisis center and referral service that the original Diggers had envisioned. They put an office in a trailer in the Yorkville area, manned it with young people who had street experience of their own, and helped build up a network of medical and dental services. Throughout the winter of '68-'69, Metro Toronto's Social Planning Council held meetings of an Ad Hoc Committee, chaired by Dr. Reva Gerstein, to consider the problems of displaced young people. During the summer which followed, the committee with no name launched Project '69, which provided transients with a night's lodging or a hot meal. The Community Service Organization at St. Paul's-Avenue Road United Church, the pioneer drop-in centre in the Yorkville area, cooked the meals.

Digger House, meanwhile, had evolved into what its director called a "group-living situation." Twelve homeless young people at a time live there, sorting themselves out with the aid of a relaxed staff. Some attend school, some find jobs, some make jewelry and leather goods to sell in Yorkville boutiques. When they leave, Digger House keeps in touch.

Financially, the House is sound. United Church, Atkinson Foundation, and Addiction Research Foundation grants are sufficient to operate the House until at least early 1970. Two other group-living homes, Oolagen and Gothic House, are not so fortunate and, in the summer of 1969, were in desperate straits. Curiously, in other parts of Canada where the need for a Digger House-like facility has been recognized, funds have been made available from provincial governments, or from the United Appeal, or from established social agencies. Toronto remains one of the few urban centres where such homes fight almost unaided for survival.

Yorkville today is a curiosity where geologists may find evidence of all the life forms that once existed there. Occasionally, but rarely, a genuine hippie saunters through; he has all he owns on his back, but he also owns himself – it shows. His visit is brief, for most hippies now are in universities, or living quietly on communal farms or in well-kept houses; a great many are artisans and merchants.

There is a scattering of motorcycle gang members in tribal dress.

The hippies, they say, turned the Vagabonds on to marijuana with a resultant improvement in that gang's violent tendencies; Satan's Choice, however, prefers beer, and there are dark stories of the gang-rapes in neighbourhood basements.

In the summer, migrant youths stop by to stare; in the winter, suburban teenagers inspect Yorkville boldly. These leave no trace; they are risking nothing, and there is vulgarity in their health and new shoes and lack of cavities.

The regulars now are those too tired to move. Plugged into drugs that are killing them slowly, they languish. They came to find love, but it's gone, and what can you do? As they decay, the police pick them over; so do the dealers who cut the product with poisons and the thugs who take the girls and sell them. The regulars watch it happening – but what can you do?

Part Two:

Little-Known Groups and Their Behaviour

1 Blacks in Toronto

Martin O'Malley

As the black population of Toronto rises to over 20,000 –
and keeps increasing – the issue of discrimination, and its
consequences, becomes more critical. How much is there,
and what forms does it take? How do the blacks view the
white majority, and what is their reaction to black power
movements south of the border? To what extent are Toronto's
Negroes united, and what methods are they using to gain
equity and equality?

The author of this piece, Martin O'Malley, talked with a
wide variety of Negro leaders and citizens in attempting to
answer the questions above. This article, which resulted from
his research, was originally titled, "A Tolerant People? Nice
to Believe. We're Really Just Polite Racists." In a few words,
the title indicates how the Canadian style of moderation and
prudence in all things, so characteristic of Toronto, shapes
racial relations in the city.

Mr. O'Malley is a well-known member of the staff of the
Toronto *Globe and Mail.* He has recently devoted himself to
a series of articles on prominent contemporary issues, in-
cluding the rise of black power groups outside of Toronto.
The following article first appeared in *The Globe Magazine* in
February, 1969.

A study titled "Perception of Discrimination among Negroes and
Japanese Canadians in Hamilton" has a rather broad category
called "differential treatment." Besides such things as a clerk
keeping a Negro waiting beyond his turn, the study says, "it
includes a landlady stealing a respondent's mail and spitting in her
soup. . . ."

131

Despite extremes, black militants and even moderates see us as polite racists. Like Canada itself, they say, our discrimination is cautious and somewhat reserved. "Like a hair across the cheek," a Negro woman told a Toronto audience, "you can feel, but can't see." Most annoying, especially to the militants, is that we insist we are so damn *tolerant*.

"The fundamental difference between Canada and the United States vis-à-vis the black man is not that you are less prejudiced – you just have fewer black people," says an angry West Indian.

The militants are a vociferous minority within a minority, but their influence is growing. Some read discrimination into the most innocuous instance of human frailty; like the Jew who applied for an announcer's job and complained he wasn't hired because of "p-p-p-prejudice." The housing problem, for example, which hits everyone, is a frequent source of racial bitterness.

There is no black ghetto in Toronto, although blacks refer to a "green banana belt" in the west-central section of the city. Many West Indians are scattered throughout the metropolitan area. Few are unemployed. Many have well-paying professional and managerial jobs.

The militants say these are blacks who have been bought off by The System. Many of the slogans have been imported from the United States. When some Detroit Black Panthers visited Toronto last December, one of them, Len Brown, "the deputy minister of education," complained on C.B.C. radio's *Don Sims Show*, "I can bet the police – the pig department – in Canada, in Toronto, is sitting around saying, 'We don't want to spark up anything.' And there are apathetic blacks sitting around thinking the whole situation is taken care of. They don't understand what's really happening. Canada is under a farce, a façade. It's a façade of being liberal. She's at the forefront of exploitation just like all the rest."

And yet at a Black Panther rally later that night, only about 100 blacks showed up – and about 500 white radicals. A *New York Times* reporter at the rally told me, "I would have been much more impressed if there were not so many whites."

This is not saying that there is no racism in Canada. If the black militants err in exaggerating, the whites err in underestimating the extent of Canadian discrimination.

Typical is the case of Myrtle Yearwood, a young Trinidadian girl who came to Toronto in 1965. On February 21, 1967, she had a co-worker, May Bothwell, phone an apartment building on Bathurst Street to ask about vacancies. She said she was calling on behalf of a coloured girl and asked if that mattered. A man told her it did not and asked her to call back next morning.

She called back, identified herself, and was told there were no vacancies. Another friend, Susan Gibson, called five minutes later and was told a bachelor suite would be available on March 1st.

Miss Yearwood visited the rental office that night and asked if there were any vacant bachelor suites. A woman said no. She asked about one-bedroom suites, and the woman said not until April 1st. Could she see a suite? The woman said it was too late. She left.

Two minutes later, Susan Gibson arrived and asked about vacancies. The woman took her to see two one-bedroom suites, one of which would be available March 1st, the other April 1st.

Hundreds of examples like this are on file at the Ontario Human Rights Commission.

In 1963-64, the second fiscal year of operation for the Commission, it received 284 complaints. In 1967-68, it received 3,673. Much of this simply reflects an increased awareness of the Commission. From April to December of 1968, however, there were 4,477 complaints, already substantially higher than for the entire 1967-68 fiscal year.

Dr. Daniel Hill, the forty-three-year-old, Missouri-born director of the Commission, does not deny that there is discrimination against Negroes in Toronto. About 50 per cent of the complaints involve Negroes, who make up only 1.5 per cent of Metro Toronto's population. But he says it is ridiculous to regard this minuscule percentage as a serious threat to law and order.

He believes Canadians should be able to cope with an increasing black population because they did not respond negatively to the 50,000 refugee slaves who fled here in the mid-nineteenth century. (His PH.D. thesis was on Negroes in Toronto, 1793-1865.) Besides, he says, human rights legislation in Canada, particularly Ontario, is much better than similar U.S. legislation.

Not all Canadians are so calm.

On the CBC-TV program *Viewpoint* last month, a Toronto newspaperman, Peter Dempson of *The Telegram*, reacted almost hysterically to what he said would be about 18,000 black immigrants to Canada in 1968. He warned that Canadians will find disturbing an increase in immigration from Africa, Asia, and the West Indies and a possible decrease in immigration from Britain and Western Europe.

"As long as we are selective and admit only the educated and skilled," he concluded, "we have no problem. But if the doors are opened to the riff-raff, then heaven help us. Watts, Cicero, Newark would be on us in no time."

Black militants say this is no way to improve race relations. "Take the bone with the meat," they argue. Jan Carew, a Toronto novelist and playwright who once was Guyana's director of culture, says Canada is in almost a unique position to do something constructive in race relations. "You are not going to solve the problem by shutting out immigrants."

He sees Canada as a wide-open country without the inherited problems of the United States or Britain. He finds healthy the self-deprecating, non-chauvinistic attitude of Canadians, as well as their apparent espousal of multi-nationalism.

So far, as with other ethnic groups, Toronto has only gained by its black culture. Our biggest Centennial event, for example, with the unlikely exception of the mayor's beard-growing contest, was a lively carnival week called Caribana '67. A week of uninhibited dancing, games, and colour added some bezazz to a generally complacent summer.

West Indian restaurants and groceries offer such specialties as curried goat, okra, saltfish, jack fruit, cho-cho, passion fruit, breadfruit, yams, mango nectar, papaya, and avocados. We can enjoy West Indian music ("rock steady") in West Indian night clubs and record stores. Toronto has black barber shops, beauty salons. People from Guyana, Jamaica, Grenada, Trinidad, Tobago, Aruba, and Saint Kitts have formed associations that make Toronto different from, say, Winnipeg. There is even a West Indian market in Scarborough run by an Italian.

Most Toronto Negroes are not militant. And they seem to prefer the terms Negro and coloured to black and Afro-American, especially the native-born. To a militant, black is a political term. Generally, it means an advocate of Black Power. (Some conservative West Indians will distinguish between black, brown, and coloured, all of which have specific meanings back home.)

Never call a militant coloured.

Despite the preponderance of non-militants, there is a growing awareness of blackness. Even whites admit black is in. Afro-wigs. African boutiques. Soul music and soul food. Eldridge Cleaver for President.

Sometimes it is clumsily expressed. A West Indian newspaper in Toronto ran an editorial last fall eschewing the word Negro, arguing it was created "by the white slave masters to separate the black race around the world," and that "it is suggestive of a head

scratching, grinning, inferior black man who lives in America."
It was followed by a notice from the Negro Women's Association.
And in a corner of the front page was an advertisement for
Norem Hairstylists – specialists in hair straightening.

Moderate blacks eye suspiciously attempts to "do a story on the
black community" (which might "stir up trouble") or compare
the black situation in Canada with the black situation in the United
States. Some deny there is racism here. Others say they are simply
tired of reading about it.

"The minute one begins to talk in Canada about race, they say
you stir up racialism," says Carew, a tall, muscular man who runs
three miles a day, winter and summer, and has a karate black belt.
"I say I *expose* it. It is there. You expose it, you put it out for
scrutiny and begin to dismantle it. You don't go through the
hypocrisy of saying you don't have it."

Even the moderates, if you talk with them long enough, will give
you examples of discrimination. Sociologists say blacks feel the
brunt of whatever racism exists here because of their "high visibility factor."

Accurate statistics are not available, but Canada's Negro population probably exceeds 60,000. Toronto has about 22,000
Negroes. In 1961, according to the census, Canada had 32,000 and
Toronto only 3,000. Dr. Hill says it is important that a better count
of ethnic groups be taken.

The main source of black immigration is the West Indies, but
more Negroes are coming here from Britain and the United States
because of increased racial tension. More are coming to Ontario,
too, from the Maritimes. Negro immigrants to Canada in 1968
numbered more than 15,000, and final figures may show about
20,000.

Dr. Hill urged the Personnel Association of Toronto last fall to
take definite action "to forestall the racial strife and divisiveness"
of the United States. He was speaking to them as employers.
Housing is another crucial area, he said.

Don't panic at Black Power. Some militants say Black Power,
in the sense of black awareness, is what prevented any serious
racial outbreaks in the United States last summer. Frustration has
been channelled more constructively into black identity. But others
will tell you it is merely the calm before the revolution.

More emphasis on black (and Indian) history in the schools
would help. Denny Grant, a Halifax West Indian, complains
bitterly of his Anglo-Saxon textbooks: "In botany, I had to study
British plants which I had never seen. The plants I knew by sight

and touch (mango, guava, sugar apples) were not even mentioned. I wrote poems about the oak, the elm, the pine tree, and the birch, which I knew only by imagination and picture."

José Garcia, secretary of Toronto's Afro-American Progressive Association, came to Canada from the West Indies island of Aruba in 1965. A stocky young man, he speaks in a deep, husky voice and lives in a small walk-up flat on Bloor Street West with his white wife and their pudgy two-year-old daughter. Canadian society, he says, is "racist to the core." Despite his militant posture, he has a rather warm, engaging personality.

Is the A.A.P.A. some sort of Canadian chapter of the Black Panther Party for Self-Defence?

"We're part of the same political line, which is a Marxist-Leninist line. Why call it a Black Panther Party? It's a nationalist thing. The struggle internationally takes different phases. Like in Vietnam. We identify with the Vietnamese. They're struggling for us. . . ."

He had never lived in an Anglo-Saxon society before coming to Canada. "I wasn't prepared for this Anglo-Saxon . . . *thing.* Christ, I used to get on a bus, and I could feel it in the air, the tension. I've been through all the stages – where the man says the room has just been rented, where the job has just been taken."

A friend of his, a young black social worker who was born and raised in Toronto, said he did not want his name mentioned because he might lose his job. Both men said Toronto has the beginning of a black ghetto, and they drew up a map of an area bounded by Queen, Bathurst, Harbord, and University.

Garcia's friend says Toronto is a great place to live, but he finds a special warmth when he visits the black ghettos in the United States. His father was a barber. He has many white friends outside the ghettos, however.

They both agree there is not enough oppression in Toronto to unite the blacks. "The general feeling of blacks here is, 'I'm all right, Jack,' " says Garcia's friend. "The quantity of blacks here isn't a threat," adds Garcia, "but it has grown five times [more like 10] since 1957. It's not a threat yet, like in England."

Like in England. Many see a resemblance.

In 1956, the *London Observer* did an article on West Indians after 17,000 had come to Britain in the first seven months of that year. It ended by saying they "tend to keep later hours than their British neighbours and landladies, particularly on Saturday nights, but they are hospitable and have found it sometimes works wonders to invite their neighbours and the landladies to join in. In short, the West Indians long ago won British affection."

On September 2, 1958, the *New York Times'* Drew Middleton began a dispatch from London: "Shouting, 'Down with the niggers,' rioters swept through the Nottingham district of London late tonight in a renewal of race riots."

At the Black Panther rally in Toronto last December, 600 jammed the Ontario College of Education auditorium on Bloor Street West. A pretty, mini-skirted girl dispensed red Che Guevara flags in the lobby. A huge, moustached Negro sold books at a table (titles: Honky-this, Whitey-that, sex, and racism). Slogans represented the latest ideological hemlines.

Three Black Panthers from Detroit sat at a long table in front of the stage. They wore khaki jackets, khaki pants, black tams, and black sweaters. Burnley (Rocky) Jones of Halifax was there. And Jan Carew. And Garcia, of the A.A.P.A., a Black Power group that is so exclusively black he is not even permitted to bring along his white wife. (About 100 show up at weekly A.A.P.A. meetings.)

Garcia opened the meeting with a short speech and the clenched-fist Black Power salute.

Rocky Jones stopped his speech once to lecture the largely white audience, which was applauding him furiously. "You're damn fools to applaud me when I call you racists." (The applause ceased.) "You're a symbol of what has happened to me. Every cop I ever came across, every teacher I ever knew, was white. . . ." (Rocky is not overly fond of white radicals.)

Ron Scott, deputy minister of justice for the Panthers' Michigan chapter, said, "They saw Watts and they saw Detroit, but they haven't seen Toronto yet." (Cheers.) "Canada has become a left-hand lackey of America," said Leonard Brown, deputy minister of education. "They get together collectively, and they become partners in crime. International thieves and thugs." (Cheers.)

After the speeches, a scratchy film on Huey Newton. Bullet holes in walls. There's Huey. (Chants of "Hugh-Eee . . . Hugh-ee.") There's Cleaver. (Cheers.) A quick shot of Stokely Carmichael. The whites don't seem to know whether he is still worth a cheer. (He is.)

A fat white policeman waddles from a building to the rear of a cruiser, amply stocked with rifles, helmets, tear gas grenades, and other riot-fighting equipment. (Snickers.) "Honky Power," grunts a voice from the balcony.

The white radicals are almost sadly alienated. They watch the black militants stroll through the crowd, and they listen to the hearty, slapping sound whenever two of them embrace. Their whiteness, unfortunately, is indelible.

While the militants blame capitalism for all racist evils, Wilbert Richardson, a successful black businessman in Toronto, sees employment opportunities in Canada as the reason for our relatively tranquil atmosphere.

"I live in a world where monetary remuneration is a driving force," he says in his office at Wayne Distributors and Advertising on Queen Street East. While he does not accept the A.A.P.A.'s Marxist-Leninist philosophy, he can understand why its members think and feel that way.

"Black militancy is misunderstood. You need some degree of militancy in any revolution. It adds impetus to the movement."

He came to Toronto from Pennsylvania in 1947, worked at Massey-Ferguson as a welding inspector, then went into advertising with Mercury Distributors, now one of his competitors. He has seven Negroes on his staff of forty-eight. His firm's annual gross is $2 million.

He once tried to buy a $45,000 house on Parkdale Road, and the real-estate man said the other homes on the block would depreciate by $20,000. Richardson went to newspapers and television for help, and the man eventually went out of business. But he never did buy the house.

"Most Negroes in Toronto would be hard-pressed to find any incidents," says Dr. Joseph Alban Liverpool, a West Indian who came to Canada in 1941. He admits that he might have had it soft as a doctor. He directs a $250,000 medical clinic on College Street, surrounded by corned-beef-and-pastrami signs, tiny real-estate offices, and the smell of warm, crusty bread. When he began practicing medicine in 1956, he was the only black doctor in town.

He was called to a house in Toronto's west-central section one Saturday night by the Academy of Medicine. He knocked on the door, a white man opened it, then slammed it in his face. He knocked again, said he was the doctor, and told the man he might as well let him in because he would be charged for the call anyway.

The man's brother was lying on the floor with a stroke. Dr. Liverpool took him to St. Joseph's Hospital, and he eventually recovered – and became one of Liverpool's patients until he died a few years ago. The man who slammed the door in his face is still a patient.

At his clinic, six black G.P.s, six specialists (two black), and a black dentist handle an average of 130 patients a day, 35 per cent white. He says the racial situation in Canada has improved greatly in the past fifteen years. "The Panthers would be hard-pressed to convince the average Negro in Toronto that he hasn't any rights."

Some accomplishments of the Ontario Human Rights Commission are impressive, especially when you consider it has hardly any legislative teeth. The Ontario Human Rights Code provides for a maximum fine of only $100. Most of the Commission's work is done by persuasion, and its most effective weapon is exposure. "People in Canada do not like to have their prejudices made public," Dr. Hill said.

Six Toronto West Indians complained in 1966 that a U.S. firm discriminated against them when it was hiring men for an Iowa construction project in the city. The Commission prepared to hold a formal enquiry at Queen's Park, and the company made a settlement with the men before the hearing. It paid them $28,600 for wages they would have earned had they been hired. Few formal hearings are required.

A formal enquiry was held into a complaint from Allen Eugene Walls, a twenty-year-old Essex County Negro who said he was denied accommodation at a Windsor apartment because of colour. He said he phoned the proprietor last April after reading an advertisement for a suite. The man told him to come and see him. Walls later phoned to ask if the fact that he was Negro made any difference.

"You know how coloured people are," the man said. Walls hung up when the man began telling him about all the trouble Negroes were getting into. He wanted a suite in Windsor because he had a job there. He finally managed to get one eleven weeks later, and he submitted an expense account of $153 to the Commission for travel costs to and from work.

The man testified at the hearing that when he said "nigger," he did not mean Negro. He meant a "destructive person" or "a person who does not live within the law." But he signed a statement that read: "I would prefer to have an empty house rather than rent to coloured people and have it destroyed." Enquiry Chairman Horace Krever recommended that the man pay Walls the $153. The man said he would appeal the decision; the appeal has yet to be heard.

Another file at the Ontario Human Rights Commission describes an incident in which a Hamilton landlord repeatedly called a dark-skinned tenant a "God-damned Gypsy Armenian Turk," slapped him in the face, twisted a towel around his neck, and tried to bite him.

Dr. Wilson Head, born in Atlanta, Georgia, came to Canada

nine years ago and says he has not come up against a single case of overt discrimination. He does not say there is no discrimination in Canada, just that he hasn't met it head-on.

He worked in Windsor five years before coming to Toronto, and now he is research director of the Social Planning Council of Metro Toronto. "I was surprised to find how little discrimination there was here. The difference between Detroit and Windsor? You can almost feel it in your hands."

Despite all this, he sees racial violence as inevitable, even in Canada. He said it will probably come from Canada's Indians. (The A.A.P.A. is considering opening its black-only meetings to the Indians in order to help them organize as part of the "oppressed" Third World). Negro racial violence is unlikely because of the small numbers, he said, but something like the housing shortage could prompt lower-income whites to strike out against such "high visibility" targets as the blacks.

Historically, there were a few hundred Pawnee and Negro slaves in Canada in the eighteenth century, primarily in the Niagara district. In 1793, the province passed An Act to Prevent the Further Introduction of Slaves and to Limit the Term of Forced Servitude Within This Province. It provided that the children of slaves be set free at age twenty-five. In 1834, the Emancipation Act abolished slavery in the British Empire.

William Lyon Mackenzie once told a meeting in Philadelphia that equality could be seen in all its glory in Upper Canada. He was referring to a coloured man named Butler in the town of York who had a white man and women servants from Europe looking after him and his black children.

Today as then, though, looking for bad examples in other countries seems rather futile. Dr. Eugene Carson Blake, then secretary-general of the World Council of Churches, said in 1963, "It is always easy to point to a worse situation somewhere else: in the United States we could always point to South Africa, and in the North to Mississippi and Alabama. I will not draw the lesson there may be for Canadians in this regard."

Militant blacks do draw the lesson: if their population is too small to be a threat, the Indian-Eskimo population is not. And they are living in conditions often worse than in some Southern states. And they numbered 125,000 in 1941, 220,000 in 1961, and about 250,000 now.

2 Alienated Youth

John Byles

Youthful alienation seems to reach its peak in urban centres, where adults never cease asking, "How do they get that way?" In Toronto, profound concern was expressed in 1966 for the city's alienated young people, symbolized by those aimless youths hanging around suburban plazas or drifting off to Yorkville. An impressive citizen's committee was organized under the chairmanship of Trevor F. Moore of the Imperial Oil Company, and a two-year study was launched with Dr. John Byles as research director.

In September, 1969, an impressive, book-length report, *Alienation, Deviance and Social Control,* was released to the public by the study's sponsoring body, the Ontario Department of Education. Using the most up-to-date statistical methods and techniques of sociological research, the study looked into the character and extent of alienation and deviance among selected samples of middle- and lower-class youth in Toronto. The study is far and away the most carefully researched and perceptive examination of urban youth to appear as yet in English-speaking Canada. The chapters of the report which follow describe its aims, methods, and basic findings.

Dr. Byles is currently teaching at McMaster University in the Department of Psychiatry. This is his first major sociological publication.

INTRODUCTION

Purpose and Nature of This Study

This research is concerned with understanding the processes by which young people become alienated from the society in which

141

they have been born and nurtured. Alienation of young people has become a most important concern, not only in Canada, but around the world. Youth in many countries are in revolt against the "establishment," whether it be political, economic, social, religious, legal, or educational. Stories about youth power, variously labelled "student," "Black," "flower," "red-guard," and others, assail us from the news media. Though there have always been a "generation gap" and a "rebellion" of youth, the present revolt takes on startling new dimensions; it is frequently well-organized and highly committed. It employs effective strategy, and it is often violent.

The backdrop of this study, then, is larger than just adult concern with alienated youth in a Canadian metropolis; it is also the self-concern of young people growing up in a world characterized by revolutionary change, a world in which rapid technological progress is endangering the very existence of our present social institutions. But for present purposes the study must be limited, for it cannot account for all the youth in the world, or even in Toronto for that matter. Nor can it explore all the ramifications of the term "alienation." It is confined to alienation of young people between twelve-and-a-half and eighteen-and-a-half years of age from the institutions of social control (family, school, church, organized recreation, work, and the law) as they exist in several communities of Metropolitan Toronto. While both "delinquents" and "hippies" were among those interviewed, this study is not primarily concerned with any types as such. Rather, it is a beginning exploration in an attempt to discover the factors or forces that contribute to the alienation of young people from society. . . .

METHODOLOGY

The Analytic Survey Method

The approach used in this study is referred to as "analytic survey," which means that data is gathered in the "field" rather than in a laboratory, and phenomena are measured in a way that permits the testing of hypotheses about the relationships between different phenomena. A "simple survey" would be simply counting and categorizing some variable, such as "religious affiliation" of families, in an area. Thus we might discover that 60 per cent are Protestant, 15 per cent are Roman Catholic, 10 per cent are Jewish, and the other 15 per cent belong to a dozen other minor sects. An analytic survey would go further, to discover whether these religious differences were related to something else, such as contributions to United Appeal.

This study is considerably more complex in that it is investigating relationships between twenty-three variables, but the procedures are essentially the same. Briefly, the procedural steps are:

1) Defining the community, or population of interest.
2) Selecting a sample that is representative of that community.
3) Collecting the data from those subjects selected from the sample.
4) Collating all the data from all subjects.
5) Analysing the data, using statistical methods appropriate to the hypotheses.

Though seemingly straightforward, this method can become very complex, as the following illustrate.

The population of concern in this study was the youth of Metropolitan Toronto. Short of spending many years and vast sums of money, there is no way of sampling and interviewing this enormous population. Some concessions had to be made.

Sampling Method and Design

The first phase, which was mainly to develop and test methodology, was conducted in a suburban community of one of the boroughs. A sample (stratified by age and sex) of 155 young people was selected randomly from a list of nearly 3,000 youths between twelve-and-a-half and eighteen-and-a-half years of age known to be residing in the community. The list was compiled from the enrollment records of the schools serving the community and included "retirements" as well as those still in school. A table of random numbers was used to ensure a "random" selection of the sample. This random selection of sample subjects is the best method known for obtaining a sample that represents the population of interest and allows making conclusions about the entire population from which the sample was taken.

A considerably larger sample of young people (508) was interviewed in the second phase, and instead of one, they represented four "communities" of Metropolitan Toronto youth. The subjects from the "North" community reside within an area of about four square miles bounded on all sides by main traffic arteries. It is a community of fine homes, pleasant parks, no industry, and has about the lowest rate of juvenile delinquency in Metropolitan Toronto. The subjects in the "South" sample live in an area of approximately the same size. It is an area of small crowded homes, interspersed with various small and heavy industries. There are few parks, though the area has several recreational facilities. Also, it has one of the highest juvenile delinquency rates in Metropolitan Toronto. Forty per cent of the fathers in the North area completed university, compared with only 2 per cent of fathers in the South; nearly 20 per cent of the North families had incomes greater than $20,000 per year, compared with 1 per cent in the South; about 60 per cent of the fathers in the North area are in "professional" or "semi-professional" occupations, compared with only about 6 per cent of the fathers in the South. Thus, North and South represent two quite different residential communities within the City of Toronto.

Again, lists of the names of youths in the North and South communities were compiled from the records of the schools serving these communities (sixteen schools in all), and stratified random samples were selected for interviewing. One hundred and seventy-one subjects representing a population of nearly 1,000 youths living in the North area and 185 out of a population of nearly 2,000 youths living in the South area completed interviews. The population density (of youths between twelve-and-a-half and eighteen-and-a-half years of age) of the South area is about twice that of the North area.

Obtaining a sample of Toronto youths confined in correctional institutions (D.C.S.) required a different strategy. Though its data processing branch, the Department of Correctional Services provided the project with a list of all incarcerated Toronto youths over twelve-and-a-half years of age. Again, a stratified sample was selected, but getting to these subjects to conduct interviews required travelling to all the training schools in the province. Youths over sixteen come under the jurisdiction of another branch of the Department, which necessitated visiting the reformatories.

Altogether different problems were encountered in obtaining a sample of the "heads" – young people who have voluntarily opted out to take up residence in Yorkville, who refer to themselves as "heads," not "hippies." This follows from their conviction that in choosing to leave the "straight" society, they were using their heads; it was a conscious, deliberate, and (to them) an intelligent decision. The term "hippie" is used by people in the "straight" society and is viewed by most "heads" as a derogatory term. In view of the fact that the audience here is mainly from the "straight" society, the term "hippie" will be employed simply to prevent confusion.

Two eminently qualified interviewers who had lived in Yorkville and worked with the hippies for several years devised a unique strategy. Armed with a table of random numbers, the interviewer would enter a "pad" (house where hippies live) and ask each person present at the time the day of the month of his or her birthday. This produced numbers ranging from one to thirty-one. The interviewer would then go down the table of random numbers until he came to a number corresponding to somebody's date of birth. If that hippie was from Toronto and within the required age range, he was asked for an interview. The only other requirement was that he was not "high" on a drug at the time. This procedure was followed until fifty good interviews had been conducted.

The "stratification" of the sample mentioned above is merely a technique for ensuring a reasonably even distribution of subjects in each cell. The meaning may be clarified by the following tables showing the samples of youth interviewed in each phase of the study.

TABLE I

SAMPLE DESIGN: SUBJECTS INTERVIEWED

PHASE I (Suburban)

	Age Group I 12.5 - 14.5 yrs.	Age Group II 14.6 - 16.5 yrs.	Age Group III 16.6 - 18.5 yrs.	Total
Boys	25	26	29	80
Girls	25	25	25	75
Total	50	51	54	155

TABLE II

SAMPLE DESIGN: SUBJECTS INTERVIEWED

PHASE II

	Boys Age Groups			Girls Age Groups			
	I	II	III	I	II	III	Total
North	25	32	30	25	29	30	171
South	27	33	38	26	28	33	185
Yorkville		4	20	1	3	22	50
D.C.S.	18	28	27	7	18	4	102
Total	70	97	115	59	78	89	508

As expected, most Yorkville youth are in age group III (16.6 to 18.5 years), though one girl was under 14 years, 6 months.

The D.C.S. girls in age groups I and III include all the Toronto girls in custody at the time of interviewing; the majority of confined girls are evidently in the 14.6 to 16.5 age range.

Every effort was made to interview each subject selected so as not to distort the randomness of the sample. The initial contact (for North and South) was a letter from the Project office to the subject requesting his or her co-operation as a respondent. Enclosed with this letter was another addressed to the parent or guardian requesting their authorization for an interview and a stamped return envelope.

As the permission slips returned to the office, they were assigned to interviewers who then telephoned the subject and arranged an appointment for the interview. Subjects who did not return a permission-to-interview slip were telephoned; interviewers would visit the home in a final attempt to elicit co-operation.

The interviews for North and South subjects were conducted in social agencies, recreation centres, and churches within the area; every effort was made to make the time and place of the interview as convenient as possible for the subject.

For this kind of survey research, the refusal rate was remarkably low, as the following table indicates:

TABLE III

REFUSALS AND OTHER LOSSES FROM SAMPLE

	North	South	Suburb (Phase 1)
Refused to be interviewed	9	24	6
Moved, or unable to locate	36	68	17
Disqualified from sample for other reasons*	1	2	1
Total "lost," all reasons	46	94	24
Number of completed interviews	171	185	155
Refusal rate	5%	11.5%	3.7%

*Includes illness, inability to understand or respond to questions, and evidence of fabrication.

Though accurate information on reasons for refusal was not obtainable, it is our guess that the higher rate in the South is partly attributable to greater feelings of suspicion and mistrust of "authority" among both the more economically deprived and the recent immigrants from Europe in the area. In the North, refusals stemmed partly from fear of invasion of privacy, as indicated by one father who wrote to the Project, "I am most disturbed with your high-handed approach directly to my daughter. . . ."

Interview Method

A part-time staff of twenty interviewers greatly helped to expedite the data collection in the final study. All had previous training and experience in interviewing and were given additional training by the Project Director in the use of the interview used in this study.

Three interview schedules were used in the second phase. One lengthy schedule was given to all 508 subjects, and two supplementary schedules were added – one for Yorkville subjects only, the other for D.C.S. subjects only. Minor revisions had to be made in the main schedule for the Yorkville and D.C.S. subjects in order to make the data comparable with the North and South groups. Questions were re-phrased to elicit responses relating to their last year of living at home in Toronto, rather than to their present condition. Neither group was asked the questions pertaining to "contact with the law," since this was explored in greater detail in the supplementary schedule. Nor were Yorkville subjects asked about their Yorkville "identification" or "participation," since they were all presumably living in Yorkville by choice at the time of interview (July, 1968).

As the interviews were completed, the information was "coded" on large sheets in preparation for key-punching. All the data were analysed by electronic computer.

Data Analyses

Several kinds of statistical analyses were made in order to answer the variety of research questions raised. The set of hypotheses regarding the interrelationships between alienation, deviance, and social control, and the relationships between each of these and the twenty independent variables, were tested by multiple regression analysis.

The set of hypotheses dealing with "similarities and differences" between the eight subgroups in the total sample was tested by (a) Bartlett's test of homogeneity, (b) one-way analysis of variance, and (c) Duncan's new Multiple Range test.

Simple correlation analyses were also made of:

1) The "like," "power," and "fairness" scores for adult authorities.
2) The sub-scores (family, school, church, etc.) that contribute to the Alienation Index.
3) The Social Control Index scores for parents and Alienation Index score for family; the Social Control Index score for teachers and Alienation Index score for school, etc.

It should be noted that all decisions regarding the hypotheses are based on these analyses; hence the selection of appropriate statistical devices is of crucial importance to research method and design. Hopefully, even readers uninitiated in statistics will find the following chapter on the findings of this research understandable. . . .

SUMMARY AND CONCLUSIONS

Introduction

This study was prompted initially by community concern for "unreached" youth. Through difficulties encountered in attempting to define the term "unreached," the focus shifted to concern with the process of alienation. We assumed that the "unreached" are those youths who have become alienated from the community's institutions of social control, such as family, school, church, and so on. We assumed, also, that the most needed and potentially useful knowledge would be that which increased our understanding of how young people come to be alienated from these social institutions. For only with this kind of knowledge can those concerned about the problem of alienation of youth develop programs that might deal with the problem more effectively.

Two other processes presumed to be related to alienation are included in the study: "deviance" (youth's proclivity to engage in deviant behaviour) and "social control" (pressure exerted on youth to prevent them from engaging in deviant behaviour). The first question, then, is whether these three processes are interrelated.

The second question is, what are the factors, forces, or conditions in community life that contribute to, or are somehow related to, these processes of alienation, deviance, and social control? Twenty variables thought to have some connection with these processes were included in the data for analysis.

We are interested, too, in how these processes develop among the so-called "normal" youth living in Toronto communities. Thus, random samples of young people from two very different communities were selected for interviewing. On the assumption that hippies and delinquents represent more extreme types of alienated youth, random samples of Toronto-raised hippies and delinquents were also included in the study. Altogether, 508 boys and girls between twelve-and-a-half and eighteen-and-a-half years of age provided the data for this study. Some rather sophisticated statistical tests were made of this abundant data (possible only with a computer) in order to derive the maximum information in the most efficient manner.

What are the main conclusions to be drawn from this plethora of statistics? We will now attempt to synthesize what seem to be some of the major conclusions about alienation, deviance, and, to a lesser extent, social control.

Alienation

The terms "alienation" and "integration" are used throughout the study to refer to the relationship between youth and a number of institutions that socialize and acculturize youth into our society. These institutions are the family, education, religion, recreation, employment, and the law. Together they create and express the collective values and standards of society. Identification with and acceptance of these values and standards are indicative of integration; rejection of and disdain for these values and standards are indicative of alienation. When we speak here, then, of youth being more or less alienated (or integrated), we mean the degree to which youth identify with or reject the values and behavioural standards represented by these institutions in our community. In other words, "alienation" can only be defined and understood within a specified context; our context is the network of social institutions mentioned above.

We have found that it makes no sense to talk about the "alienated" as if they were some easily distinguishable type of youth; they do not fit neatly into any kind of pattern. Although the hippies tend to be typed in this way, they are undoubtedly only a small fraction of the alienated youth in a city like Toronto. In every community there are non-hippies who are as alienated from society's institutions as any hippie. They are not recognizable, though, by their dress, hair, or behaviour. At the other end of the continuum are the extremely integrated youth; these, too, are a minority. The majority of youth are alienated to some degree from at least one of the six institutions included in this study. Some alienation, then, is "normal."

The varieties or patterns of alienation are dependent on the number of institutions being considered. There are, for example, sixteen varieties of alienation-integration possible if we limit our social system to four institutions (e.g., family, school, church, and recreation). All sixteen were found to exist. Since the frequency distribution of all 508 scores on the Alienation Index was found to resemble the "normal curve" distribution, the picture of alienation among youths generally in the community can be thought of as illustrated below. At either end are the extremes, those who as a result of the integrative or alienative forces impinging on them have become either extremely integrated or alienated. About two-thirds of the population would be in the middle, "normal" range, integrated in some institutions, but at least partly alienated from others.

Our more immediate concern, though, is with a better understanding of what contributes to these alienating or integrating forces.

The first and perhaps most obvious conclusion from the findings is that we cannot talk about the alienation of youth; we can only

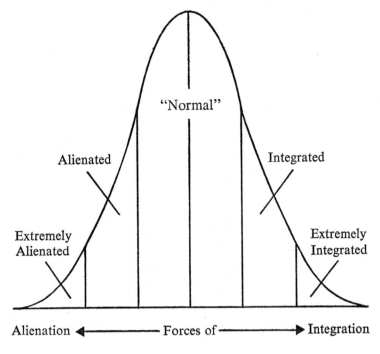

talk about the alienation of boys or of girls. This is true not only of alienation, but of other processes (deviance and social control) as well. Girls are very different from boys in ways other than biological; the factors or conditions that relate to the alienation of boys have very little influence on girls.

Boys tend to become increasingly alienated as they get older; girls do not. Also, conflict with parents and being called derogatory names by adults apparently contribute directly to the further alienation of boys, but not to the alienation of girls. As boys become more alienated they frequent Yorkville more often and form an identification with the Yorkville subculture. Girls tend to form an identification with Yorkville but do not frequent the area more often as their alienation increases. These findings apply only to the young people in North and South areas, nearly all of whom are in school and living at home. Youths who eventually become delinquents or hippies stand out in contrast with community youth; the girls, particularly, have reacted to conflict with parents. It may be that for girls, conflict with parents is tolerable up to a point, but beyond that "critical point" it becomes unbearable and requires decisive action, such as rebellion or escape.

The sense of powerlessness, of not having sufficient power or authority to make choices and decisions, is also likely a cause of boys' alienation, but this, too, is unrelated to the alienation of girls. Perhaps in our culture girls do not expect to have the same freedom for self-determination accorded to boys; they expected to be more obedient and submissive, and they are. Girls seem to be more sensitive and reactive to social approval given by adults; their alienation may be intensified when these needs for adult approval are not adequately met.

Girls are equally alienated (or integrated) at all levels of social class, whereas the prevalence of alienation among boys increases as social class level increases. Alienation is not a product of poverty; if anything, it is nurtured by affluence. The most alienated group included in this study, the Yorkville hippies, come predominantly from middle- and upper middle-class families in the community.

Finally, the processes of alienation and deviance are related but separate processes. Whether alienation causes an increase in deviant behaviour or deviant behaviour causes an increase in alienation is problematic; very likely it is a bit of both. As a youth becomes alienated from an institution (e.g., family), he is less influenced by the control attempts made by the adults (parents) and may thereby be more susceptible to opportunities to deviate.

Indeed, much deviant behaviour can be attributed to the desire to "put down" or retaliate against adult authority. This kind of deviance only adds fuel to the fire, creating a response in adults that alienates the youth even more. Each process, then, serves to escalate the other.

Deviance

The deviant behaviour of youth is of far greater concern to adults generally than is their alienation. Indeed, it is really only the deviant behaviour that arouses anxiety and creates consternation among adults. If hippies, for example, did not look or behave so differently from other youth, they would not constitute a "problem" for adult society.

The process of deviance (developing patterns of deviant behaviour) is different from, but related to, the process of alienation. Not all "alienated" youths are deviant, nor are all "deviant" youths alienated. Just to clarify the picture, the process of "delinquency" should also be included in this discussion. Deviance is often confused with delinquency, but the terms are not synonymous. "Delinquency" is used here to mean the process by which a youth becomes a delinquent; this includes, in part, being apprehended, tried, and convicted for committing some form of illegal behaviour. We have found that while delinquents tend to be more deviant than the average, many if not most of the more deviant youth are not delinquents.

Although we have stated that putting youths into categories is dangerously misleading (and it is), the diagram of these three

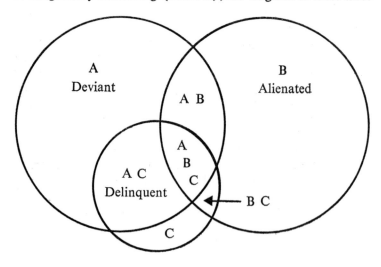

categories (alienated, deviant, and delinquent) is presented simply to clarify somewhat the interrelationships between them. Thus all the following "types" are possible:

A: Deviant, but not alienated or delinquent
B: Alienated, but not deviant or delinquent
C: Delinquent, but not deviant or alienated
AB: Alienated and deviant, but not delinquent
AC: Deviant and delinquent, but not alienated
BC: Alienated and delinquent, but not deviant
ABC: Alienated, deviant, and delinquent.

It is little wonder that attempts to categorize youth only add to the confusion. If "alienated," "deviant," and "delinquent" were three clearly definable and distinguishable entities, there would be seven possible pure and mixed "types" resulting. But they are not definable entities, as we have seen. A youth is not simply a "deviant" or "non-deviant"; the only valid questions are, in what ways is he deviant and to what extent is he deviant?

Which brings us back to the process of deviance. We find that age (just getting older) is significantly related to the increasing deviance of boys, but not of girls. The tolerance for deviant behaviour of both boys and girls, however, increases as their deviance increases; this is about the only characteristic shared by both sexes. In contrast, the more deviant boys (in North and South communities) go to Yorkville less than the not-so-deviant; girls (North and South) tend to visit Yorkville more often as their deviance increases. We cannot conclude that Yorkville "causes" deviance, but it seems to provide a safer place for girls to express their deviance. Boys from non-English-speaking families are not as deviant as boys from English-speaking families, but with girls there is no difference. There is no support for the contention that "cultural conflict" is related to the deviant behaviour of either sex. Among boys in the community (North and South), deviant behaviour increases slightly with increasing family mobility and socio-economic status. The latter (greater affluence) is possibly related to the greater prevalence of drug use by boys in the middle- and upper middle-income families. The deviance of girls increases directly with the amount of derogatory social typing (name-calling) by adults that they experience; this again seems to indicate that girls are more sensitive and reactive to valuations made of them by adults. Indeed, this process of typing appears to play an important role in the development of delinquent girls.

Social Control

We are not able to formulate any firm conclusions about the process of social control on the basis of the measure (Social Control Index) used in the study. Just what it measures is difficult to determine, and the measure is too unstable to give confidence in the findings. Whatever it measures has little to do with behavioural conformity, obedience, or other indicators commonly thought of as part of the concept of social control. The difficulty created by this measure is likely a result of the way in which the scores from three scales were combined to create the Index. Greater reliability can be placed in the scales taken separately. Thus we find that "liking" for adult authorities is related to the alienation or integration of both boys and girls. Also, the more integrated youth tend to attribute greater power to adult authorities. Surprisingly, only girls react negatively to the "unfairness" of adults; this further confirms the idea of girls' greater sensitivity to adult authority.

It is quite possible that in spite of the difficulties inherent in the measure of social control, the picture presented by the findings is congruent with reality. The findings indicate a significant but modest relationship between social control (perceptions of adult authority) and both alienation and deviance; that is, as perceptions of adult authority become more negative, alienation and deviance both increase. However, as a group, the delinquent boys had the highest positive perceptions of adult authority.

It may be that among youth generally there is only a slight relationship between deviant behaviour and perceptions of adult authority. That is, most deviance and delinquency may develop in spite of, rather than because of, relationships with authority. Other studies of deviant behaviour among boys, such as the Sherifs',[1] suggest that most deviant behaviour develops out of the interaction (status-striving, etc.) that takes place in the peer group.

Virtually all existing literature on the subjects of social control and deviance is concerned only with boys. It is abundantly evident that there is little similarity betwen boys and girls in the manner in which these processes develop. Although the rates of delinquency may be lower for girls than for boys, our findings indicate that girls tend to be more alienated, and that the consequences of both deviance and alienation are much more severe for girls in our society than for boys. It is about time, we think, that some attention be given to the problems of girls.

The findings revealed many significant differences between the two deviant groups (Yorkville and D.C.S.) included in the study and between these deviant groups and the community-based (North and South) groups.

Both deviant groups manifest significantly more deviant behaviour than either North or South groups, but their patterns of behaviour also differ. The deviance of the Yorkville group leans toward drug use – a "social" and non-violent pattern, whereas the deviant behaviour of the D.C.S. youth is more expressively violent. Although both deviant groups are more alienated than North or South groups, the Yorkville youth are significantly more alienated than the delinquents. Further, the perceptions of adult authority held by the delinquents were similar to those held by North and South youth, but Yorkville youth viewed adult authority much more negatively.

These findings lead us to suggest that the cause-effect relationships between alienation, deviance, and social control function quite differently among youths destined to become hippies than among youths destined to become delinquents.

We suggest that the hippies become alienated from society's institutions partly as a consequence of their everyday transactions with adult authorities (parents, teachers, etc.) but probably more as a consequence of developing differences between their values and the values of the "establishment." With them, deviant behaviour is not a contributing "cause" of alienation but, instead, is a symptom or a consequence of their alienation.

Conversely, it is suggested that deviant behaviour is a contributing cause of delinquency, but alienation is not. The deviant behaviour of the delinquent group correlates significantly with their perceptions of adult authority and may be viewed partly as a reaction to negative feelings toward authority. With the delinquents, though, these negative feelings toward adult authority are not related to their alienation. Their alienation is more a consequence of their deviant behaviour, which in turn causes them to be officially labeled "delinquent" and forcibly separated from the community and its institutions.

Thus, with the delinquent-prone youth, deviance is viewed as a "cause" and alienation as a "consequence" in the sequence, whereas with the potential hippie, the sequence is reversed. Also, the potential hippie tends to react to conflict with authority by withdrawing or "opting out," whereas the potential delinquent tends to react more by aggressive retaliation against persons or property.

Conclusions

Some of the gaps in present research have already been alluded to. It should also be recognized that this study is concerned only with urban youth; there are as yet no comparable studies on small-town or rural youth. Further, there is a tendency to assume that Canadian culture is identical to American culture, and that Canadian youth problems (e.g., delinquency) are the same as the problems of concern in the United States. Much of the research and literature on delinquency, for example, is based on studies of delinquent gangs in large American cities.

It is our contention that Canadian and American cultures are not identical, and our problems are not the same as those encountered in large American cities. This means that to understand the Canadian situation, we must do our own research, formulated on the problems as defined here.

Although it is the manifestation of deviant behaviour that arouses the ire of the "establishment," we believe that the deviant behaviour – whether student rebellion, violence in the streets, or use of hallucinogenic drugs – must be viewed as symptomatic of deeper underlying problems. These problems are exceedingly complex, and they are not problems of youth, but of the whole society.

It is fallacious to begin any assessment of these problems from the premise that the disturbing and disruptive behaviour of young people is simply an indication of "something wrong" with youth. Their behaviour is a reflection of the problems of the society in which they live.

Nor can we assume that all alienation is "bad" or "wrong." As Keniston says, "alienation may point more to a society that needs 'treatment' than to an individual in need of therapy."[2] It is quite possible that the extremely well-integrated youths are in a potentially more dangerous condition from a mental health point of view than are the alienated disturbers of the status quo. For society is changing at an ever increasing rate of acceleration. Our institutions are currently in a state of revolution, largely under pressure from youth. Those who cannot adapt to change may become, eventually, the most alienated.

The important questions, perhaps, are whether our institutions can change rapidly enough to meet the demands and needs of young people – not for today, but for the future – and whether this change can be brought about without severe dislocation of the entire institutional network or excessive alienation of youth.

Hopefully, this and further research into the process of alienation will provide some helpful clues as to how this change can be accomplished so that our social institutions can better prepare youth to make their maximum contribution to the world they will soon inherit.

3 Sex at York University

W. E. Mann

In 1959, with the encouragement of the University of Toronto, a new university was begun in Toronto, taking upon itself the hardly unusual name of York. For several years, its first independent campus was in a north-eastern suburb at Bayview and Lawrence. In 1965, a large new campus was opened at Keele and Steeles Avenues, and it opened its doors to a massive influx of students while the original campus, Glendon, was limited to about a thousand undergraduates. Located on the northern boundary of Metro, the new school has gained a reputation with the public for liberal, if not radical, innovations.

Its students, too, like students elsewhere in Canada, have engaged themselves in the transformations of our era. Among these transformations is that of the traditional codes of morality which fall within the scope of the "sexual revolution." In this article, Professor W. E. Mann, editor of this anthology, analyses that revolution and its effect at York by contrasting sexual mores there in 1969 with those he studied at other Canadian campuses earlier in the decade.

Although for some years certain investigators were unwilling to call it a revolution, it is well-recognized that a new climate of attitude and conduct in sexual relations is emerging in our universities. Due to the lack of careful studies of non-college youth in North America, it is impossible to claim scientifically that similar changes have occurred among unmarried working people, although this is certainly probable. But we can state with certainty that widespread moral uncertainty and confusion, along with a profound questioning of traditional sexual behaviour and attitudes, has infected the country's youth. And, of course, this phenomenon is not confined to North America but applies to practically all the leading Western nations.

Before studying sexual mores at York University, I had previously examined sexual norms at the University of Western Ontario, Glendon College (York), and the University of Calgary. In addition to comparing findings from a commonly used questionnaire administered to a random sample of students at these institutions, I had tried to ascertain the major variable associated with more liberal sexual behaviour patterns. Something of the findings of this inquiry were summarized in the conclusion of my study, *Canadian Trends in Premarital Sexual Patterns*. One discovery of special relevance to Toronto was the following:

> Students with big city and metropolitan residential backgrounds, having parents of high income and managerial and allied upper middle-class status, displayed more permissive attitudes and behaviour than those with small city or lower social rankings. Confirmation of such correlations is fairly common in the literature, including studies made in Sweden, Britain and the United States.[1]

Analysis of the data from these three studies suggests that it is not simply the social environment of the big city itself that generates more liberal thinking and behaviour, but certain "intervening variables." These include such conditions as: 1) greater secularization, reflected in the dearth of contemporary religious piety, the slacking off of church-going, and the rejection of Christian ideas on sex; 2) greater affluence, leading to more money for dates, greater access to a car; and 3) higher frequency of permissive middle- and upper middle-class family experiences. It was indicated in the data that students from the homes of affluent businessmen and men of professional standing tended to adopt more liberal ideas and practices. The same homes were less likely to be wedded to church and to specific religious norms. Many more attributes and characteristics of affluent family living and of the big city milieu need to be analysed more thoroughly before we can be certain of the precise dynamics inherent in this correlation between liberal sex behaviour and metropolitan residence, specifically with middle- and upper middle-class families.

Before looking at the patterns of sexual behaviour discovered at York University in 1969, it is interesting to glance briefly at two other Toronto campuses where "abbreviated" sex surveys were carried out in the late 1960's. The first of these, based on a mailed-out, thirty-seven-item questionnaire at the University of Toronto, was organized by students in the medicine and zoology faculty in 1968. Of 1,200 questionnaires sent out, 511, or 42 per cent of the total, were returned. Since this is less than half of the selected sample, certain findings likely represent a biased picture of the views and actions of the 26,000 full-time students at the university. It might be noted here that various studies, including my own investigations at the University of Western Ontario, indicate that those who volunteer to answer sex questionnaires often tend to be more liberal in their ideas than a strictly randomized sample.[2]

Quoting from an article in Toronto's *Globe and Mail* of November 14, 1968, it is possible to provide here some of the more interesting "findings" of the University of Toronto survey:

> More than 20 per cent of the unmarried students at the University of Toronto have sexual intercourse occasionally or often. . . . The survey also shows 36 per cent of unmarried respondents have had sexual intercourse at least once – six per cent fewer than results of surveys made at Cambridge University and at three New York City area colleges in the past year.
>
> Of the one in twelve unmarried coeds who have sex relations often, 42 per cent use birth control pills and 25 per cent use no contraceptives. . . . Of the one in nine males who have sex often, 35 per cent have relations with girls using the pill, and 14 per cent use no contraceptives with their partners. . . .
>
> The survey shows 42 per cent of students raised as Protestants no longer consider themselves as such. Of students raised as Catholics, 27 per cent left the Church. Of Jewish students, 18 per cent no longer consider themselves Jewish. While only 11 per cent of the respondents were raised as atheists or agnostics, 35 per cent now list themselves as such.
>
> Of lapsed Jewish unmarried males, 78 per cent have had sexual relations at least once. For lapsed Catholics the figure is 69 per cent, and for lapsed Protestants the figure is 43 per cent. Among lapsed Jewish unmarried females, none remains a virgin. Sixty per cent have sex frequently. Among lapsed unmarried Protestants, 53 per cent have had intercourse. Among lapsed Catholics, single females, 78 per cent are non-virgins. . . .
>
> Significantly more Protestant-reared students have lost their religion than have Catholics or Jews and almost all such students now list themselves as atheists or agnostics. Jewish-reared men and women students who are unmarried and have

lost their faith are more prone to have lost their virginity than are ex-Catholics and much more prone than are ex-Protestants. Unmarried Jewish men have frequent sex in more than twice as many cases (31 per cent) as do unmarried Catholic or Protestant men, while unmarried Jewish girls have a higher virginity rate than Catholic girls (78 per cent), Protestants (75 per cent) and atheist-agnostics (46 per cent). . . .

On questions about legalized abortion, the biggest pro-abortion response went to the case of a mother who would be harmed by giving birth. Abortion in the case of pregnancy through rape received the next strongest majority support. Then the case of a possibly deformed baby. Votes were almost split in the cases of "unwanted child" and "economic inability to support child." The only minority vote of the respondents went to the case of abortion because of out-of-wedlock pregnancy. There were 261 against abortion and 214 for it.

While Jewish women favored legalized abortion in all cases, Jewish men favored only three cases – pregnancy through rape, possible deformity and likely harm to mother. Both male and female Protestants and male Catholics approved abortion only in the same three cases. More than 70 per cent of Catholic female respondents opposed abortion even if the child were possibly deformed.

Of 499 students responding on the first source of sex education, 229 listed "friends" while only 131 listed "parents." Only two of the 499 learned from a doctor or nurse, only three from a clergyman and twenty-three from a school program. While personal experience was cited as the strongest influence on their sex attitudes by 240 or 49 per cent only 70 credited their parents with main influence and only 22 credited their church.

It is interesting to relate the degree of secularization – as indicated by the proportion of respondents of lapsed religious faith – to the high rates of pre-marital activity. This has been the standard finding of sex surveys in other places and countries for years. What is significant about the Toronto study, however, is the high lapsed rate among Protestants. One must add a caveat here, though, to the effect that it is most likely that the questionnaire respondents did not represent an accurate sample of the students on that campus – one cannot scientifically support the high lapsed rate produced in the 42 per cent sample.

In March, 1969, an economics instructor at Ryerson Polytechnical Institute (a downtown Toronto college with an enrollment of over 6,000 students) carried out a non-randomized survey among male students in some ten different classes. The 164 students surveyed came from the business, engineering, and arts faculties of the college. They filled out a short questionnaire in the classroom after being told that it would help compare Ryerson's sex attitudes and behaviour with that of other colleges. Such an opening statement, while serving to explain and justify the experiment, could easily have acted to bias the results in the direction of non-virginity; this may account for the high rate of premarital activity "discovered."

Quoting from an article in the Toronto *Star* of April 2, 1969, here are some of the main results of the Ryerson investigation:

> Sixty-six per cent [of the respondents] have had premarital intercourse. . . . Of these male non-virgins, 54 per cent said they had their first sexual intercourse at age eighteen or younger. Nearly 40 per cent said they had sexual relations at least once a month and 16 per cent at least once a week. Of the virgins, the largest group, 36 per cent said their chief reason for sexual abstinence was "lack of suitable opportunity." Twenty-three per cent said they had abstained from intercourse for fear of getting the girl pregnant.
>
> Only 23 per cent said they abstained because it was "morally wrong" and only one person – less than one per cent of the sample – said he had refrained . . . because it was "against the teaching of his church." For many people the most significant part of the survey may be the evidence of the massive erosion of fundamental religious beliefs among some students and the relative lack of religious influence on sexual conduct. To the question, "Do you believe in a Supreme Being?" 56 per cent of the students said yes, 13 per cent said no, and 29 per cent said they didn't know.
>
> There was hardly any difference between virgins and non-virgins on the question of the existence of God. Fifty-eight per cent of the virgins said they believed compared to 55 per cent of the non-virgins. To the question, "Do you believe in a life after death?" only 20 per cent . . . said yes, 46 per cent said no, and 32 per cent said they didn't know. Again, on this question the difference between virgins and non-virgins was very slight.

Commenting on the reason for the rather high rate of non-virgins at Ryerson, Mr. Fandrich, the instructor-investigator, suggested that it

> may be linked to the type of curriculm it [Ryerson] offers and the kind of student it attracts as a result. "The Ryerson student tends to be more work-oriented," he said. "He's more pragmatic in his approach – what kind of job will this course get me? The university student, on the other hand, tends to be more idea-oriented, interested in education for its own sake. Is it the case that the idea-oriented person is more inclined than the work-oriented one to refrain from premarital sex?"

Mr. Fandrich added that the work experience of some of the students, a large percentage of whom spend at least a year in a factory or other work situation before entering the college, could be another factor. Such experience, combined with a background closer to that of the working class and embodying less ambitious occupational goals, may tend to strengthen the Ryerson students' identification with working-class values, including the norms of that class with regard to sexual activity. It must be noted, however, that Mr. Fandrich's observation about the idea-oriented university student tends to be more true of the arts student than those in certain other faculties, such as law or business, where financial gain is often the major goal.

Moreover, when we compare our 1969 study of sex at York University with that from Ryerson, some of the results are not that different, and we are led to wonder at the necessity of postulating a working-class or pragmatic value orientation as distinguishing Ryerson from York students. Thus, some of the crucially interesting data from the York study are summarized in the following table.

TABLE I

PERCENTAGE OF 153 YORK STUDENTS WHO, IN THEIR
DATING BEHAVIOUR, HAVE ENGAGED IN:

	Necking	Petting A*	Petting B	Petting C	Coitus	No Answer
In the past three months, with someone being dated regularly or fairly regularly:						
Male	20.4%	7.5%	2.2%	24.7%	25.8%	19.4%
Female	15.0%	8.3%	8.3%	33.3%	21.7%	13.3%
In the past three months, with anyone:						
Male	17.2%	10.8%	3.2%	26.9%	29.0%	12.9%
Female	20.0%	10.0%	6.7%	35.0%	16.0%	11.7%
In whole lifetime, with someone really liked or loved, and on more than one occasion:						
Male	9.7%	8.6%	6.5%	26.9%	40.9%	7.4%
Female	8.3%	8.3%	6.7%	40.0%	30.0%	6.7%
In whole lifetime, with anyone:						
Male	7.5%	6.5%	3.2%	22.6%	50.5%	4.3%
Female	5.0%	8.3%	6.7%	40.0%	36.7%	1.7%†

* The definitions of Petting A, B, and C are as follows: A, contact with breasts over garments; B, contact with breasts under garments; C, further.

† The balance of 100 per cent, in each case, has gone as far as holding hands or kissing only.

Two other items on the York questionnaire throw additional light on the students' coital behaviour. One asked, "In your lifetime, with how many different partners have you had sexual intercourse?" The results here were as follows:

TABLE II

LIFETIME NUMBER OF SEXUAL PARTNERS

	Males	Females
One partner	18.0%	16.0%
Two partners	11.0%	13.0%
Three partners	4.0%	1.7%
More than three partners	19.0%	3.0%

The balance had not had intercourse. The results of the other question examining the frequency of premarital coitus within the past year follow in Table III.

TABLE III

FREQUENCY OF INTERCOURSE IN THE PAST YEAR

	No Answer	Once	Less than monthly	About monthly	About weekly	More often than weekly
Male	7.5%	5.4%	14.0%	10.8%	7.5%	3.2%
Female	5.0%	5.0%	8.3%	6.7%	5.0%	5.0%

The "No answer" group here raises some questions; could they not fit their relations into one of the five categories or had they some guilt over this question or did they wish to suggest – or pretend – premarital coital activity without actually having coital experience? The remainder of the sample had not experienced intercourse.

With this simple comparison of the York data with Ryerson and Toronto, it is appropriate now to describe the sociological procedures used at York. The aim was explicitly to examine a scientific random sample of 4 per cent of the total student body. The procedure used was as follows: the student directory was secured and every twenty-fifth student's name was noted. The student was then invited by letter to one of three opening questionnaire sessions, scheduled for after lecture hours in selected rooms on the campus. Those who failed to show up at these sessions were then telephoned and invited to newly planned sessions in succeeding weeks. For those (fifteen students) who had moved or could not be reached by phone, new names were drawn from the student directory by a random method. After more than a dozen questionnaire sessions spread over five weeks and scores of phone calls, a total of 153 questionnaires had been filled out. The approach of April final exams then ruled out further attempts to reach the others. The 153 completed questionnaires represented 85 per cent of the original 180 students sought for the survey; this is not a perfect or near-perfect percentage, but it is reasonably adequate and is clearly more reliable than the 42 per cent sample secured at the University of Toronto.

As indicated earlier, previous work by the author[3] and by others has demonstrated that volunteers tend to be more sexually permissive than non-volunteers. In short, it can be assumed that the 85 per cent who volunteered to answer the questionnaire are somewhat more permissive than the non-answering 15 per cent. Some of this latter group may have failed to show up either because they were more guilt-ridden than the average student or because a sex questionnaire might reveal their failure to measure up sexually to accepted standards – that is, it would reveal to them that they were sexually less active than conventional expectations. (Of course, some who failed to show up were simply expressing laziness or disinterest in the questionnaire process itself.) In brief, if the missing 15 per cent had all shown up, it is likely that our percentages for non-virginal males and females would be somewhat smaller. By how much, unfortunately, the present state of our investigation of sexual behaviour does not allow us to say.

The questionnaire which the York students were asked to answer had some 130 questions. Except for a few new questions, it had previously been used at four other Canadian campuses: University of Western Ontario, Calgary, University of New Brunswick,[4] and Glendon College at York. It will thus be possible to make some interesting comparisons between York and other universities, although the bulk of such analysis must wait for another article.[5]

At the outset of our analysis of the findings, it is essential to note the kind of students embraced in the York sample. Of the 153 respondents, males represented 61 per cent and females 39 per cent. Ninety-three per cent of the total were then unmarried; those married were asked to answer on the basis of their premarital experiences. In age, 44 per cent were over twenty, 27 per cent were twenty, 17 per cent were nineteen, and 10 per cent were only eighteen years of age; one per cent was sixteen years old. By faculty, 88 per cent were in arts, 9 per cent were in science, and 3 per cent were in business. Again, 45 per cent were in first year (a somewhat disproportionate number), 34 per cent in second, 16 per cent in third, and 4 per cent in fourth, with 1 per cent engaged in graduate work. The high percentage for first year may signify that freshmen at York are less blasé about questionnaires than older students and thus more prepared to answer them.

Overwhelmingly, the York students sampled were urbanized, secularized, and middle class. While 75 per cent had lived ten years or more in a city with a population of 350,000 or more (e.g., Toronto) and 10 per cent in a fair-sized centre (population 25,000 to 350,000), only 1 per cent had a farm and 6 per cent a small-town (population 1 to 4,000) background. Secondly, indices of church-going, prayer-saying, and attendance at week-day religious meetings indicate that these students have little use or time for organized religion. Only 22 per cent attend church or synagogue regularly (at least twice a month), 21 per cent say prayers regularly (75 per cent of the time, nights or mornings), and 10 per cent regularly attend one week-day church meeting or more. By religious affiliation, 15 per cent claim to be Anglican, 37 per cent Protestant, 20 per cent Jewish, 20 per cent Catholic, 3 per cent "other," and 5 per cent unattached; some 3 per cent admit they have no serious religious beliefs. In comparison with students at the other colleges previously surveyed, these percentages indicate a much higher degree of secularization.

In terms of family income, while 54 per cent say their parents gross over $9,000 a year, another 22 per cent say the family income ranges between $6,000 and $9,000 yearly. Only 5 per cent come from homes where the annual income is less than $4,500; seven per cent said family earnings were unknown to them. Parents' occupational background included 23 per cent in the semi-professional and professional category, 29 per cent in the managerial, top-executive, or business-owner category, 14 per cent doing skilled labour, and 7 per cent holding manual or unskilled jobs. Some 18 per cent claim a father of lower middle-class occupation, such as clerk, office worker, or salesman.

Another set of questions reveals that on some significant counts our sample at York was relatively typical of Ontario's youth, as known through statistics or conventional observations. Thus, by ancestry, 62 per cent are Anglo-Saxon, 22 per cent are of continental European origin, 7 per cent have mixed Anglo-Saxon and French blood or mixed Anglo-Saxon and other European blood; 7 per cent have another ancestry, and 1 per cent are French-Canadian. Their family lives are not untypical. Some 42 per cent say they got along very well with their parents during their 'teens, while another 44 per cent managed fairly well, 8 per cent fared less happily, and 5 per cent experienced a great deal of friction with one or more parents. Three-quarters of our respondents resided at home while attending the university, while 13 per cent were in college residences, 7 per cent in apartments, and 2 per cent either in rooming houses or in the home of a friend or relative. Exactly half the respondents report their parents to have been happy together; 18 per cent described their parents as "fairly happy," 21 per cent noted that "there were stresses, but these seemed rather natural," and only 7 per cent reported a great deal of quarrelling, to the point where the marriage seemed *often* on the verge of collapsing. Of the entire sample, 3 per cent came from divorced households and 1 per cent from separated households.

Only about a quarter of the sample felt that the sex instruction their parents had offered had been at all adequate: 6 percent described it as "entirely adequate," 10 per cent said "reasonably so," and another 10 per cent said, "It was all right." Thirty-five per cent received no sex instruction at all, and 40 per cent of the respondents found it either somewhat or very inadequate. Judging from other campus studies done in Canada, these figures are not extreme. In terms of school courses in sex education, only 25 per cent of the sample felt that these had been of either some or great help, while 42 per cent of the sample had received no such instruction at all.

In their responses to a broad range of questions, the York students generally exhibited a decidedly secularized and liberal or permissive attitude, which was in keeping with their rather permissive behaviour. Thus, some 55 per cent are not happy or satisfied with the social codes of our society with regard to premarital sexual relations, 31 per cent are uncertain on the issue, and only 12 per cent expressed satisfaction with these codes. Twenty per cent of the respondents said that they had once tried to keep to the teachings of the churches (or synagogues) on premarital behaviour, but that they had *lately* stopped trying, while 63 per cent claimed never to have paid any attention to the religious teachings which are still observed by 12 per cent of the respondents. Only 5 per cent of the sample believe that such religious standards provide a satisfactory and realistic guide for behaviour with the opposite sex. At the same time, while 7 per cent clearly admit they are confused as to the ethics of sexual behaviour, another 32 per cent confess to at least partial uncertainty or confusion.

Two questions in particular indicate something of the York students' attitudes toward realistic issues.[6] When asked, "How far is it all right for a young couple who are very fond of each other and have exchanged a pin, ring, or other token of affection (excluding an engagement ring) to go in expressing their affection?" 9 per cent of the respondents answered that necking activity was acceptable, 4 per cent chose Petting A, 7 per cent chose Petting B, 24 per cent chose Petting C, and 33 per cent answered that intercourse was acceptable. Nineteen per cent were uncertain. The most significant difference between the sexes on this question came at the choice between Petting C and coitus, the girls favouring the former as a stopping point, the men the latter: thus, 21 per cent of the men and 27 per cent of the women said that Petting C was the proper place to stop, while 38.7 per cent of the men and 25 per cent of the women said coitus.

The second question asked, "How far is it all right for an engaged couple to go in expressing their affection?" Here the figures are: necking, 4 per cent; Petting A, 2 per cent; Petting B, 2 per cent; Petting C, 10 per cent, and sexual union, 58 per cent![7] Again, 18 per cent admitted no clear or definite views. As with the earlier question, more girls than boys felt that the couple should stop at Petting C: only 7 per cent of the men chose this alternative, compared to 20 per cent of the women, while 64 per cent of the men and 46.7 per cent of the women opted for coitus. It is interesting that these percentages are from ten to fifteen percentage points higher than the figures secured in answer to the same question at other Ontario campuses only four years previously. Doubtless only a small amount of this difference can be attributed to the passage of time; the rest of the variation must be ascribed either to York's more liberal student outlook or to the inadequacy of our 85 per cent sample of its student population.

On homosexual relationships, an area not examined in previous surveys by the author, the findings are interesting. Only 17 per cent of the respondents considered such relationships to be inherently wrong or sinful; 7 per cent described homosexuality as "physically or mentally harmful if engaged in frequently." Twenty-seven per cent of the sample regarded such relationships as not a good idea, although not sinful, 19 per cent said they were all right for adults under certain circumstances, 5 per cent thought them quite natural, and 23 per cent were uncertain how to regard them. Only 1 per cent admitted to having engaged in homosexual actions during the previous two to three years; another 2 per cent failed to answer the question, a failure which makes one wonder.

Let us look now at certain salient aspects of the actual premarital behaviour of our sample. It is significant that three-fourths of our respondents have gone steady at least once. This pattern usually begins between the ages of fifteen and seventeen, somewhat later for boys than for girls. Half of the respondents had gone steady at least once or twice, but only 20 per cent more than twice. At the time of the survey, 48 per cent were not going steady, 15 per cent were going steady exclusively, 10 per cent were going steady but going out with others as well, 8 per cent were pinned, and 7 per cent were engaged. A quarter of the group said that they would have intercourse with their steady date on occasion, and about one-third would stop at Petting C. When asked what prevented them from going further with someone they loved, 19 per cent answered "fear of pregnancy," 13 per cent answered "respect for the date," and 13 per cent answered moral considerations. Thirty per cent of the respondents found this question impossible to answer; insignificant percentages named other considerations.

A number of "men only" questions dealt with items especially relevant to males, like visiting a burlesque show. Fifty-three per cent of the men had gone to a strip show, averaging between two and three visits. Ninety-one per cent had looked through picture magazines featuring nude or nearly nude women, and 60 per cent had done so more than ten times. Almost half (48 per cent) had used these pictures to stimulate masturbation, but only 4 per cent said that perusing such magazines led them to uncustomary sexual intimacies. Forty-seven per cent of the men had purchased contraceptives, sources being a drugstore, a friend, or a poolroom, in that order. Interestingly enough, only 31 per cent admitted to using the contraceptives they had purchased. Only 8.7 per cent of the men had used a motel for sexual purposes; 10 per cent admit to intercourse with a prostitute, but only 3 per cent have gone to a brothel.

With the women, some of the above questions and other particularly relevant questions were asked. While only 12 per cent felt that they fell in love too easily, 23 per cent were worried about maintaining their attractiveness for men and having enough dates, and 35 per cent worried about going too far on dates. Another 22 per cent have these doubts on special occasions. Some 15 per cent worried about holding the boy they were dating, and another 33 per cent are so concerned only occasionally. Although 95 per cent of the women admitted to looking at nude picture magazines, the practice is much less frequent among them than among the men; only 25 per cent of them had looked over ten times at such publications, and only 2 per cent had found them stimulus to masturbation. Some 6 per cent claimed to have been aroused by them to sexual fantasies. Just over a quarter (27.6 per cent) have purchased contraceptives, nearly all from a doctor. Another question inquired about their knowledge of abortionists; while only a miniscule percentage knew one by name or hearsay, one-third thought they knew someone who could locate an abortionist should the need arise.

A special section of the survey inquired into those situations which apparently favour or encourage petting and intercourse. For instance, what is the role of the drive-in theatre, the so-called "passion pit"? It was found that 14 per cent of the respondents had experienced Petting A at least once at a drive-in; 8.5 per cent had reached Petting B, 20.3 per cent had gone as far as Petting C (31 per cent of the males but only 3 per cent of the females), and 2.6 per cent had achieved intercourse. The role of the car – the modern mobile bedroom – parked in a secluded place was much greater. Some 20 per cent of the respondents had experienced Petting A, 10 per cent Petting B, 30 per cent Petting C (37.6 per cent of the males and 18 per cent of the females), and 16.3 per cent had had sexual intercourse. In short, roughly half of the girls who admitted premarital coitus and about one-third of the boys had experienced this at least once in a parked car.

Baby-sitting has also been accused of providing important opportunities for premarital sex, and our findings generally supported such assumptions. Some 4.6 per cent of the respondents had gone as far as Petting A at the home of a friend (presumably when there were no adults around), 8 per cent to Petting B, 25 per cent to Petting C, and 30.7 per cent to intercourse (31 per cent of the males and 30 per cent of the females). Just under 1 per cent of the sample had engaged in homosexual acts in this situation.

Asked about being alone, or virtually alone, in one's own home, a somewhat similar pattern emerged from the group's answers. Seven per cent had participated at least once in Petting A, 5 per cent (1 per cent of the males and 11.7 per cent of the females) in Petting B, 27 per cent in Petting C, and 21.6 per cent in sexual union.

Since the use of contraceptives may be construed as permitting intercourse, respondents were questioned about the effect of their use on their sexual practices. Some 30 per cent of the males and 26.7 per cent of the females said they had used them; 2 per cent of both sexes mentioned use of contraceptives only once, 11 per cent of the males and 3 per cent of the females several times, and 17 per cent of the males and 18 per cent of the females more than five times. (Over 3 per cent of the women failed to answer this question, in a fashion consistent with the previous one.)

To conclude the analysis, it is fascinating to consider how our respondents evaluated their relationships with the other sex and their tendency to experience sexual guilt. Forty-eight per cent (44 per cent of the males and 55 per cent of the females) considered their sexual relationships of the previous twelve months to have been both satisfying and happy, 16 per cent (18 per cent of males and 13 per cent of females) classified them as occasionally satisfying, and 21 per cent of the group described them as a mixture of satisfying and unsatisfying experiences. Only 7 per cent (9.7 per cent for the men and 3.3 per cent for the women) said that their sexual relationships had *not* been really satisfying or happy, and 3 per cent of the men described their relationships are generally unhappy or not satisfactory. Not quite 5 per cent avoided answering this enquiry. Over-all, one may wonder how honest these respondents were being in such evaluations.

In terms of guilt, the results are consistent with the general trend reported above. While 42 per cent of the sample said they had experienced some guilt or shame, only 3.3 per cent – mostly girls – admitted to a considerable amount of guilt, while another 2.6 per cent confessed to "a great deal." Practically half of the sample (49.9 per cent) claimed to have experienced no guilt or shame over their sexual behaviour! The major focus of guilt, where admitted, seemed to be on masturbation, involving 24.7 per cent of the males and 10 per cent of the females, and on Petting C, involving only 4 per cent of the males but 23 per cent of the females. Only 5 per cent of the men and 13 per cent of the women admitted much guilt over sexual intercourse. (The actual question read, "Which activity has aroused the most guilt feeling?") Reading erotic books or looking at nude-type magazines aroused most guilt in 7 per cent of the men, and homosexual acts came first with another 2 per cent. Interestingly enough, the percentage who admitted to feeling no guilt fell from 49 per cent in the earlier query to 43 per cent on this question.

On the matter of homosexual actions, the questionnaire first asked, "Did you have more than fleeting homosexual desires in your middle 'teens?" The question was aimed at that period when girls develop "crushes" and boys find other boys sexually desirable. The question is probably too pointed in saying the middle 'teens, and perhaps it is otherwise poorly worded. Regardless, 7 per cent of the boys and 1.7 per cent of the girls answered yes, and another 9.7 per cent of the former and 5 per cent of the latter declared themselves uncertain, suggesting that they had had some such experience, although perhaps very minor. Three per cent of the males admitted to having homosexual desires in the *present* – but no girls – and another 11 per cent of the males and 1.7 per cent of the females checked off "just occasionally." If the next question was answered honestly, then these desires are well-checked; only 2 per cent of the men admitted that they had engaged in one or two homosexual acts during the previous two or three years. No one admitted to more frequent homosexual activity.

In concluding this preliminary survey, three things need to be said. Much valuable information may be obtained by further computer analysis of the data which will correlate many of the background and attitudinal variables with each other and with behavioural items. This analysis has yet to be completed. Such a questionnaire probe as this was admittedly a less than perfect method either to obtain completely accurate answers or to investigate many subtle and significant aspects of attitude and behavioural motivation and change. At the present stage of sociological research, the questionnaire is but a crude first step, necessitated largely by the limitations imposed by lack of money, time, and trained interviewers. Undoubtedly, there will be some distortion in our York study, partly because of the relatively crude questionnaire approach, partly because of the lack of a more perfect sampling of the student body. For example, a 95 per cent sample, which was our goal, would have yielded considerably more certain statistics.

What is the over-all significance of this general profile of attitudes and behaviour at York University? Allowing for distortion in the results, it seems that York students, both male and female, are substantially more permissive in attitudes, norms, and behaviour than those on some other English-speaking campuses. Assuming that our findings at Western Ontario and Calgary are roughly accurate and that no significant change has occurred there since 1965, then it would seem that York students belong toward the more permissive end of the university continuum in sexual conduct. (The assumption of little change is, of course, not scientifically admissible.) It is possible that investigation of two Albertan and two British Columbian universities would find them even further along such a continuum. Of course, it is possible that there has occurred a significant liberalization since my original investigations four years ago and that the higher

York figures indicate a strong movement towards increasing permissiveness.

At the same time, the percentage of respondents at York favouring intercourse with anyone was forty-five, placing it very close to the figures secured recently in studies in New York and Cambidge; it is, in fact, a little higher. The most impressive difference between York and other Canadian universities, however, is the higher degree of liberalism among its women students. For instance, the percentage of women who had experienced intercourse at Western and Calgary was between thirteen and fifteen; at Glendon, in 1965, some 22 per cent of the women students had experienced intercourse, but the figure leaps to 35 per cent at York in 1969.

This liberalism and the higher percentage of men who have experienced intercourse than is ordinarily reported in Canadian studies of the subject may be attributed in part to a combination of three factors. First, there is the fact that 75 per cent of York students come from metropolitan urban backgrounds, a proportion twice as large as that found on most campuses outside Toronto. The significance of this, of course, is that these students are exposed to a high degree of secularizing and liberalizing forces. Secondly, 7 per cent of our sample live in apartments, which, other studies have shown, tend to favour sexually permissive behaviour. Thirdly, some 13 per cent of our sample lived in residences on campus, and this kind of environment, it has been noted, favours liberal attitudes towards heterosexual relationships. Moreover, York's residences seem to exhibit an unusually free atmosphere in which controls on sexual pairing-off are rather minimal. According to some student reports, it was possible for men to live in a woman's residence for months without being discovered and asked to leave.

Taken together, these three social background factors may well have been crucial in determining the figures reported in our study. Only much more controlled testing of the data still untabulated and more comparative studies on other Canadian campuses can provide the scientific foundation on which to base a definitive statement of the situation.

4 Student Radicals

Stephen Langdon

Large, big-city universities have lately generated organizations of radical students demanding profound changes in the administration and teaching processes of their institutions. To some extent, these student radicals constitute a separate and hidden world, but they often have great influence on the thinking and behaviour of the major student groups. This has been true at the University of Toronto, with its 25,000 daytime students, although less so, so far, at the much smaller and newer York University.

In this article, Stephen Langdon, a leading member of the 1968-69 Student Administrative Council at the University of Toronto and a prominent spokesman for the radicals, writes of the various departments singled out for criticism, describes some of the radicals' plans for 1970, and predicts a continuation of confrontations. This article first appeared in the Toronto *Globe and Mail* in March, 1969, and was entitled, "Why Student Activists are Zeroing in on a New Target." During the summer of 1969, Mr. Langdon was on the staff of the editorial page of the Toronto *Star*.

The university revolution is not nearing an end. In fact, it has hardly begun. In spite of the wide-spread inclusion of students on high-level governing bodies in most Canadian universities, student power has not lost its impetus. The student power movement is only beginning a long fight.

This partly reflects the growing base the movement is building in high schools that will assure increasing support in the universities. In terms of protest action, there is a generation gap even between high school students and university student activists.

High school students today are doing things university students would never have dared when they were in the secondary education system.

More immediately important is the shift of focus within the university. During the last year, students have gained major changes in the top-level structure of university government. Only two years ago, the major issue was whether one student would be on the Board of Governors of the University of Western Ontario. Today, at the University of Toronto, a commission of which students comprise four of nine voting members is working on creating a new structure which will almost certainly eliminate the board and replace it with an over-all governing body, likely with equal faculty-student membership.

At other universities, student members of the senate are the rule, and students help choose university presidents. At Toronto, colleges have incorporated students into their governing councils, and such service committees as housing now maintain a student majority. Almost everywhere, university governing bodies are beginning to meet openly, even allowing the press to attend their sessions.

In spite of horrified predictions of disaster from wise administrators when such ideas were first suggested several years ago, universities still manage to operate.

Students have begun to realize, though, that such upper-level changes are not very significant. The involvement of a student élite does not reduce the feeling of powerlessness and unimportance that students as a group feel. Student representatives often come to accept the slow pace of university change and become unwilling to try to force major changes through the governing bodies of which they are members.

It can become easy for students in such a situation to accept underlying assumptions of the faculty and administration and to speak only in such terms. Finally, upper levels of university government are usually unable to effect any real changes where they seem most immediately important to the student – in the classroom and department.

Universities are made up of faculties, such as engineering, medicine, and arts and science. Within these faculties are departments corresponding to particular areas of study; in arts and science at Toronto, these include political economy, sociology, East Asian studies, and about twenty others. Tremendous autonomy is left to the departments in determining what is taught and how teaching is done.

It is this level which is becoming the centre of attack for most student activists as they seek to change the methods used to educate them.

It is difficult to relay the uninspiring, pedestrian, and uncreative reality of education at the University of Toronto. Boredom and cynicism are predominant throughout the student body. In a statement adopted March 12 by a vote of twenty-five to three, the Students' Administrative Council at Toronto said:

> The style of education at this university does not accept the student as an active participant in a self-development learning process, but sees him simply as a recipient of knowledge. Rewards are given for the latter pattern of response; the structure of learning – lectures, courses laid out by professors, stereotyped labs, major crisis examinations – is patterned for passivity.

Creative citizens, able critically and independently to evaluate and influence their environment, are not turned on by such a system.

The conformity of teaching methodology is reflected in the complacent status quo orientation of much course content. Contrary to popular opinion, university classrooms are rarely places of radical thought. Rather, in terms of the emphases and omissions of some departments and of the direction and approach of many courses, the university teaches its students the conventional wisdom of mid-century capitalist society.

The Department of Political Economy at the University of Toronto does not offer a single undergraduate course in socialist economics. The History Department offers no history of the Canadian Indian. Medicine builds in profit motivation; English becomes picayune; sociology concentrates on problem-solving within the status quo; law doesn't question the assumptions of our legal system – it memorizes them.

Many students on campus have read *The Dissenting Academy,* an anthology of academic criticism edited by Theodore Roszak, and have found that their university courses reflect the inadequacies exposed in this book. Not only does much content apologize for and explain away the status quo with its inequities and anti-humanism, but content either cuts itself off entirely from social realities, refusing to become relevant for the thinking student, or it becomes directly tied to the needs and demands of the present power structure. Regarding the latter possibility Martin Nicolaus, a sociology professor at Simon Fraser University, described his discipline at the last meeting of the American Sociological Association as owing "its prestige in this society to its putative ability to give information and advice to the ruling class of this society about ways and means to keep the people down."

Students are afraid Mr. Nicolaus may be only too right and that university education has to be challenged and changed in content and purpose before the university can become the exciting and critical part of society which it should be. The growing Americanization of faculty and curriculum add to this concern. Thus the classroom and department become the focus of attempts to change content, style, and the relations between faculty and student which flow from these.

Several developments this year have marked the shift of focus. At the University of Toronto, the Students' Administrative Council established a Free University of Toronto in which about 600 students participated. Various non-credit courses were given, some by senior students, some by professors, some by persons from outside the university.

All rejected the traditional authoritarian style of university education, and many acted as counter-courses in content. One group studied non-authoritarian medicine, discussing an end to the traditional power of the doctor in hospital relations. Another group approached Canadian history from the perspective of the labour movement, and another discussed the engineer in society, considering, among other things, the role of engineers as a new working class.

At the same time, students in many departments have begun to organize course unions aimed at changing departmental decision-making structures, effecting educational changes, and, in some cases, breaking disciplines down into broader, less-specialized divisions. About ten to thirteen arts and science departments now have developing course unions.

Most are doing major course evaluations for next year. Some, such as that in history, have held regular seminars at which the philosophy of history and the biases of present course content have been discussed. The Psychology Course Union organized a counter-course in clinical psychology to challenge the white-rat orientation of their department. The Sociology Union has published a newspaper called *Anomie* that critically assesses the discipline and analyses élitism in departmental decision-making. Recently the Political Economy Union held an all-day teach-in on the content and purpose of political science.

Such events have been the impetus for major confrontations elsewhere and will almost certainly be at Toronto. At McGill, political science students occupied the department and staged a sit-in until major changes were made in the decision-making structure – including establishment of committees with one-third student membership to consider the hiring and tenure of professors. At the University of Windsor, the firing of a professor in the Theology Department led to a successful ten-day occupation. Student demands were similar to those at McGill. The result was inclusion of students on hiring and tenure committees throughout the university – to as great a proportion as one-half in theology.

Much of the struggle at Simon Fraser University has occurred at the departmental level, especially in the departments of politics, sociology, and anthropology.

Such structural changes are much closer to the average student and of much greater immediate significance to his life and education at the university. They consequently mean much more to him. He knows that an equal role with faculty in hiring and setting the tenure for professors will enable him to shape the style and content of his education. He wants an equal role in deciding which courses are to be offered and the regulations under which they will be taught.

A system implemented at Simon Fraser and supported at Toronto by the Students' Administrative Council sets up a parallel decision-making structure which demands that the shape, direction, and personnel of any department be approved by separate open meetings of all students and all faculty in that area of study. This system gives students clear equality in their relations with faculty, challenges the passivity of present education by having everyone participate in decisions which will affect them, and begins to build a truly involved university community.

It also makes changes in the style and content of education much easier. It is the extension of student power which will mean the most to students in their classrooms.

It is also this extension of student power to which faculty members react most defensively. This is hardly surprising, since they are the target of such changes. When students attacked the Board of Governors, faculty often went along with them.

Such cannot be the case when students challenge the power of faculty over its own department. Some junior faculty members may support such demands (at the risk of retaliation in promotions, etc. from their colleagues), but the faculty generally resists change on this level. This is especially true when it comes to the questions of hiring and tenure. The faculty is vitally affected, and many liberal professors have been heard to mutter that they just don't trust students when it comes right down to it. At the same time, students know they will have to gain power in such decisions if they are to really influence education in their areas of study.

Another point in the resistance of many faculty members is the restrictions on outside consulting work which they know students wish to institute. Many professors spend much time and make much money consulting in their specialties for outside corporations and government. This is often at the expense of time spent on learning with students and doing independent, original research work. Students will try at least to limit such non-university activity, and some professors feel financially threatened.

This hard-line resistance means that confrontations on campus are inevitable and bound to increase in number next year. Such a situation will require militant student tactics. Strikes, sit-ins, and the occupation of university buildings will occur, just as they have occurred because of similar issues at McGill, Windsor, and Simon Fraser.

Violence, such as that at Sir George Williams University, will not arise, however. The Sir George situation was not typical. The racism issue heightened tension, and the violent atmosphere of present-day Montreal made physical destruction a more believable option than it would be for students anywhere else.

Instead, campus protest will continue to be non-violent. It will use direct action, but the chances of its resorting to physical violence are slight.

People outside the university must remember this. They must also realize that major issues are being fought within the university. Student protest is not a conspiratoral product of outside agitators aligned with the Communist Party. It is a serious attempt to change education to meet the needs and desires of the students involved in it and eventually to change the university to meet the needs of the ordinary men and women of Canada.

It may be hard for some to understand why students temporarily occupy a building. In such cases, real issues are always involved, and the public should not jump to hasty anti-student conclusions. They should remember that the buildings are, after all, part of the university of which the students are a major part, and they should not demand that police take action. They must be tolerant about the conflict which seems to them to be hurting the universities for which their taxes pay.

For students are not trying to destroy these institutions, but to change them greatly, and for the better, so that the people who come out of them and the people who teach in them will be critical-thinking individuals, creative citizens, persons aware of their social responsibilities to the millions of people in this country.

5 Unity and Disunity in Two Ethnic Groups in Toronto

Clifford J. Jansen and J. Gottfried Paasché

To the outsider, ethnic groups in Toronto appear as mono-lithic and integrated communities, revolving around natural leaders who speak for all in their community. Two sociologists examined Toronto's German and Italian communities to test this common assumption and found that it differed widely from the reality of the situation. Their article is a valuable contribution to an understanding of ethnic assimilation as well as the specific "world" of German and Italian immigrants to Toronto.

The authors of this article are both professors of sociology at York University. Professor Jansen took his doctorate at Bath in England, where he studied "sociological aspects of internal migration." His interest in Italians dates from the mid-'60's, when he did a study of sociological developments in Italy. Professor Paasché, born in Japan of German ancestry, took his PH.D. at the University of Michigan, where he studied school desegregation in the southern United States.

The following article represents but part of a larger study of ethnic groups in Toronto, their strengths and problems, being directed by Professor Anthony Richmond of York University and funded by The Canada Council and the Central Mortgage and Housing Corporation.

INTRODUCTION

Because of large scale immigration since the Second World War, Toronto has become a highly cosmopolitan city; in 1961, close to 40 per cent of its population was not of United Kingdom ethnic origin. The proportion may be even higher now (1969), since immigration on a large scale has continued since 1961, immigrants

182

coming principally from continental European countries. Thus, it is not uncommon to hear social scientists, government officials, people connected with various social service agencies, and others refer to "ethnic communities," and specifically the "Italian community" or the "German community."

The theme of the present paper is that the use of the concept "community" and the related concept of "institutional completeness"[1] is misleading and possibly based on incomplete assessments of the situation. These conclusions are based on studies undertaken during 1968 on organizations involving German- and Italian-speaking Canadians. The investigators were struck early in the research with the marked tendencies toward a lack of unity and cohesion among organizations and among the people themselves.

There is, of course, much variation among sociologists with respect to a definition of the term "community," ranging from purely ecological to normative and moral conceptions. With respect to groups of people of similar ethnic origin, a definition provided by J. P. Fitzpatrick,[2] although not rigorous, probably catches what is meant when the term "ethnic community" is employed. He writes that a community is

> a group of people who follow a way of life or patterns of behaviour which mark them out as different from people of another society, or from other people in the larger society in which they live or to which they have come. They ... have generally come from the same place, or ... identified with the particular locality where they now live. ... They speak the same language, probably have the same religious beliefs. They tend to "stick together," to help and support each other. They have expectations of loyalty one to the other and methods of control.

The dominant note in such a definition is that of a certain unity within the ethnic group which is different from any other unity which may cut across ethnic groups. It is this assumption of unity with respect to the German and Italian ethnic groups which is questioned in this paper.

Observations made in the process of studying organizations and the people involved in them will be examined in the light of the question concerning unity and disunity of ethnic populations in Toronto. The approaches taken to the analysis of observations in the two ethnic-origin groups under study differ somewhat from each other. However, both provide information relevant to an examination of the issues in the context of the particular ethnic group.

The study will begin with brief reviews of background characteristics of the two ethnic groups, in order to place the subsequent studies in their proper perspectives.

BACKGROUND CHARACTERISTICS

Italians

The 1961 Census of Canada shows that there were 140,378 persons of Italian ethnic origin living in the Metro Toronto area. Since an appreciable immigration has continued in the years following the census, estimates of the group now range between 200,000 and 250,000. In 1961, Italians represented 7.7 per cent of the population of Metro Toronto and were the second largest ethnic group after the British (60.7 per cent).

However, a large majority of Italians are recent immigrants. In 1961, about seven in ten persons of Italian ethnic origin were born in Canada. This is an important factor to bear in mind when considering assimilation and integration of the group. Another important factor about Italians in Canada and on the North American continent in general is that a large majority have originated from the poorer rural parts of Southern Italy and the islands of Sicily and Sardinia. Figures from Italian statistical publications[3] show that in two post-war years (1959 and 1963) as many as eight in ten Italians who emigrated to the Americas originated from the area south of Rome or from Sicily and Sardinia. This means that a large majority of immigrants are of rural or small-village origin, and, as one spokesman of the group put it when interviewed, "The only large city a majority of Italians have seen is Naples, which they passed through on their way to board ships or planes for the New World." Yet, the 1961 Census of Canada shows that after the Jews, the Italian ethnic group is the most urbanized, with about 95 per cent of Italians in Canada living in urban areas.

Another feature about Italians in Canada is that large proportions of immigrants have been sponsored. Again comparisons from the Italian publications show that (in 1958 and 1962) while only 11.5 per cent and 4.5 per cent of Italian emigrants to European countries were "Non-Active," as many as 67.7 per cent and 57.6 per cent of emigrants to Canada were "Non-Active," that is, were not in the labour-force. There is reason to believe, however, that this high rate of sponsorship has dropped (and this has been supported in interviews with Italian travel agents in Toronto) since October, 1967, when the Canadian government introduced an immigration policy based on a points system involving many other factors (like age, qualifications) besides sponsorship.

In making comparisons of the age and sex characteristics of Italians and of Torontonians in general, from the 1961 census it was seen that while Italians had an identical proportion (63.2 per cent) of persons in the fifteen to sixty-four age category, they had 5.5 per cent more children (0-fourteen) and 5.5 per cent less older persons (sixty-five and older) than the Toronto average. And the number of males still exceeded that of females in the group, especially in the older ages. For those aged fifteen to sixty-four, there were 117 males per 100 females; for those over sixty-five years, the ratio was 126 men per 100 females. The respective proportions for males in Toronto as a whole were only 98 men per 100 women and 75 men per 100 women. This situation is probably indicative of the fact that the early Italian migrants were mainly males.

Toronto has a distinct and clearly definable "Italian area" (on the contrary, one cannot speak of a German area in Toronto). Indexes of Residential Segregation indicated that for Italians to be distributed in similar fashion to all ethnic origin groups in Toronto, 51.7 per cent would have to move from their present place of residence; this is one of the highest segregation indexes.[4] However, there are two areas outside the major Italian area where persons of Italian ethnic origin have tended to settle. Interviews revealed that almost all Italians living in these two areas originate from two specific areas in Italy, thus giving support to the idea of chain and sponsored migration.

Given that a majority of Italian immigrants have originated in the rural south of Italy, it is not surprising to find that they are of low educational level. A rank order correlation of census tracts by ethnic origin and elementary school only, revealed that Italians had a coefficient of .76. Almost a quarter (23.4 per cent) of Italians in Toronto in 1961 spoke no English at all: no other ethnic group had more than a tenth of its members who spoke no English.

This low level of education is reflected in types of occupations and average incomes. Two-thirds (67.4 per cent) of Italian males were classified as labourers or craftsmen in the 1961 census. Only 7.9 per cent (compared to a Toronto average of 24.8 per cent) were in managerial or professional occupations. The few Italians who did get into high-status jobs appear to have been born in Canada (of Italian origin parents); among those born in Italy, only 4.2 per cent were in managerial and professional occupations, while almost three quarters (73.2 per cent) were labourers or craftsmen. Of all ethnic groups, Italians (both male and female) had lowest average incomes ($3,189 males and $1,592 females). The Toronto average for males was more than one-and-one-half times higher, while Jews had an average more than twice as high.

There did, however, appear to be more and more Italian females entering work in Canada. For the whole of Metro Toronto, the proportion of females in the labour force compared to all women aged fifteen to sixty-four was 44.9 per cent. This proportion among Italians was 41.5 per cent, while it was 45.0 per cent for British and only 30.9 per cent for Jewish women.

Germans

Persons of German ethnic origin numbered 80,300 in 1961, comprising 4.4 per cent of the population of Metropolitan Toronto. More than half (55.4 per cent) were foreign-born. On the basis of natural increase and some continued immigration, the total in 1968 may be over 100,000 persons of German ethnic origin in the area. The heaviest immigration occurred in the 1950's, prior to which there were less than 20,000 persons of German ethnic origin. Thus the Germans as a population category experienced tremendous growth in a relatively short time in Metropolitan Toronto.

Among the ethnic groups, one of the outstanding characteristics of the Germans is their relatively even distribution over the Toronto area. Among Metropolitan Toronto's twenty-four planning districts, the percentage of Germans ranges from 2.5 to 8.4 per cent with the modal figure being 4.2 per cent.[5] The index of segregation for this population is the lowest of all ethnic groups. For Germans to be distributed similarly to all ethnic groups in Toronto, 13 per cent would have to move, whereas 30 per cent of the British, the next lowest segregation index, would have to move.[6]

With respect to occupations and income, the Germans compare favourably with the British ethnic groups. Occupationally, the Germans have almost an identical percentage categorized as labourers as the British, but they have a significantly smaller proportion in the managerial, professional, technical, clerical, and sales categories. Instead, the Germans have a high proportion of their male labour force in the craftsmen and production occupational categories (43.6 per cent compared to 27.7 per cent for the British). With respect to income, the Germans are second only to the British (excluding the ethnic category "Jewish").

All ethnic-origin groups are characterized both by differences in mother tongue (they all have varying proportions whose mother tongue is English and French) and by the proportion whose birth place is Canada. The German ethnic-origin group, however, is characterized by another differentiating characteristic which is somewhat unique to it. Many people of German ethnic origin were born neither in Canada nor in Germany. For instance, among those whose mother tongue in 1961 was registered as German, 3.6 per cent were born in Canada, 61.4 per cent in Germany (using the political boundaries after the First World War), and the rest, about a third of the total, were born in other European countries.[7] Since those Germans whose mother tongue is German are the most relevant population with respect to German language organizations, this phenomenon must be kept in mind.

UNITY AND DISUNITY

Italians

When studying the Italians in Toronto, persons in various key positions were interviewed. Choice of respective interviewees was based on their importance to the present Italian ethnic group. Thus, included in interviews were church leaders, a majority of Italians belonging to the Roman Catholic faith, persons in charge of social-assistance organizations catering particularly to the needs of Italian immigrants, labour leaders, for a majority of employed Italian males are labourers, real-estate agents, for a major problem facing Italian immigrant families is the housing problem, travel agents, who could give some insight into problems involved in the actual immigration, and the Toronto Italian press (there are two weekly Italian language newspapers in Toronto). When interviewed, these persons were asked about their own concern for Italian immigrants in Toronto, how they rated concern by other persons or groups for Italians as well as for the names of those whom they thought of as leaders or spokesmen of the group. A number of these "named" leaders were also interviewed.

Community or Group

Twelve "named" leaders were asked if they thought of Italians in Toronto as a "community." Only three replied affirmatively. Typical replies were: "The Italian is an individualist: this is truer of Italians than of others – Jews are at the other extreme." "Not an organized community but individuals, for organization is not a strong point of Italians." "No, we are individualistic members of some future Italian community." "Very individualistic, regionally oriented; there are close-knit groups who are proud of their *paese* [village of origin]." "Sadly, we are only a community to a certain point – in the same way as all immigrant groups are a community – we're not very united." An apt description of the group was, "We're a group of communities with a common language," and one other respondent said, "A group but not a community; for example, no one politician can swing all Italians to vote one way."

In their study of Italians in New York, Glazer and Moynihan state that, "The two keys to understanding the role of Italians in America are the Italian neighbourhood and the Italian family."

> When the immigrants settled . . . they tended to congregate with others from the same province or even village. Illiteracy seriously hampered the development of these diverse settlements into a single ethnic group for differences in dialect, which in turn engendered mutual suspicion, tended to endure in the absence of widespread written communication.[8]

There are indications of a similar situation among Italians in Toronto. And it would appear that this is not only the view of the outside observer, but of the majority of their leaders as well. However, three respondents did feel that Italians were a community, and they explained, "They couldn't be anything else because the group is so huge, so commercially important that everyone who needs their business plays up to them in their own language, thus setting them apart as a community." This definition of "community" seems to come from outside the group – the way other groups "see" and "treat" Italians – and not from within the group. Another respondent said, "Yes, they are a community, but divided in church and politics," while the third said, "Yes, they came because of the possibility of a better future – but they should keep some Italian customs, though this is difficult."

Leadership

As mentioned earlier, when the first interviews were carried out, respondents were asked to give the names of leaders or spokesmen of the group. But there was a general pessimistic attitude when the subject of leadership came up. Of the fifty-five respondents interviewed, twenty-one (37.2 per cent) could not give the name of a leader.

Comments about leadership among priests were as follows:

"There aren't any real leaders. There are self-appointed men taking the lead, but they aren't looked upon as leaders by other Italians. The ones who have most power and impact are those in the labour movement – they have done most for Italians. Self-appointed leaders could never organize the Italians because of petty rivalries and policies. There is no real need for leaders as such. The labour movement and priests are the ones closest in touch with the people." "Unfortunately, there are no leaders: the self-styled ones are only interested in their own betterment. A non-Italian would have more support than an Italian – they do not trust their own." Among four priests who couldn't give a name, one was very proud of the fact that Italians living in Eastern Toronto had not produced any leaders, while another said that Italians did not trust anyone – they would prefer a Canadian representative; a third said that there were self-appointed leaders, but none capable of leading all Italians – even though this is necessary.

Similar negative attitudes were expressed by respondents in social assistance organizations. One said, "You don't talk to Italians about leaders. Each Italian speaks for himself – they're individualists," while another said, "Italians aren't influenced by anybody." However, one person did describe what a leader should be: "An educated Italian of recent immigration with a modern way of thinking."

Among trade union representatives, three simply did not know anything about leaders, for they were "not much involved in these things." Others replied that there were no real leaders, but many self-appointed ones. One respondent said that Italians should be in different sectors but do not need one leader to represent them.

Comments by real-estate agents were that there were no leaders as such, but spokesmen who represented a small section of Italians and having small influence; the problem, they said, was precisely that Italians could not get a leader, no one stood out. Two others were not sufficiently involved with Italians for they were very pro-Canadianization and felt that there were a lot of smart fellows among Italians, but that ethnic origin did not come into it.

Only one of nine travel agents interviewed mentioned the names of leaders, but others expressed many comments like, "There are so-called leaders who try to do something to improve the position of Italians and protect them, but there are many who are merely ambitious." Another felt there were too many chiefs and not enough Indians: most leaders here further their own interests, not that of the community. A third said that many just think about money and don't care – they claim that Italians don't give them much support – there is no trust in our people. While one respondent was not sure if one could speak of leaders, another was sure that "we don't want any bosses," since they're just in it for themselves.

This pessimistic attitude towards leadership was accentuated when leaders themselves were asked about persons playing a leading role in their relations with Canada. Of the twelve interviewed, five felt that "no Italian" played a leading role, two mentioned themselves exclusively, while a third mentioned himself along with others.

The twelve leaders interviewed were shown a list of the names of the other eleven leaders and asked about their relationship with each. When a relationship with another leader was considered "very friendly," a score of three was allotted; "friendly," two; "spoken to, but not friendly," one; and "no relation or unknown," zero. Thus, if a respondent said he was very friendly with every leader, he would score a maximum of thirty-three (11 x 3). Likewise, the popularity of a particular leader could be measured: if every other leader thought of him as a best friend, he would score a maximum of thirty-three.

Only one respondent, a television producer, considered himself "very friendly" with ten and "friendly" with one other leader. The majority of others were fairly well spread among "very friendly" and "friendly," but one respondent scored as low as fifteen, not mentioning a single other leader whom he considered to be a very good friend. Two respondents had not heard of as many as three other "leaders," and one commented, "They can't be important, for I've never heard of them."

The highest "popularity" score was twenty-eight, with three others scoring twenty-six. However, there appeared to be very little reciprocity among the twelve leaders, thus giving little support to the idea that these named leaders were forming cliques. A general feeling of mistrust towards each other was felt throughout the interviews; for instance, at least four leaders interviewed claimed to have initiated the "Sicilian Disaster Fund in Toronto" early in 1968.

Concern by Different Groups

The various subgroups (i.e., priests, real-estate agents, etc.) were asked to comment on the concern, from their own group and others, for Italian immigrants in Toronto. Using a similar scoring system to that used for leaders, after deducting scores of a group about itself, priests were considered to be the most concerned about Italian immigrants, and they were followed by social assistance organizations, newspapers, clubs, Italian employers, trade unions, travel agents, leaders, and real-estate agents in that order.

As well as replying directly to the question, comments were made about the different groups. Comments made by leaders were: that they would like to believe that priests were concerned; that some political leaders were sincerely concerned; that regional Italian Clubs (based on village of origin of immigrants) were killing the idea of Canada; that both trade union leaders and travel agents were a bunch of crooks, and that most of these (trade unions, newspapers, real-estate agents, travel agents, and employers) put business first and were only incidentally concerned about Italian immigrants.

Respondents in social assistance organizations felt that leaders, trade union representatives, and newspapers had their own interests at heart first; employers were considered as exploiters of cheap Italian labour; real-estate agents were out to skin their fellow Italians, and travel agents were worse – they overcharged for every service given. Only a few priests were really concerned.

One real-estate agent said they were concerned themselves, for they had cleared up all speculators. Another felt that priests were concerned, but that they overstepped the mark – they got more "reverence" from the immigrants than they deserved. Social assistance organizations got no co-operation from the people; newspapers provided a service, but Italians still used the English language press for quicker results.

Trade union representatives felt that the church was never "for" the workers; that leaders were strictly businessmen; that clubs created partitions among Italians; that real-estate agents were robbers, and that Italian employers were exploiters: many had refused to allow their workers to join a union.

Travel agents felt that priests were concerned only about religion – nothing else, except money: in Italy they help you without having to be asked, here they want your money first. Leaders were "in it" for personal benefit. Most persons join trade unions to get higher wages, but they have to pay for it – it's $160 to join. Real-estate people are really making a large profit because most Italians are obliged to buy a house.

Germans

The German-Canadian organizations included in this study were the multi-activity "community" type associations, small clubs, and associations organized around more restricted interests such as churches, language schools, and business and professional associations. In addition, two other areas relevant to German-Canadian life were investigated. The first was the communications media, specifically German language newspapers and radio programs. The second was German-Canadian commercial life.

Through a variety of sources, including informants, lists of associations, clubs, churches, etc., were compiled. An effort was then made to interview the top personnel in each organization. In some cases, several interviews were conducted either with the same person or with two different ones. Finally, the participants in the study involved themselves as observers in the activities of some of the organizations.

The interview schedule included questions asked of all informants as well as questions tailored to the specific organization involved. Interviews lasted about one hour, but they often ran longer and consisted primarily of open-ended questions. Tape recorders were used wherever possible, and the choice of language (German and/or English) was left to the informant.

This present paper deals with some of the little known aspects of the group, resulting mainly from questions concerning relationships between German-Canadian organizations and the kind of membership served by each. Very early in the research, we were asked by respondents to distinguish between *Reichsdeutsche* and *Volksdeutsche*. The former refers to Canadians who have emigrated from territories which make up German national states and the latter to those coming from other states in which there were German language minorities. This distinction, we discovered, was only the first aspect of disunity among German-speaking Canadians, and it was prominently reflected in their organized life: German-speaking Canadians as well as their organizations were separated along these lines.

National Origins

The most obvious and clearest basis of disunity among German-speaking organizations was found to be the differences in the national origin of German-speaking immigrants in Canada. We found that almost all the organizations we had undertaken to study could be separated into six nationality categories: Austrian, Swiss, German, Sudeten, Danubeswabian, and Baltic.

The Austrian and Swiss organizations we studied served people from those countries only and took pains to indicate that they were not "German" organizations. Both indicated actual plans or the desire to be further independent of the initiatives of other German-speaking organizations (e.g., both Austrians and Swiss spoke of forming their own language schools). Some of the organizations of other German-speaking national-origin categories were cited as examples of what they did not want to become.

The organizations of the Austrian and Swiss national-origin categories were the only ones in which a close and cordial relationship with the consulates and embassies of the "mother" countries was highlighted by the informants (consulates provided names of new arrivals, for instance).

One clear difference between the organizations in the German national-origin category and those in other categories is that some of the former saw themselves as, and to some extent were, pan-German; those who didn't see themselves thus limited themselves to serving people from regions within Germany. However, pan-Germanism often went hand-in-hand with an open-door policy to Canadians in general. For instance, the most prominent German organization is officially bilingual, and many of its main events are conducted in English and in German. Another prominent organization considers English its official language. In the process, the most prominent organization has taken in large numbers of non-English and non-German mother-tongue Canadians as members. Thus it seems that a pan-German policy goes hand-in-hand with a pan-Canadian policy, and pan-German organizations are thereby separated even more from organizations in the other national-origin categories than they would have been simply by virtue of being German.

A similar process is seen with respect to an organization which has taken on a large-scale German language training program. Partly in attempting to serve all German-speaking parents, it has recently become highly "professional" in its approach to the German language, i.e., avoiding history and culture and focussing on standard German with an eye on the Grade Thirteen certificate in the high schools as well as the equivalent certificate in West Germany.

The rest of the national-origin categories have much in common with each other in that they include German-speakers who were in a minority in their country of origin and who were uprooted by German political and military policies. This, however, does not mean that there is co-operation between the organizations involved. In fact, they have very little else in common. Each has different reasons for feeling an antipathy towards the major

German-origin category organizations. The Sudeten German organization is politically left of center and feels uncomfortable in associating with the German organizations. The Danubeswabian organizations feel that their interests are not met by the major German organization, in addition to feeling looked down upon as "outsiders," and the Baltic organization feels that their keen concern with culture is neglected by the major German organizations.

Regional Differences

Organizations based on regions within the country of national origin have existed, exist in embryo, or actually do exist, depending on the specific national-origin category.

Such organizations are most prevalent in the German national-origin category, numbering about ten. They are looked down upon by the larger, central organizations, and they are also viewed as competitors in certain instances. These small clubs do not use the facilities of the big clubs, making their own arrangements instead. They are looked upon as divisive. On the other hand, the small clubs see themselves as meeting a need for sociability among people of similar dialect and background which the large organizations, partly due to their very size, cannot meet.

Also regionally based are some churches in which most of the congregation comes from one particular town. Such situations, when they are not specifically noted in the name of the organization (e.g., "Berliner Club"), are difficult to spot and were probably neglected in this study.

Differences in Aims and Undertakings

A basis of disunity among German-speaking organizations is differences in goals making the organizations incompatible. An example of this is the relationship of the German language training organization to its sponsoring multi-activity social organization. The language training organization was attempting to disassociate itself from the other organization because that organization was a profit-making venture which had some very strong interests in appearing to be interested in supporting German culture. The language training organization, in attempting to appeal to all German speakers, independent of national origin, considered its tasks hampered through association with a profit-making German organization.

Another example of disunity based on differences in tasks may account for some of the separation among the national-origin categories. The Danubeswabian organizations and, to a lesser extent, the Baltic ones have a cultural goal in their organizations – they are interested in cultural survival. The organizations in the German category seem very disinterested in any cultural goals.

Rivalries

In addition to the bases of disunity discussed above, several others were noted. For one, there was no doubt that competition for members helped to sharpen some of the differences. Would the Austrian club or the German club attract the German-speakers to its restaurants and to its dances and other activities? Secondly, class considerations, with the attendant differences in style of living, seemed to also play a role in differentiating organizations. Some groups, which could have operated under one roof and did at one time, no longer felt the association was good for their status. On the other hand, others felt that same organization was too sophisticated and not interested in "the working man," and a small regional organization was therefore considered better. Finally, the most prominent organization came under attack because it did not fit the image of what the most prominent German-speaking organization should be like. It was upsetting to some that it should be so commercially oriented, that so many non-German-speakers participated, that it didn't take wider responsibility for German immigrants, and that it wasn't more culturally oriented.

CONCLUSION

Though ethnic groups in various places are referred to as "communities," it is doubtful whether the term as commonly used could be applied to immigrant groups in Toronto. The concept "community" usually invokes the idea of a cohesive group which is represented by a few leaders and organizations.

Studies of two ethnic groups in Toronto reveal that, though the term "community" is in common use, members of these groups tend to emphasize the lack of unity and community cohesiveness rather than to promote it. Among Italians, few leaders thought of their group as a community, and most regretted their lack of unity. Most persons in the group who were interviewed believed that they had no real leaders or persons who could represent them as a whole in their dealings with other groups. Few leaders had any respect or confidence in other leaders, and they tended to emphasize differences rather than similarities. Different subgroups tended to be following separate courses and emphasized rivalries rather than making a concerted effort to help new immigrants. Many social clubs were based on the village of origin of the immigrant. Among Germans, it was found that "community" is an elusive matter which may exist within subsectors of the German ethnic category, but certainly not among German Canadians as a whole. The demographic information suggests divisions which are confirmed by the over-all organizational structure. It is doubtful that even among subsectors of the ethnic population one might discover "community," since one of the chief complaints of all organizational leaders was the general disinterest that they perceived among German-speaking Canadians in German-oriented organizations.

The absence of unity among organizations within and between the various divisions in the German ethnic-origin category does not mean that the organizations are not active or that they do not serve the interests of some people. Nor does this disunity prevent outsiders from acting as if there were unity among German-speakers, with the consequence that sometimes the organizations act as if they were representative of a unified population. Canadian political life and public sentiment seem to require this, and the organizations will not disappoint these expectations.

That two such different populations as the Germans and the Italians in Metropolitan Toronto should be so similar with respect to their disunity is remarkable and should prompt a more realistic appraisal of ethnic social life and the consequences for urban studies and for policy makers in public and private agencies.

This study suggests that it is not very useful to think in terms of the extent of "institutional completeness" of ethnic communities without a much more careful examination of the communities. It is perfectly true that in Toronto there are both German and Italian churches, services, newspapers, commercial enterprises, etc. However, these are "available" to people of Italian and German ethnic origin *only in the eyes of the outsiders* who have not realized that the various institutions cater to a *selective clientele* within the ethnic groups and are thus not available to *all* members of the Italian or German ethnic groups.

6 Changes in Toronto's Élite Structure

Merrijoy Kelner

In the expansion of a large community, it is customary to expect some significant changes in the composition of its leadership or élite structures. In theory, if key élites resist entry of new elements over a long period of time, the community will suffer in significant ways. Some theorists have claimed that urban industrial communities are more inclined than other kinds of societies to make way for newcomers, including members of low-status ethnic groups, to enter their élites.

This article, based upon a doctoral dissertation done at the University of Toronto, examines some key élite groups in Toronto to see to what extent they have really been opened in the last twenty years to non-Anglo-Saxons of ability and talent. Its conclusions suggest that the Family Compact syndrome, born in the early nineteenth century in Ontario, has yet to give way substantially, in spite of Toronto's rapid expansion.

The author, Mrs. Merrijoy Kelner, is an assistant professor of sociology in the new Department of Behavioural Science at the University of Toronto. In abbreviated form, the article was first given as a paper to a meeting of the sociology section of the Learned Societies' meetings at York University in early June, 1969.

The emergence of Canada as a modern industrial nation has involved profound modifications in the structure of the whole society. Nowhere can these changes be more clearly seen than in Toronto, an urban community in the forefront of social change.[1] During most of Toronto's history, it was a small provincial capital, solidly Anglo-Saxon and markedly Tory in character. Leadership roles were inevitably filled by members of the majority group, so that European immigrants, who began to arrive in some numbers by 1900, found a community in which the strategic institutions, such as the banks and the government, and the profitable trade activities, such as merchandising, were controlled by entrenched Anglo-Saxons.

Since the end of the Second World War, however, overseas immigrants to Canada have shown a pronounced preference for settling in Toronto, and this influx of newcomers has transformed the social character of the city. Today it is a decidedly multi-cultured community, providing a home for a broad range of ethnic and religious groups.[2]

Associated with the large influx of newcomers is the explosive growth and prosperity the city has experienced since the end of the Second World War. The increase in population that has brought Metro Toronto to the two million mark represents two-and-one-half times Canada's total growth rate.

In addition to skyrocketing physical and commercial expansion, the city has experienced dramatic cultural development in the post-war years. The support and involvement of European immigrants have been important factors in the flowering of opera, ballet, theatre, music, and painting that has enriched the city.

The new arrivals have also been associated with a marked change in attitude toward the British Empire. The old, almost automatic alignment with Britain no longer exists. The steadfast devotion to British traditions and life-styles which formerly characterized the citizens of Toronto is no longer predominant. The heterogeneous ethnic composition of the city has made this shift easy, perhaps even inevitable, since the loyalties of the European immigrants who now form such a significant part of Toronto's population are to the traditions of their own motherlands.

The presence of so many people of various ethnic origins in a rapidly expanding urban centre must act to release new forces in that community. The pace of technological development and the thrust of industrial expansion carry many new opportunities for advancement in their wake. In a community experiencing such rapid growth and wide-spread social change, it can be hypothesized that a greater number and variety of leadership roles will be created; as a consequence, access to positions of power and prestige will widen and increase, and the social backgrounds of those who occupy these positions will be more diversified.

This hypothesis provided the focus for a recent study of changes in the élite structure of Toronto in the period between 1948 and 1968.[3] The specific aim of the study was to examine whether élite positions have become more accessible to non-Anglo-Saxons within the last twenty years. This required systematic analysis of the ethnic origins of Toronto residents occupying positions of power and prestige, as well as investigation of the career patterns which led to these key positions. The primary emphasis of the study was on the relationship between ethnic origin and élite status.

Two distinct levels of élite status were delineated. The bottom level of the élite structure was seen as consisting of persons who have achieved key functional positions in Canadian society. This level, which includes labour leaders, corporation presidents, cabinet ministers, and the like, was defined as the *strategic* élite, following Keller's classification.[4] Members of strategic élites are selected primarily on the basis of achievement since it is their functional contributions to society which are the crucial consideration.

The upper level of the élite structure, a much smaller group, was seen to consist of persons who not only filled key functional roles but were also accorded high social status in the community. This select group, found at the apex of the élite structure, was defined as a *core* élite. Its members form a socially homogeneous group which is distinct from, and superior to, the strategic élites from which it is drawn.[5] It is, in short, more élite than other élites.

Using the conception of two distinct levels of élite status and following the positional model employed by John Porter in his study of the distribution of power in Canadian society, élite groups residing in the Toronto community were identified for each major institutional sphere.[6] A corporate élite, a labour élite, a political élite, a civil service élite, a communications élite, and an academic élite were identified; their ethnic composition was then analysed in order to assess the degree to which non-Anglo-Saxons have risen to functionally important positions – that is, membership in strategic élites – during the past twenty years.

The data indicated that although non-Anglo-Saxon representation in strategic élites had definitely increased since 1948, in no major institutional field had it reached the same level as non-Anglo-Saxon representation in the total community.

Currently, non-Anglo-Saxons constitute approximately 7 per cent of the corporate business leaders residing in Toronto.[7] In the labour sphere, they constitute 21 per cent; in the political sphere, 19 per cent; in the civil service, 10 per cent (mainly in the research branch) ; among the owners and directors of the mass media, 5 per cent; and among academic leaders, 19 per cent.

Changes in the ethnic composition of strategic élites has clearly not taken place at the same rate in each institutional field. The major thrust of upward mobility has taken place in the interstitial, innovative fields, which had no entrenched aristocracy in control, and in those spheres requiring a high degree of technical specialization. The greatest non-Anglo-Saxon penetration into top positions has occurred in dynamic fields like mining, construction, entertainment, psychoanalysis, and the new universities that have sprung up since the Second World War.

Changes in the élite structure of Toronto can also be analysed from the point of view of prestige or reputation. Such an approach affords a broader perspective than exclusive concentration on formal position and encourages consideration of dynamic processes. Developments are occurring at the present time which may create future changes in the ethnic composition of the élite, and these new trends also merit study.

New patterns have recently been established in the corporate sphere which will eventually have a significant impact on the ethnic constitution of the corporate élite. Within the past ten years, new trust companies and savings and loans associations have been formed or taken over by non-Anglo-Saxon businessmen. As yet, these financial institutions have not achieved the size or stature of some of the older, established financial corporations, but they nevertheless represent a definite breakthrough in the ethnic composition of the financial community. The club-like atmosphere of the city's financial world is being somewhat diluted through the entrance of a few non-Anglo-Saxon competitors.

Real-estate development in Toronto, which has enjoyed tremendous growth since the end of the Second World War, is a form of enterprise that has become vitally important to non-Anglo-Saxons as a way up the commercial ladder. The building business has offered fresh opportunities to many who found more established commercial fields, like banking and insurance, closed to them. It is a high-risk enterprise which requires little equity in order to operate on a small scale. By borrowing from the banks on the basis of personal worth and by skilfully manipulating payments to the trades, many small-scale, non-Anglo-Saxon builders, particularly Jews and Italians, dramatically widened the scope of their activities, moving from the manufacture of a few houses to the production of complete subdivisions and apartment complexes.

Similarly in other fields, non-Anglo-Saxons are clearly moving up toward positions of power and prestige. In the labour field, the increasingly large number of Italian labourers has been reflected in the recent inclusion of Italians in the leadership of local trade unions. In the sphere of politics, non-Anglo-Saxons have been putting themselves forward as political candidates in increasing numbers as they become more acculturated to Canadian society. Eight of the city's twenty-two federal Members of Parliament and seven of the twenty-nine Provincial Members are currently non-Anglo-Saxons. A few non-Anglo-Saxons have also succeeded in becoming high-level officials within the political parties themselves. Substantial influence over the policies and decisions of the Progressive Conservative Party has been attributed to a non-Anglo-Saxon Toronto lawyer; he has worked his way up within the party hierarchy and is currently reputed to be one of the three most powerful Conservatives in the country.[8]

Until the post-war period, the civil service did not attract many non-Anglo-Saxons, either through design on the part of the bureaucrats or because the salary scale and prestige rewards were too low. Today, however, the greatly expanded scope of government activities has brought with it an increasing need for highly qualified people, particularly in the research branches. The increased salaries and higher prestige of government employees are making the civil service more attractive to ambitious and qualified non-Anglo-Saxons, who find they are more welcome at the higher levels in government than they are in business. The net result of increased acceptance plus higher compensation for government service should be to increase the extent of non-Anglo-Saxon penetration into the top levels of the civil service.

When the definition of the élite group in the communications sphere is extended to include not only the owners and directors of the mass media but also the leading creative people in the field, it is evident that there has been extensive non-Anglo-Saxon involvement in top positions. The two members of Canada's most famous comedy team are both sons of Eastern European Jewish immigrants, as are several of the leading producers and directors on the two television networks. In the last decade, an important and beautiful theatre in Toronto was saved from demolition and completely renovated by a local Jewish merchant. Approximately 80 per cent of the private art galleries in the city today are owned and operated by non-Anglo-Saxons. It is clear that even though the major instruments of communication are largely owned by Anglo-Saxons, the leading writers, producers, directors, and artists come from a variety of ethnic groups.

Before the Second World War, the hiring of people for university posts, both administrative and academic, was restricted largely to Anglo-Saxons. Since the war, however, there has been such rapid expansion in higher education that the demand for trained academics has been difficult to fill. The combination of increased demand and greater rewards, coupled with the emphasis placed upon higher education by many ethnic groups, has had the effect of opening up the academic field to non-Anglo-Saxons.

The rate of increase in the proportions of non-Anglo-Saxons admitted to strategic élites has not been uniform for all ethnic groups. To date, Jews have been more successful than other non-Anglo-Saxons in reaching leadership positions in major institutional hierarchies, due to their urban background, high educational level, and a generally longer period of acculturation to Canadian society. The cultural sphere has drawn a significant proportion of its leadership from the Jewish group, while the labour movement, on the other hand, is currently attracting Italians and Ukrainians to its top-ranking positions. A wide variety of non-Anglo-Saxon groups are represented in the research and planning branches of the civil service.

Variations were also found in the types of routes to élite status that were followed by members of different ethnic groups. Analysis of the avenues of ascent followed by members of strategic élites reveals that in contrast to Anglo-Saxons, who rise *within* the bureaucratic structure, non-Anglo-Saxons typically achieve prominence *outside* it, through more individualistic and high-risk paths. The usual pattern is to start one's own business and to build it up into an important corporate structure, at which time it is customary to add some Anglo-Saxon names to the board of directors to ensure legitimacy.

Omitted from Porter's study of élite groups in Canadian society was consideration of leaders in the social, cultural, and professional spheres. Particularly important, it appears to this investigator, is an examination of the ethnic origins of *social* leaders in the community. The power of social leaders consists of deciding who shall be included in the membership of the "best" clubs and who shall be invited to the most exclusive social gatherings. The basis of this power is upper-class status, which derives from a composite of many factors, including old family prestige and a particular lifestyle.

Litle change was found in this study in the ethnic origins of Toronto's social leaders during the past twenty years. Either by expressed policy or long-standing custom, the city's high-status social clubs make it clear that they do not welcome non-Anglo-Saxon members. The purpose of these clubs is to limit social interaction to the "right" people, the "people one knows," and these are rarely members of non-Anglo-Saxon groups. Few Anglo-Saxon leaders make close friends among people of other ethnic groups. Social relations between upper-class Anglo-Saxons and others in the community were found to be categorical and formal in nature, restricted almost entirely to public occasions.

This social exclusion has important repercussions for the hierarchical structure of the society. Social restrictions have the effect of containing power and prestige within a select circle, even though this may not be the primary motive for exclusion. Membership in the leading men's clubs, for example, is a tacit prerequisite for advancement to top positions in many fields, particularly in the professions and in large corporations. It is in the relaxed club setting that many major decisions are made, and it is through the camaraderie of the club atmosphere that younger men are recognized and selected for future leadership roles. Personal relations are cemented in common social experiences, and those who are excluded from them are at a serious disadvantage in their attempts to reach and maintain top positions. One respondent in the study suggested that Jews are rarely hired by banks because young bankers on the way up must belong to the "right" clubs, and these clubs do not welcome Jewish members.

It is important to note, however, that there are powerful forces within the various non-Anglo-Saxon groups which also act to limit social interaction. Their leaders encourage them to maintain a distinctive identity, and, in doing so, they discourage them from close social relations with members of the general community, thus imposing serious limitations upon the degree of upward mobility that can be achieved.

Exclusion from intimate social interaction with the Anglo-Saxon upper class imposes certain practical limitations on advancement into key functional positions – that is, into membership in strategic élites – in the ways suggested above. Such exclusion is also a crucial factor in restricting the entry of non-Anglo-Saxons into the small inner circle designated here as the core élite. This élite nucleus, whose members combine leadership roles in major institutional spheres with high social status, is the most powerful and prestigious group in the community, and it is this group which has proven almost impervious to non-Anglo-Saxon penetration.

The growing need for skilled specialists and executive talent occasioned by the increasing complexity of management and the constant development of new techniques, combined with the influx of New Canadians into the society, has resulted in freer access to membership in Toronto's strategic élites. Positions of power and prestige have become more accessible to qualified non-Anglo-Saxons as ascriptive criteria become increasingly less important in recruitment.

This democratization process has been shown, however, to have definite limitations, contrary to Keller's thesis that as industrialization creates larger and more complex societies, ruling classes, or core élites (as they are described here), will disappear and be replaced by strategic élites.[9] The élite nucleus is still very much in evidence, and it is still almost completely reserved for upper-class Anglo-Saxons. In sum, the shift from criteria based on ascription to those based on achievement is far from complete.

Sociologists have not been noticeably successful in predicting the direction of social change. Nevertheless, they feel an obligation to try. Some, like Baltzell, have warned that élite groups which fail to assimilate new and able members due to considerations like ethnic background and social class are destined to degenerate in time.[10] Baltzell regards a core élite restricted to upper-class Anglo-Saxons as an anachronism which can no longer fulfill its leadership function.[11]

This prognosis highlights one of the major problems of exclusivity. The continuing development of élites is an essential aspect of an expanding, democratic society. A core élite that continues to restrict membership to one particular ethnic group runs the risk of suffering eventual replacement by a new élite group. It seems evident that if the core élite in Toronto is to retain its control, it must eventually incorporate some of the most powerful members of other ethnic groups. They will not only provide fresh sources of talent and training, but their inclusion also puts members of the core élite in a position to exercise social control over these new men of power. Once they have become members of "the club," they are not likely to break the rules.

Part Three:

Little-Known Institutions

1 Rochdale: The Ultimate Freedom

Barrie Zwicker

Contemporary student protests against various aspects of our universities have caused, as a side-effect, the emergence of free universities. Usually controlled by students and offering a wide variety of new and radical courses, such institutions are attempting to devote themselves to more liberal teaching methods and freedom from authoritarian or impersonal administrative procedures. Following the example of institutions in San Francisco, New York, and elsewhere, Toronto saw the opening of its first free university, Rochdale, in the fall of 1968.

Barrie Zwicker, who tells the story of Rochdale's aims and its first year of operation, has been education editor for both the Toronto *Globe and Mail* and the Toronto *Star*. He has also served as chief of the *Globe's* Queen's Park bureau. He is currently a consultant for the Province of Ontario Council for the Arts, helping develop a pioneer kind of arts activity centre for a regional city to be built near Metro. This article first appeared in November, 1969, in an American magazine, *Change*.

It's not easy to get a grip on Rochdale College. I hope this isn't taken entirely as a plea for sympathy for the writer, which partly it is. But Rochdale doesn't lend itself to polite discourse or even, really, to print.

Rochdale is an experimental, residential free university, run by students and housed in a $5.8-million, student-owned, eighteen-storey building in downtown Toronto. Of the more than 300 free universities on this continent, Rochdale is perhaps the most ambitious. It opened last year with good press, high ideals, and its building unfinished. It now houses about one thousand persons – fewer than one-third of them original residents – of unusual diversity, especially in dress, background, and education. Little formal learning is taking place there.

The reality of Rochdale – the graffiti, the open use of drugs, the sounds, smells, conversational styles, and way of life – shatters most conventional yardsticks by which colleges are measured: degrees offered, faculty renown, quality of student clientele, facilities, course descriptions. It will, if it survives, be measured in part by the attainments of its alumni, a criterion also applied to conventional universities. Otherwise it is the antithesis of their image. Unconventional dress is the norm; bizarre behaviour is tolerated; until recently chaos was honoured over *any* substantial rule. (How else explain that one "head of security" for the Rochdale building was a "biker" [a motorcycle gang member] addicted to pink shirts and tough talk?)

Some writers have rummaged deep into a Kandy-Kolored, incense-filled urn of psychedelic modifiers in an attempt to zap their readers with Rochdale. I was asked to write "a tough, concise portrait of Rochdale and its student-faculty clientele." After a year's acquaintance with Rochdale, I still haven't one of those. Rochdale rejects labels as a faulty vending machine rejects coins. Rochdale does not comprise a "hard" story.

The place offers no degrees, cannot be said to be recognized academically (although two students were given credit for their Rochdale work at a department of Simon Fraser University), has no faculty and few courses which last very long. Programs for screening applicants come and go. One scheme was to have one person, by more or less common consent, do all the interviewing and use his judgment. The day I talked with him about his criteria, in an off-campus attic with eighteenth-century atmosphere, his first words were, "Have some dope," as he offered me a smouldering corncob pipe. Five or six others, relaxed around a heavy rectangular wooden table, were bathed in near silence. One, wearing heavy boots, absently and expertly drew a haunting, muted melody out of a beaten-up concert guitar. I settled as unobtrusively as possible into a deep chair and tried not to disturb the luxuriousness of the occasion. "I just use my judgement, like anyone else would," the admissions officer said, before taking another long drag from the pipe. Had he turned anyone down? "Yes, three." Why? "Because they would have been complete disasters." A girl offered a more particular explanation: "If someone comes in waving a gun, you turn him down."

As President Claude Bissell of the University of Toronto says, it is too early to tell about Rochdale. Serious students of the phenomenon agree that the first year is a shakedown for such an institution and that the second year will be telling. Rochdale is fascinating; it could be significant. Already there are signs that certain arts – music, weaving, sculpture, drama – may flourish well, that Rochdale may produce more humane, more socially-conscious graduates, that it may have lessons to teach about the place of drugs in the society of the future. There are dark omens, too. Tough elements have infiltrated; some carry guns; hard dope, such as heroin, has been pushed; motorcycle gangs like the Detroit Renegades have paid visits. Over the summer, a much harder policy toward such activities developed, and, at the time of writing, Rochdale is cleaner and "straighter" than it probably has ever been.

More than any other university I know, Rochdale is its students. More than any other university I know, Rochdale is about the outside world, because the strongest thread of commonality among Rochdalers is that they have rejected the world. Rochdale is pervaded with reaction to that world. Therein lies its fascination, its promise, and, perhaps, the seeds of its dissolution. The joys and problems that consume the energies of Rochdale are primarily those of human interaction, rather than learning in the conventional sense. The question, then, is: How relevant to life in the remainder of the twentieth century will the learning-by-living offered by Rochdale turn out to be?

The name "Rochdale" comes down through the years from 1844, when twenty-eight workers in the little town of Rochdale, England, formed one of the world's first consumer co-operatives and laid down the tenets of co-operativism. In 1936, a divinity student, inspired by a Student Christian Movement conference in Indianapolis, established a student-owned and operated residence in Toronto. By 1945 that house had grown, after several evolutions, into Campus Co-operative Residence Inc.; it owned ten houses near the University of Toronto, and by 1968 it had 400 members, most of them students at the University of Toronto, living in thirty-one buildings.

In 1965, the Canadian government, recognizing a serious shortage of student housing, passed legislation enabling the Crown-owned Central Mortgage and Housing Corporation to loan up to 90 per cent of the cost of co-operative student dormitories. During the following two years, the education committee of Campus

Co-op was in a state of ferment about the purposes of university life. The debate focussed on the proposal to create Rochdale. Those who conceived Rochdale, including doctors of philosophy, faculty members, and doctoral candidates, were very much of the intellectual community, although profoundly ill-at-ease in the conventional university setting. They also were the heirs of thirty-two years' successful experience in student-operated college living quarters.

A Statement of Aims[1] was approved in principle by the Rochdale Council in November, 1966, and these aims were further articulated in the charter[2] granted by the Ontario Provincial Secretary and Minister of Citizenship on July 17, 1967. Financial and construction arrangements were made,[3] and although the building was not completed in time for the September, 1968 opening, people began moving in.

This is not an insignificant point, as anyone who has lived in a partially-finished building or one being renovated can testify. Residents wove their way around workmen bobbing on air hammers and leaning on power drills. Live wires hung from gaping holes in ceilings, and piles of dust, broken concrete, cardboard boxes, and rubbish were everywhere. Furniture was months late in arriving. There were serious floods from vandalized plumbing. And much idealism, couched in the form of imagery about pitching in to sweep the floor, was frustrated.

Rochdale's soaring concrete tower could be just another high-rise apartment with red curtains flapping from windows in the soft breeze. It stands on the rim of the stylish Bay-Bloor district of boutiques, fur salons, and expensive shops, overlooking the University of Toronto's Varsity Stadium and the well-heeled Medical Arts Building. There are a bank branch and some offices on the main floor. But Rochdale's outer lobby is usually peopled with an assortment of beings groomed and dressed suitably for roles in the hippie party scenes of the movie *I Love You, Alice B. Toklas*.

The "communications desk," a big wooden affair in the inner lobby, comes and goes. When functioning, it is covered with papers and handbags. Two harried souls answer an endless stream of questions: *Where can I find Mary so-and-so?* and telephone calls: *Is Mary so-and-so there?* Of an evening, a permanent crowd of twenty adolescents, youths, and adults, two infants, and three pets waits at the four elevators, one of which is evidently out of order. The three functioning lifts pause for mysteriously long intervals at each floor. A happy young man in buckskin plays a guitar, singing tolerably well.

On the second floor is a lounge wherein take place council meetings, folk concerts, visits from Jerry Rubin and Marshall McLuhan, and lounging. Here also is the L.B.J. Suite, which derives its name from the first-name initials of big-moustached former manager Bernie Bomers, his practical former assistant Linda Bomphray, and clean-shaven, business-suited former registrar Jack Dimond. Rochdale goes into the current school year with no one assigned these jobs.

On the walls are painted messages: Rochdale Doesn't Like Weekend Slobs. Are You A Slob? Wandering through the building is a young man with flowing blond hair and tight blue jeans whose head is twitching; he is on a "speed trip" induced by an overdose of methedrine. A girl with long straight black hair paces like an animal back and forth on a stair landing. The smell of marijuana is strong on weekend evenings, and the red-carpeted halls are commonly strewn with cigarette butts. The music is mainly acid rock, although one occasionally hears Bach on record or, here and there, live. Music is one pursuit that is alive and well and living in Rochdale.

Into Rochdale's beginning last year plunged about 400 University of Toronto students, perhaps fifty from the New School of Art and the Ontario College of Art, 100 to 150 students from Ryerson Polytechnical Institute, and about the same number of full-time Rochdale members. Mingled in were a dozen "resource persons," the Rochdale equivalent of faculty. Two of them, English honours graduate Dennis Lee and Anglican minister Ian MacKenzie, were full-time and paid as such. Eight to ten other resource persons got $2,000 to $7,000 in the form of rent rebates or cash. "They tended to get what they said they needed," Lee says.

Jim Garrard, for instance, head of Rochdale's promising dramatic endeavours, was (and is) excused from paying half his rent. Stan Bevington, head of artistically-prestigious Coach House Press, is affiliated with Rochdale by virtue of an arrangement under which he does all the college's printing for a price which includes the cost of paying off his machines. He invites some students interested in graphic design and printing to work with him. Other resource people – photographers, psychologists, weavers – are helped with room or board, get small bursaries, or raise funds for themselves. Each case is considered personal and unique. "It's very messy and unsatisfactory," Lee says. "But if you step back a pace, it's attractive in principle. We just don't know how to make it work yet."

Rochdale's first wave of inhabitants was attracted by a variety of fare. Some were familiar with Campus Co-op and visualized a great big happy modern co-operative residence. Some were fed up with the ways and content of traditional university education and visualized self-starting seminars of intellectually-committed people growing together. Some, like high school teachers Joan Doiron and her husband Henri, sought respite from the massive, persistent conformism of their middle-class suburban schools. Ryerson journalism student Arnold Rapps, twenty-six, says many came because they were lonely; like Arnold, they had a vision of experimental living. Many were university students breaking away from stultifying backgrounds. "They saw Rochdale as a little Europe in Toronto where they could get away with a lot of things," Rapps says. *Freedom.* All hoped Rochdale would be different from the world they knew.

Dozens, perhaps more than 100, are Americans. One of them is Jennifer Michaels, twenty years old and a cool-eyed blonde. A native of Chattanooga, her husband so far has avoided the American Selective Service System. She wants to model and found that Toronto, as a fashion centre, is now giving New York City competition. A fashion photographer and other people she met "and would be friends with anyway" were living at Rochdale, and so she and her husband decided to move in.

Initially, high expectations characterized the Rochdale mood. But as the long gray winter set in, as physical problems with the building continued, and as interpersonal problems emerged, Rochdalers were forced to examine themselves and their new institution. "It's positively beautiful to see the initial euphoria," Lee recalls. "But then people run into difficulties. There are junctures which are enormously painful. A number who leave, leave at these junctures, seeing the distress as the end of their hopes. To others the distress is just a beginning." Lee himself moved out, "not by choice but to preserve myself. I just couldn't spread myself as thin as the situation was forcing me too." And in May he resigned from Rochdale, as a number of the founders have.

Most of those who moved out were students from the universities and colleges who couldn't stand the dirt, noise, frustrations, lack of privacy, way of life, or the other Rochdalers. Art Hendricks, an ex-Rochdaler studying journalism at Ryerson, remembers Rochdale as

> lousy – people decide what they want to study and then get a group together to form a seminar. They only study what they agree with, they never meet opposing views, and education degenerates into nothing more than the reinforcement of what they already think and believe.

By the end of February – after the equivalent of one semester – the turnover rate was 6 per cent a month.

Moves within the building, from room to room and floor to floor, reached a similar pace. I met one youth who was badly dissatisfied with his life in a fifteenth-floor Ashram Suite (eight rooms whose residents share a common lounge, kitchen, toilet, and bath) [4] and who said he was "getting out." I asked where he was going to escape. "Down to the thirteenth floor," he replied. If Rochdalers don't find Utopia on one floor, they look for it on another. Some have shifted as many as six times, like human sand.

The replacements for those who have left altogether have been mostly young working men, typically high school dropouts with $55-a-week jobs driving bakery trucks. The average age and level of education thus is dropping, as is the proportion of women students. The turnover has vitiated Rochdale in two ways, by downgrading its population and by robbing it of an effective collective memory, thereby lowering the level of intellectual exchange that does occur and stretching out the period Rochdalers require to arrive at a consensus on major problems. Trial-and-error solutions are applied to continuing problems, such as whether to keep out "crashers" – uninvited guests – and, if so, how. Even repetitive exercises are carried out with strain and strife because almost every new Rochdaler goes through months of fanatically rejecting or avoiding every whiff of organization or authority. Rochdale's governing councils have oscillated between stalemate and issuing unrealistic *diktats*. Example: writers intending to write about Rochdale *must* contribute money to the college. (A *Time* man was "ordered" to pay $3,000.) The council governs only in so far as those who happen to learn of its legislation happen to agree with it.

The most persistent and severe problem is that of "crashers" who, in the winter, stream to Rochdale for food and shelter. Runaways, mainly teen-age girls from the suburbs, are a year-round phenomenon. And, by mid-April, the good-weather wanderers present themselves at the communications desk in the lobby: young men in leather jackets who motorcycled from Nova Scotia, British Columbia, or the United States. All of these are "crashers." Slight, red-mustached Peter Turner, twenty-three, a well-liked and respected American who worked for a year on Eugene McCarthy's national committee, told of the "crasher" problem:

> Thirteen [the thirteenth floor] had a "community." At the beginning of last year, there were all these extremely enthusiastic people on thirteen. It was totally idealistic. There weren't really any hassles to be resolved. A few people had pets, and they got adopted by everybody. And if a couple of people did things, others would come along and pitch in. And everybody would sit up until all hours. . . .
>
> And then there started to be a lot of people crashing. It started in the middle of October. To the end of October, idealism prevailed to the extent that everybody agreed that the kitchen shouldn't be locked and no doors should be locked. Then it was decided that crashers couldn't take food from the kitchen. One group felt crashers are a group that has been rejected by society and must be helped. *Society has failed. These are children; be friendly to them.* It is part of the *raison d'être* of Rochdale. Another group didn't want crashers because they thought they'd be detrimental to Rochdale. When crashers come in, it disrupts the whole feeling of community. You come in to eat breakfast in the morning, and here are these ten bodies all stretched out on Chesterfields.
>
> It was then decided that crashers would have to find places to sleep in people's rooms if they wanted to stay for the night. This was decided in the second week of November. [But] there were a lot of crashers who were "speed freaks" who would just sit around for hours like this – just sitting – not making any attempt to involve themselves with the residents. So it was decided that crashers who were people's guests would be allowed, but people who just sat there would be kicked out. Then people started locking doors. . . .

By early last summer, a consensus had hardened in the building that a screening and "crasher" policy was necessary. Much rent was going uncollected, although a $31,000-plus monthly mortgage payment had to be met. Rochdale was housing drug pushers, "greasers" (those from tough neighbourhoods where violence, cheating, theft, manipulation, and endless excuse-making are accepted ways of life), and "bikers" (those with motorcycles and leather jackets). The concerns of these groups cannot be construed as educational if the word is to have any semblance of meaning. Among the pushers were "big dealers" who got "ripped" (had their "stuff" stolen or strong-armed away). "Ripping" led pushers to arm themselves, which made Rochdale residents uneasy because it led to the presence of armed "rippers."

In the public mind, sex, too, is closely associated with Rochdale, which has a strictly-no-questions-asked policy about relations between the sexes. The Ashram Suites consist of three double rooms and five single rooms, a kitchen, common lounge, and bath, with no segregation by sex. One survey, by a University of Toronto sociology student living at Rochdale, found that of thirty-two persons questioned, 80 per cent preferred relations with the one person with whom they were deeply involved (regardless of his marital status); 10 per cent were less selective in choosing sexual partners; the rest were living with prospective mates or were refraining entirely. Details on the city's venereal disease clinics are posted in the Rochdale lobby.

Over the summer, a "get-tough" council took charge, so far as it could. Many "heavies" were ejected. "Speed evicting parties" were held; according to Mr. Bomers, sixty-five speed freaks have been "permanently graduated." Some were charged with trespassing when they tried to return. Informers are paid to put the finger on speed and heroin pushers, and informers are no longer timid about coming forward. Rental and rent collection procedures have been tightened; food is being made less accessible to wanderers; the cafeteria and restaurant are being turned over to a private catering firm. Guns are required to be deposited in a safety deposit box. An agreement has been reached with the local police, under which the police are called in for particular disturbances but not for general surveillance.

Signs printed in bright red over every fire alarm box in the college read: "Anyone guilty of knowingly submitting a false fire alarm with this device will be required to await questioning by legal authorities and will vacate Rochdale within twelve hours of the offence." A new fee and admission policy acts somewhat as a screen. There is a trial membership of two to four months which costs $10. If the member is judged acceptable by the council, he pays a minimum of $25 for the school year (toward which the $10 is counted), plus any combination of $40 or forty hours of work (cleaning, manning the communications desk, and so on).

One gets the impression that nothing by way of education takes place at Rochdale, but this is inaccurate. The most invisible activities, such as a seminar on violence and a printing group, are comprised of members who are happy with their numbers and composition, and who therefore do not advertise themselves.

A nursery school, Indian Institute, *Théâtre Passe-Muraille,* and weaving classes have exhibited staying power. The Indian Institute, subsidized by a federal grant, is an educational-residential center where Indian people can study and teach in their own languages. The theatre group produced *Futz* at the downtown Central Library Theatre last spring. Before morality officers arrested the producer, director, and complete cast – a first for Ontario – the play received fine reviews. Over the summer, an arts festival was staged. The performances, seminars, and displays were well-received and well-reviewed. An intimate theatre is being constructed inside a ground-floor office of the Rochdale building.

Other learning activities which have taken place with some continuity include the history and theory of jazz, classical music theory, folk singing, folk and pop song-writing, yoga, poetry, life drawing, Judaism and religious existentialism, cosmic history, the drug seminar, social journalism, a magic school, an outing society, Jungian psychology, sculpture, primitive religions, painting, films, ceramics, Confucianism, a seminar on revolution, silk-screen processing, and sensitivity training. A clearing house for information on the interests and skills of Rochdale people and scheduled activities was established this year. A library has taken shape, its backbone consisting of a collection of science fiction donated by Judith Merril, the American writer.

Affiliated with Rochdale – affiliation meaning there is a relationship ranging from sympathy to co-operation – are the House of Anansi (Dennis Lee's publishing house, which made a name for itself with *The University Game),* the Modern Dance Theatre of Canada, Superschool (a "free" school for about thirty students between the ages of three and twenty), the Coach House Press, and the Centre for the Study of Institutions and Theology (which conducts the violence seminar).

Rochdale is a magnet for the alienated. Will their gropings illuminate new paths for the university and society? The lack so far of social commitment at Rochdale – beyond "legalize marijuana" petitions – is curious, for one of the failures of North American society in the eyes of its alienated is an insufficiency of social commitment. Perhaps nascent in Rochdale are leaders who will inspire some of their fellows to use their freedom in socially relevant ways. Or is inspiration unacceptable to the alienated and therefore unworkable? Certainly the Rochdale ethos leaves little room for the "great leader."

Rochdale may simply be a partial vindication of McLuhan's aphorism that "the future is with us," and it may prove only that significant numbers of the young generation would rather try primitive freedom and suffer degrees of chaos than suffer even reformed campuses. One cannot evade the hope, however, that out of this maturation cell called Rochdale will come a few Real People who will be able to show what lies beyond alienation. Such young citizens of the future may recommend against further Rochdales. If their views spring from their Rochdale experience, then Rochdale will have served a noble purpose.

2 Life and Death on the Telephone

Elizabeth Kilbourn

Loneliness and anomie are endemic phenomena of the big city and can often be part of the process leading to emotional depression and suicide. In recent years, the official suicide rate in Toronto has climbed significantly, and this has led to efforts at its prevention. While Los Angeles has a sizable, highly trained, psychiatrically focussed Suicide Prevention Bureau, Toronto has so far restricted its efforts to church-related services.

The Toronto Distress Centre, originated by concerned persons associated with Holy Trinity (Anglican) Church and operating out of one of the church buildings, is the most widely known of such organizations in the city. Through the telephone, its volunteers minister to the lonely, the disturbed, and the suicidal, twenty-four hours a day. Since it has proved impossible to tell how many suicide attempts are actually made in Toronto each year – though the figure is known to run into thousands – one cannot gauge the actual achievements of the Distress Centre. But Mrs. Kilbourn, a well-known Canadian art critic and author as well as a volunteer at the centre, brilliantly depicts its work and problems; in doing so, she illustrates something of the alienation and despair which is locked inside many of the citizens of the big city. The article originally appeared in *Saturday Night* in May, 1969.

> "I GET BY WITH A LITTLE
> HELP FROM MY FRIENDS"
> – *Sign on Distress Centre*
> *wall, Holy Trinity Church*

218

It's almost eleven o'clock. You drive down Yonge Street. At Dundas, the lights of Toronto's Strip advertise skin movies, topless go-go girls, alcohol, and various other attractions for the lonely, frustrated, and alienated people who move up and down the streets of the inner city. You turn into Trinity Square towards a grubby old church that announces it was built in 1847 – a year when there was nothing here but the trees and fields of the village of Teraulay. Now, the hulking black forms of Eaton's warehouses loom dark and forbidding in the night. Beyond them, you can glimpse the radiance of the new City Hall and hear the sounds of the music for the skaters on Nathan Phillips Square. As you park, you look up at the big red sign of the Ford Hotel, where a guy you know slit his wrists and then called you. Just across the parking lot there is a light on at Street Haven, where the prostitutes and lesbians and female junkies who work Dundas Street from Sherbourne to Bay can go for love and acceptance and a chance to find something of the home they left or never really knew.

From the antique Parish Hall across the street, now a theatre, some actors emerge. Members of a psychodrama group come out of the old house next door and pass you on the way to their cars. You go inside the grimy, grey-brick house which was once a country rectory.

The volunteers on the eight-to-eleven shift are glad to see you. You plug in the electric kettle and make yourself a cup of instant coffee, the first of several you will drink during the long hours before nine o'clock, when the night shift ends. If you are a woman, you will have another female volunteer with you; if a man, you may have to be alone.

Outside, you can hear the night sounds of a big city: voices of people pouring out of the theatres and the bars, and the cars parked around Trinity Square speeding off to the suburbs. There is almost always somewhere the wail of police or ambulance sirens rushing to the emergency departments of the Toronto General or St. Mike's or Mt. Sinai. Sometimes you can hear the voice of an old man, known on lower Yonge Street as God (because of his long white hair and beard), as he roars in fury his paranoid fantasies to a silent universe. There is the reassuring rumble of a police motorcycle circling the darkness of the square.

It's eleven. You sign the log book which means you are officially on duty. You check Standing Orders, which gives you any special directives about repeat callers. You check who is on Home Call, an experienced volunteer to whom you can refer any major decisions and who will be responsible for sending out the Flying Squad if there is a suicide emergency. You feel the adrenalin rise and the hollow feeling in the pit of your stomach which comes no matter how many times you have done a shift as a Distress Centre volunteer.

The phone rings, and, as you pick it up, the sounds of the city and the cosy room fade rapidly away. You are alone, alone with the voice on the other end of the line.

The telephone is an extraordinary instrument. Marshall McLuhan insists that "the telephone demands complete participation . . . with it there occurs the extension of ear and voice that is a kind of extrasensory perception." Nobody knows this better than a Distress Centre volunteer. "Befriending," in the jargon, over the telephone, is a totally different experience from listening or communicating with a person face to face. Every volunteer has to learn how to project sympathy, empathy, encouragement, and warmth without the use of eyes or hands or facial expression; all the resources and clues of non-verbal communication are unavailable. He must learn a new language and vocabulary. He must master ways of telling a total stranger, simply by means of his voice, that he is open, unshockable, firm, sympathetic, non-judgemental, patient. The number of inflections you can find for *uh-huh* and *umm* is quite remarkable.

The volunteer and the caller to the Distress Centre operate on three crucial rules: anonymity, confidentiality, and client initiative. Anonymity is an indispensable protection for the volunteer. He is known simply to the caller by his first name and the number he is given when he finishes his training and is accepted as a volunteer ("Helen 11"). The caller is also free to remain anonymous, and many do. Anonymity lends an intense poignancy to the telephone interchange. The masks and façades which cloak most social intercourse are no longer relevant. They meet simply as human beings.

Confidentiality is an obvious necessity, springing from the ancient rule of the secrecy of the confessional. And in some ways a Distress Centre volunteer, whether he's a medical student, housewife, retired druggist, nursing supervisor, Jesuit seminarian, or mother of three, is, in fact, operating very much in the role of the priest in the confessional – except that his authority is bestowed not through a hierarchical institution but by his own personality.

The third rule is client initiative. Volunteers are asked to remember that, even if the person calling is reporting the attempted suicide of another, it is in fact the *caller's* distress that must first be considered. Client initiative is, indeed, one of the most important elements a volunteer can use to help a distressed person. The ability to recognize his need and to reach out to another person to cry "help" in his anguish is a strength with which the volunteer can identify. Every successful volunteer has at some time reached out in agony and been met and touched deeply by another person.

Over one of the telephones, there used to be a sign, "This is not a problem-solving agency." One of the first tendencies to be overcome as a volunteer is the urgent desire to find a solution, *any* solution. Apart from the fact that solutions for anything important are very hard to come by, or require months of work, the problem which the caller presents may often be a fiction, an excuse to call in the first place. Instead of making a hasty referral to get an awkward caller off his hands, the volunteer patiently tries to help the client unravel and explore his feelings about himself so that he can begin to look for his own solution. When this happens, a galaxy of organizations and resources are available throughout the city.

The first move towards setting up a suicide prevention organization was taken by a man who had experience himself with the gap in the available resources for the distressed. Graham Cotter, an Anglican priest, as director of the Anglican Information Centre, a volunteer referral agency, was impressed with the amount of despair and helplessness he found among many of the people his Centre tried to serve. He realized the need for help available on an emergency basis without the lengthy screening processes and restricted hours of most welfare agencies. Many of the problems the Centre met required a willing ear and the kind of time to listen that most agencies are unable to provide. In the early 1960's, Cotter went to England to visit Chad Varah, the founder of a suicide prevention group called The Samaritans. He wrote a lengthy report on what he had learned and tried to interest the Anglican Church in the idea. For a while, nothing happened.

Then, early in 1966, James Fisk, the rector of Holy Trinity Church (whose Parish Hall was being used by the Information Centre), called together a group of people who for months had discussed what they wanted for the Centre. They formed themselves into a board, and, in April, 1967, appointed Andrew Todd, the director of the Leicester, England, branch of The Samaritans, as their director. Todd set up the administration of the Centre and interviewed and trained seventy volunteers – the minimum required to staff the Centre twenty-four hours a day, seven days a week. The Centre opened in November, 1967, and found that in one month it was getting over 500 calls. (This was phenomenally high, compared with the number reaching the Samaritan branches in England. It may be partially explained by the habits of Canadians, who use the telephone more than any other people in the world.)

When Todd left in the early spring of 1968, he was replaced as director by Gordon Winch, a United Church minister who was sometimes called the Padre of the Pubs. McLuhan has observed that the telephone caused a profound change in the styles of prostitution. Before the telephone, street walkers made their contacts by direct confrontation in streets and bars; after the telephone, call girls made their contacts through it. In one respect, Gordon Winch's career is similar. As Padre of the Pubs, he used to haunt the bars and pubs of the inner city, trying to relate to some of the thousands of lonely and isolated men on skid row. Now he makes his contacts through the telephone. Much of his time is spent in giving support and training to the volunteers already with the Centre, but even more is required for the two lengthy interviews-in-depth which any prospective volunteer has to pass before he is accepted. After acceptance, preparation consists of four evenings of sensitivity training involving role-playing on the telephone. Under Winch's direction, the volunteers function as a comradely and co-operative team with full freedom to take initiative and responsibility.

The Board of the Distress Centre now includes two priests, a psychiatrist, two lawyers, a university professor, two housewives, and a doctor. Its most pressing responsibility at the moment is raising funds. The budget for the first two years was made up of $16,000 each from the Anglican and United Churches, $1,000 each from Metropolitan Toronto, the Council of Catholic Charities, the Addiction Research Foundation, and Holy Trinity Church (which also rents the two rooms to the Centre at a nominal cost).

But not only are new sources of funds badly needed; new sources of volunteers are also necessary. At the moment, there are just enough to keep the two lines going, even with minimal advertisement of the phone number. There were 600 calls in January this year, and Winch is certain there is enough need for five lines to be kept constantly busy; obviously, there is enough distress.

Perhaps the client most convinced of the value of the Distress

Centre is that hard-headed corporation, Bell Telephone, which asked that it might include the number of the Centre on its directory cover page along with the police and fire department numbers. Bell thus elevated the Distress Centre to the status of a civic institution.

When a volunteer picks up the phone and says, "Distress Centre, can I help you?" the chances – according to statistics gathered in the first year of operation – are one in two that the call will involve a suicide factor (though only 10 per cent will require direct intervention).

Three out of every five calls deal with sex and marriage breakdown. A quarter involve alcohol and drugs. In a society as open and exploitative of sex as ours has become, it may seem strange that Gordon Winch believes that sex, along with suicide, should be the two greatest areas of distress in our society, but his experience in the Centre confirms it. Where, for instance, he asks, does a man turn to ventilate frankly his deep sexual frustrations, his dissatisfactions with his marriage, his homosexual proclivities, his uncertainty about his sexual identity? Where can he have these anxieties taken seriously?

Obscene calls are familiar to a volunteer. Sometimes a caller uses the volunteer's voice as a fantasy lover in his masturbating. Most women volunteers find that, once through the initial shock, they can stick with the masturbator until they can be of real use to him. One volunteer said to her new sexual partner, "Now that we have that out of the way, you can tell me what is really troubling you," and they were off on a frank exploration of the caller's marital frustrations. For male volunteers, this kind of call can present other anxieties. One young Roman Catholic seminarian told me that when his voice was used for masturbation by a homosexual, he was forced to face, for the first time, his own homosexual feelings. The same seminarian had his celibacy tested – in a way to which he is not usually exposed in his protected role as a priest – when a highly aroused woman attempted to seduce him over the phone.

Another kind of sexual difficulty was revealed in the call of a highly respectable, late middle-aged man who had been found naked with a male prostitute. Apparently he had had a homosexual experience in his youth which had been successfully repressed in his married life until the onset of his wife's menopause had allowed the feelings to rise again to the surface. With the help of the volunteer, he was able to face his situation and talk openly to his wife, and for this he was very grateful. But this is one of the good calls. Very few of the 8,000 calls the Distress Centre has handled have provided the volunteers with the comforting feeling that they have actually been permanently helpful to the client. Usually, the only reward available is the sound of a voice lessening in anxiety, the depressed tones lightening and becoming more animated, the hysterical voice growing calm and reasonable.

Suicide is something else. One of the most dramatic aspects of the Centre involves the suicide attempt. A voice announcing slit wrists or an overdose of pills, the address muttered, and then unconsciousness. The hurried call to the resource volunteer on Home Call. The Flying Squad pressed into action. The ambulance to the hospital. The life restored.

Or is it? The Centre is not equipped to follow through on treatment of its emergency suicide calls, and hospitals tend to take the suicide casually. Indeed, they often pass along society's disapproval and deny the right of the patient to his intentions by disguising attempted suicide as an accident: it saves a lot of trouble for everybody.

Critics of the Centre insist that there are two kinds of suicide cases, the doers and the attempters. Obviously the Centre gets many hundreds of calls from people in the latter category, those who use a suicide attempt as the most powerful way to dramatize their feelings, the ultimate cry for help. According to some critics, the true suicider would never call the Distress Centre. Winch disagrees. He says they have had some calls, not many perhaps, from people who talk quite calmly about their intention to commit suicide. One man phoned to announce his intended suicide. He talked politely with ease for two hours about any subject the anxious volunteer could think of – and then, his icy determination quite untouched, said he was off to jump from a bridge. Then why did he call? Perhaps the most taboo subject in our lives is death itself. The need to report to someone, to have at least one other human being in an indifferent world recognize your leaving of it, gives to a suicide some kind of dignity, some recognition of his responsibility for the act he is about to commit.

For most of us, certainly for me, the anxiety provoked by death can be at times unbearable. It is difficult to remain calm and to recognize the right of another person to be fully responsible for his life and his death. Suicide is probably the ultimate act of hostility, but it can also be seen as the ultimate act of self-affirmation. Our own anxieties about death and abandonment, about violation and deep betrayal, can trigger us into high gear. We rush out and mobilize all the available resources to respond to the cry for help of another human being in anguish. But perhaps a more difficult and demanding task is asked of the volunteer who grants to another person the dignity and respect he requires – to bestow, in fact, extreme unction. To affirm the paradox that at death we are most alive.

3 A True Life Drama

Betty Lee

Enforcement of the law often means the arrest, conviction, and punishment of thousands of persons whose offences are of a minor character. The majority of such persons tend to be from the lower- or working-classes, and their encounters with the law are seldom understood by those of higher income. In Canada, petty offences are generally handled by the Magistrates' Courts, where the justice is speedy, rough, and ready. Something of past traditions and mores is revealed in how such courts are run and the identity of those who receive summary treatment.

In the following article, based on notes taken in four such courts by the author, one encounters a cross-section of Toronto's petty offenders in the process of meeting the law and its sanctions. To the discerning reader, a sizable residue of Victorian Puritanism is visible in the way these courts operate.

Betty Lee is a staff writer with the Toronto *Globe and Mail*. Her article first appeared in *The Globe Magazine* in August, 1968.

CAST

Magistrate Donald Graham
Magistrate Peter Wilch
Magistrate S. Tupper Bigelow
Magistrate Charles Drukarsh

Crown Counsel, lawyers, police officers, clerks of the court, witnesses, and an unending procession of The Accused

226

SCENE 1

The scene is 23 Court in the cheerless basement of the old City Hall in Toronto, one spot in Metro's magisterial complex where The Accused – guilty, innocent, warily hep, or just plain bewildered – get their first glimpse of Canadian justice in action.

No. 23 Court is popularly known as women's or morals court. If the audience could examine its calendar for the day, it would see the tribunal deal with such matters as vagrancy C (prostitution), drunkenness, abortion, indecent exposure. New cases are tried on the spot if the alleged offender pleads guilty, remanded to a later date or different court for trial if he or she doesn't. The court sets bail, will sit in judgement on not guilty pleas if there is any time left during its morning session.

The room in which all this happens is small and overcrowded, with three rows of black benches, a press table, desks for counsel, accommodation for court clerks, and a high bench for the magistrate. There is a narrow, caged dock against one wall. It has a door leading to the cells and one exit into the courtroom.

When the curtain rises, the dock is stuffed with about thirty persons, an average morning's bag of arrests and remands in custody. (In fairness to these people, we will not use their names or the actual dates involved in their cases). The Accused are all standing, because there is no room to sit. There are some teen-age girls in the cage, a few men in shirt sleeves, several ladies dressed in blue jeans, sporting black eyes and crew cuts, three or four sad-eyed, middle-aged women. A young police guard with a billy tucked into his back pocket joshes briefly with a policewoman, then turns his attention to the back benches.

OFFICER *(to a matronly woman sitting in the second row):* Take that gum out of your mouth!

WOMAN *(astonished):* What gum?

OFFICER *(impassively):* Take whatever you've got out of your mouth. Now. *(There is some activity at the door of the court.) (Magistrate Donald Graham walks briskly into the court. He is a tanned, athletic-looking man who often does not wear magistrate's robes. Today, he is dressed in slacks and a cool summer jacket. He seats himself in his swivel chair, glances at the cattlecar dock, then nods good-humouredly at the Crown Counsel. An air of zap-zap-zap settles over the courtroom. Talk is fast, sometimes unintelligible, papers fly back and forth between counsel, clerks, and magistrate, The Accused are shuttled efficiently in and out of doors.)*

CROWN COUNSEL: Number three on page one, Your Worship.

CLERK OF THE COURT *(in a high-pitched, tired drone):* You are charged that on or about the twelfth day of July in the Municipality of Metro Toronto, County of York, you were found in an intoxicated condition in a public place, to wit, Queen Street East at 7:30 A.M. Contravention of the Liquor Control Act. How do you plead, guilty or not guilty?

VOICE FROM THE DOCK: Guilty.

MAGISTRATE *(his chin cupped in his hand):* Ten dollars or five days. *(The Accused shoves her way back to the door of the dock, and someone lets her into the cells.)*

CROWN: Number four.

CLERK *(his words begin to run into each other, but the audience can hear snatches of what he is saying):* ... intoxicated condition ... contravention of the Liquor Control Act. How do you plead?

THE ACCUSED: Guilty.

MAGISTRATE *(leaning back in his chair):* Ten dollars or five days.

THE ACCUSED: Can I have time to pay, Your Honour?

MAGISTRATE: Two weeks to pay.

CLERK *(this time, the name of the accused and most of the charge cannot be heard by the audience. But the last words are clear):* How do you plead, guilty or not guilty?

THE ACCUSED: Your Worship, I didn't do anything.

MAGISTRATE: You were drunk, weren't you? *(To the Crown counsel)* She's in here all the time. *(Cupping his chin)* How do you plead?

THE ACCUSED: Guilty, Your Worship.

MAGISTRATE: Ten dollars or five days.

> *(The next Accused, who is not in custody, is ushered into the court. She is a large woman, in her fifties, wearing a cheap cotton dress. She stands before the bench and raises her hands above her head.)*

ACCUSED: I'm guilty. All the way.

OFFICER: Take a seat. *(The woman ignores him.)*

MAGISTRATE *(staring down from the bench):* What did she do?

CROWN: Causing a disturbance and shouting, Your Honour.

MAGISTRATE: Put her on the bottom of the list. *(The woman is led out of the courtroom.)*

CLERK *(snatches of the charge can be heard as he reads to man standing in dock):* ... you are charged ... living off avails ... on this charge you can elect to be tried by a magistrate, a judge without a jury, or a judge and jury. What do you elect?

ACCUSED: Magistrate.

CLERK: How do you plead?

ACCUSED: Guilty.

CROWN: The facts are these, Your Worship. The accused was working at this club, and Kitty was also working there.

MAGISTRATE: Who's Kitty?

CROWN: The, er, woman, Your Worship. The accused and Kitty met at the club, then decided to move in and live together. According to the charge, he suggested she go out and hustle. During four years, she handed over sixty-seven hundred dollars to the man. She was supporting him. At one time, she was giving him a hundred dollars a week. *(He pauses and looks expectantly at the lawyer appearing for The Accused.)*

LAWYER: I have a witness, Your Worship. A police officer. *(A man in plain clothes walks to the witness box, swears he will tell the truth, and gives his name. He says something to the magistrate, but the audience cannot hear a word.)*

MAGISTRATE: In other words, you're saying she was not a girl to be led up the garden path?

WITNESS: No, she wasn't.

MAGISTRATE: What's this girl doing now?

CROWN: She's working as a strip wrestler in the United States, Your Worship. *(The witness leaves the box.)*

LAWYER: Your Worship, the man is married now. He's working, and his wife is expecting a child. Kitty was not led into prostitution. I think we've shown that. She had four years to complain, but she only came forward when this man married. Now, we admit he got into some trouble years ago, when he was sixteen. But I think we can regard this as a first offence. I might add he has been in custody for one-and-a-half months awaiting this hearing. He's done nothing to be proud of, but he didn't lead the woman into this sort of life.

MAGISTRATE: An offence such as this calls for a term of imprisonment. It isn't an offence for which I can impose a fine. He was living off this woman. He's guilty of it.

LAWYER: I'm sorry I took your time, Your Honour.

MAGISTRATE: No, you did the right thing. Sentenced to two months. It's a short sentence for this kind of thing. *(He glances at his watch.)*

CROWN: . . . Your Worship. *(A thirty-ish woman dressed in an orange miniskirt and green stockings stands before the court.)*

CLERK *(speeding it up)*: . . . intoxicated condition . . . contravention of the Liquor Control Act. How do you plead?

ACCUSED: Guilty.

MAGISTRATE: Ten dollars or five days. *(He looks at his watch again.)*

(Blackout.)

SCENE 2

The scene is 21 Court on the main floor of the old City Hall, another spot where The Accused in Toronto first encounter the Canadian judicial system. Twenty-one Court works in approximately the same way as 23, except that it specializes in male alleged offenders. A typical day's calendar lists such charges as theft of an auto, forgery, possession of stolen goods, assault. But even alleged murderers get into 21 for a first appearance before contesting their case in the more rarefied atmosphere of a higher court.

When the lights go up, the audience sees a larger room than No. 23 in the basement. There are the usual desks for counsel and clerks, a high magistrate's bench. The caged dock stands in the centre of the room, blocking the public benches. The Accused must climb stairs from the cells below and enter the dock through a trap door in the floor. Prisoners scheduled to appear in 22 Court, next door, use the same cell entrance. During proceedings, there is continual shuttling and scuffling around The Accused appearing in 21.

OFFICER *(to an elderly man in the public benches):* Take that gum out of your mouth. *(He turns his back.)* All rise.

(Magistrate Peter Wilch walks into the courtroom. He is a mild-looking man who is wearing his red-trimmed magistrate's robes. He also has a mild voice which can be heard only with difficulty, even though 21 Court has microphones installed at various points. As the audience soon hears, however, trucking activity behind City Hall drowns out much of what is being said in the courtroom.)

CROWN COUNSEL *(with let's-get-going zip):* Number five on page five, Your Worship. John X *(audience does not hear).* Suggest July 30 to set a date for trial and $2,000 bail.

DEFENCE LAWYER *(duty counsel for legal aid):* Your Honour! This boy is only seventeen years of age. He's working steadily, and he's living with his parents. The bail is prohibitive!

MAGISTRATE *(without looking up):* Five hundred dollars in cash and July 30 to set a date.

CROWN: Thank you, Your Worship. Next. Suggest July 29 to set a date for trial. *(The Accused stands in the dock. He is a well-built man. An interpreter helps him understand what is going on.)*

DUTY COUNSEL: Your Honour! This man has been in custody since June 6 waiting for trial. He cannot raise bail. He's Italian, and he's from Montreal. I ask you to let him out on his own bail.

MAGISTRATE *(looking at his papers):* Crown?

CROWN: One officer we want to call is on leave, Your Worship. The other one died. The man is charged with vagrancy and possession of burglar tools. He has a previous record, Your Worship. *(He hands a paper to the clerk.)* Suggest we set a date for trial on July 29.

DUTY COUNSEL: At least let him out on his own recognizance, Your Honour!

MAGISTRATE: No. We'll set a date on July 29. *(The interpreter whispers to The Accused, who cries out, tears his hair, and thumps down the stairs to the cells.)*

CROWN *(cheerfully):* Your Worship. Suggest July 31 to set a date for trial and no bail. This man has been picked up twice for bench warrants.

DUTY COUNSEL: Could the matter proceed on July 31 or earlier, Your Worship? This is only a matter of causing a disturbance. It shouldn't be too difficult a matter for the Crown. The matter should proceed at an early stage.

CROWN: I repeat that this man has been picked up twice for bench warrants, Your Worship. I would also ask that we set the date on July 31.

DUTY COUNSEL: I ask that we proceed with the trial on July 24, Your Worship. This man is employed at the moment. His problem is alcohol. He tells me that when his case comes up, he will ask to be sent somewhere for a cure.

MAGISTRATE *(folds his hands and deliberates):* Two hundred dollars bail, and we'll set a date on July 31.

CROWN: Thank you, Your Worship. In this case I also suggest July 31 to set a date and no bail. This man is charged with illegal possession of narcotics. He has a record, Your Worship. It's a long record. I strongly recommend no bail for this man's own protection.

DUTY COUNSEL: Your Worship, this man is living in Toronto with his sister and her family. His record is admitted, but he has never skipped bail at any time. He's now working. By denying bail, you are presuming this man will commit another offence. And I do suggest you take into account he has kept bail before.

CROWN *(handing some packets to the clerk):* These exhibits were found in his sweater and pants pocket. For the accused's own good, I strongly suggest no bail.

MAGISTRATE: No bail. Come back on July 31 to set a date for trial.

CROWN *(grabbing at another paper):* Thank you, Your Worship. *(A man, not in custody, comes from the back of the court.)* You got a lawyer yet? *(The man shakes his head.)* Well, you've had a month. Better get on with it. July 30 to set a date for trial. Thank you, Your Worship. Come back then with your lawyer *(to The Accused).*

(Blackout.)

SCENE 3

The scene is 24 Court in the basement of the old City Hall, a place where male Accused first tangle with the machinery of Canadian justice if they happen to be charged with an offence under the Liquor Control Act of Ontario.

When the lights go up, the audience sees 24 Court is even smaller than its basement neighbour, 23. There is the familiar court furniture, a high magistrate's bench, three rows of seats for the public or accused who are not in custody. The dock is a narrow cage built along one wall, and this morning it is crammed with alleged offenders. Few wear ties or jackets.

OFFICER: Quiet! All rise!

(Magistrate S. Tupper Bigelow walks deliberately into the courtroom. He is a severe-looking man who is also wearing the red-trimmed magistrate's robes. He has a flat, cold voice which can seldom be heard clearly in the tiny room. Crown Counsel Martin Kelso, who regularly prosecutes L.C.A.O. cases, also has an inaudible voice. As the audience will soon see, Accused standing a few feet from the bench often stand in bewilderment after their fate is decided until a police guard tells them what has happened.

There is a sameness about the cases in 24 Court. Intoxication. Drinking in a public place. Charges of selling liquor from a car or apartment. Drinking under age. The clerk of the court reads the charges somnambulistically.)

CROWN: The name is listed as St. Peter, Your Worship. *(He turns to The Accused).* Is it St. Peter or St. Pierre?

ACCUSED: It's the same thing. One's English, one's French.

CROWN: It's not the same thing. St. Peter, Your Worship.

CLERK *(in an expressionless voice which effectively masks most of his words):* . . . intoxicated condition in a public place, contravention of the Liquor Control Act of Ontario. How do you plead?

ACCUSED: Guilty.

CLERK: You are further charged . . . consume liquor in other than the residence of the purchaser or of a bona fide donee thereof. . . . How do you plead?

ACCUSED: Yes. Yes.

CLERK: What?

ACCUSED: Yes, I was guilty.

MAGISTRATE: Twenty-five dollars or ten days.

DUTY COUNSEL: Your Worship, this man is married, has five children, and is now employed in a restaurant kitchen. It's true enough that he has a previous conviction. But he does need a little time to pay.

ACCUSED: I can get the money tomorrow.

MAGISTRATE *(flatly):* Twenty-five dollars or ten days. *(He does not look up.)*

DUTY COUNSEL: One day to pay, Your Honour?

MAGISTRATE: No time to pay.

DUTY COUNSEL: But he's lived at the same address for some time.

MAGISTRATE: I've made up my mind.

CROWN *(ignoring the previous protagonist):* . . . Your Worship.

MAGISTRATE *(looking up as a witness tip-toes from the court):* There's a great deal of disturbance in this court. Who is that man? It's a mad-house!

CLERK: . . . you are charged . . . .

(Blackout.)

SCENE 4

The audience sees it is 23 Court again. A clock on the wall shows that twenty minutes have elapsed since the previous blackout. Magistrate Donald Graham lounges back in his chair and observes a chunkily built sixteen-year-old dressed in a green miniskirt as she is directed to stand before him.

CLERK: You are charged . . . no apparent means of support. . . . How do you plead?

ACCUSED: Not guilty. *(A police officer in uniform walks from the back of the court, swears to tell the truth, and states his name. He glances at his notebook.)*

OFFICER: I saw the accused standing in the doorway of a church. I asked her about herself, and she told me she had no job, no money, no friends. She said she was just hanging around. She also said she had left home and refused to go home. I arrested her for vagrancy. *(A young, earnest man wearing spectacles rises from the defence counsel's chair.)*

DEFENCE: I wonder if you could state the conversation you had with her?

OFFICER: She just stated she was hanging around. It was the only statement she made to us.

DEFENCE: But I wonder if you could give more details about the conversation.

MAGISTRATE *(annoyed)*: He's told us that. We're not going through all the evidence again!

DEFENCE: But during the conversation, were her answers spontaneous?

OFFICER: I asked her questions. One of the questions was, "Do you have a place to stay?"

DEFENCE: She answered yes?

OFFICER: I don't recall her exact words.

DEFENCE: Did you have this particular girl in mind when you picked her up?

OFFICER: Yes, among many others.

DEFENCE: Do you know whether she had been in the church?

OFFICER: She was loitering in the doorway.

DEFENCE: Do you recall whether or not anyone else came out of the church?

OFFICER: It may have happened.

MAGISTRATE: Look, all he's expected to remember is whether she had a home, a job, and money. *(He stares at the young man.)* Who are you? Nobody but solicitors are supposed to appear in my court. You don't have any status here.

DEFENCE: I'm a student.

MAGISTRATE: You have no status in this court. Ask relevant questions only.

DEFENCE: Well, in response to the question as to whether she had been in the church, what did she say?

MAGISTRATE *(leaning forward)*: Vagrancy is a matter of status. The police are supposed to find out whether she had any home, job, money. I'm not interested in any further details apart from this. If there are any other details, put her in the box.

DEFENCE: Was it possible she was in the church?

MAGISTRATE: What else do you want to ask? Put the girl in the box! *(He looks down into the courtroom.)* The Salvation Army wants to say something. Yes. *(A woman in Salvation Army uniform*

*marches to the witness box, swears she will tell the truth, and
states her name.)*

WITNESS *(severely)*: The accused woman admitted to us she had
no place to stay. She has been staying with us.

MAGISTRATE: Then she had no place to go and no money! *(He
nods. The Accused walks to the box and is sworn in.)* Now, the
only issue is where does she live, work, and does she have a
place to go.

DEFENCE: How old are you?

ACCUSED: Sixteen.

DEFENCE: How long is it since you left home?

MAGISTRATE: I don't care how long ago she left home!

DEFENCE: What were you doing when you were arrested?

ACCUSED: I had been inside the church at a dance.

DEFENCE: Is it customary to have dances in the church?

MAGISTRATE: I don't care whether it's customary for the church to
hold dances. I want to know whether she had any place to go!

DEFENCE: Did you pay to get into the dance?

ACCUSED: Yes, a dime.

DEFENCE: Were you working?

ACCUSED: Yes, the Monday and Tuesday before I was arrested. As
a waitress. I was going to stay with a girl friend.

MAGISTRATE: *(with a long sigh)*: Where is she going now?

ACCUSED: A place on Sherbourne Street.

MAGISTRATE: Now, get a job and a permanent address. If you're
back in court another time, you'll be in trouble. *(He stares at
the young man.)* Case dismissed.

(Blackout.)

SCENE 5

*The scene is 22 Court on the main floor of the old City Hall,
another forum where Toronto's Accused first come in intimate
contact with the workings of Canadian justice. Twenty-two is a
twin of its neighbour 21, but it is twice as noisy. It is furnished in
familiar court fashion, except that its walls are decorated near the
ceiling with a faintly Bacchanalian design of grape vines. Accused
in custody are accommodated in a caged dock against a wall. The
traffic from the cell entrance in 21 adds to the Union Station
atmosphere.*

OFFICER *(to a young man in the public benches)*: Take that gum
out of your mouth! All rise!

(Magistrate Charles Drukarsh walks into the courtroom. He is

a compact, unsmiling man who seems to like to wear his official robes. His voice is strong, but the clatter in the street below often overrules what he has to say. As in 24 Court, The Accused can be seen to hesitate or crane forward to listen. The Crown Counsel sometimes bowls along with the next case before alleged offenders know they are free or required to wait longer for trial.)

CROWN *(briskly):* Set a date for trial.

LAWYER: I appear for the accused, Your Worship. He has been charged with possession of an automobile. He was arrested July 12. But I'm surprised to see his bail was set at $1,000. He can't raise that amount, Your Worship! I ask that he be released on his own recognizance. This man has lived in Toronto for many years. He has no record except one arrest some time ago for sleeping in a boxcar. He has been steadily employed. Another thing: there are some questions about this case. He drove to work with the owner of that car for weeks before his arrest.

MAGISTRATE *(pausing for the crashes in the street to subside):* Bail reduced to two hundred dollars cash.

CROWN: Yes, Your Worship. *(He ignores the man in the dock and picks up another sheaf of papers.)* Set a date for trial, Your Worship.

LAWYER: This man was arrested in company with . . ., Your Worship. His bail also now stands at one thousand dollars. We admit the accused has a previous conviction for auto theft, but Magistrate Bigelow gave him a suspended sentence. *(There are some wry smiles among officers of the court.)*

MAGISTRATE *(without expression and without looking at The Accused):* Five hundred dollars cash or one thousand dollars in property.

CROWN: Thank you, Your Worship. *(A nineteen-year-old steps forward. The calendar says he has been accused of dangerous driving.)* Have you got a lawyer yet?

ACCUSED: No, I haven't. But I want to, as soon as I can afford to get one.

MAGISTRATE: When did this incident take place?

ACCUSED: In early June.

MAGISTRATE: Do you realize it's now July?

ACCUSED: I've been out of work.

MAGISTRATE: Do you expect the courts to wait while you fiddle around?

ACCUSED: I can't afford a lawyer.

MAGISTRATE: Well, when do you think you can afford one?

ACCUSED: By September, I think.

MAGISTRATE: September? Well, this is a serious charge. Snap into it. It's for your own protection. Come back August 2, and we'll set a date for trial. You'd better have a lawyer then. *(The duty counsel for legal aid looks briefly at The Accused, then at the magistrate, and turns his back.)*

CROWN: . . . Your Worship. *(A short, thick-set man steps forward.)* You got a lawyer?

ACCUSED *(with a heavy accent):* No, I am here alone. I plead guilty.

MAGISTRATE: Do you know the charge?

ACCUSED: That I did such a thing that I wasn't supposed to do.

MAGISTRATE *(shielding one ear from the street noises):* What did he say?

CROWN: He says he did a thing he wasn't supposed to do.

CLERK *(almost unintelligibly):* You are charged . . . did steal merchandise not exceeding fifty dollars. . . . How do you plead?

ACCUSED: I am guilty.

CROWN: These are the facts, Your Worship. A store investigator in Honest Ed's observed this man for some time. He put a fishing reel and a hunting knife under his jacket. The investigator followed him out of the store and went with him to a car. There, he found two other reels. The total value of the merchandise is twenty-seventy-six. Are those facts correct?

ACCUSED: Yes.

MAGISTRATE: There will be a conviction. *(He looks down at the Crown Counsel.)*

CROWN: No previous convictions, Your Worship.

MAGISTRATE: Tell me about yourself. *(More traffic noises. The Accused speaks, then has to repeat himself as the magistrate shakes his head.)*

ACCUSED: I work in a factory. I make eighty dollars a week.

MAGISTRATE: Married?

ACCUSED: Yes. I have two children.

MAGISTRATE: You're setting a fine example for them, aren't you?

ACCUSED: I took the reels for the boy and myself.

MAGISTRATE: Three reels? You figured Honest Ed's wouldn't miss them, I suppose. Well, you realize I could send you to jail for this?

ACCUSED: Yes, I think you could.

MAGISTRATE: Can you give me any reason why not?

ACCUSED: No, I can't.

MAGISTRATE: I've got no sympathy for you. *(Looking down at his papers).* One hundred and fifty dollars or ten days.

CROWN: . . . Your Worship. *(He looks at the previous Accused, still standing uncertainly in the dock.)* One hundred and fifty dollars or ten days! Next, Your Worship. We don't have an interpreter, so maybe one of his friends in court will help out. . . .
(Blackout.)

SCENE 6

The audience sees the scene has returned to 21 Court. The magistrate, Peter Wilch, is sitting at his bench. A police officer stands in the witness box. The Crown Counsel is fingering his papers. Two Accused, dressed in working clothes, stand on the floor of the courtroom.

FIRST ACCUSED: We tried to get a lawyer, Your Worship. We were turned down by legal aid because they said it was a small infraction. They advised us to pay the fine.

CROWN *(to the magistrate)*: Two brothers, Your Worship. Causing a disturbance. They plead not guilty.

FIRST ACCUSED: We're innocent!

CROWN: I have this constable present, Your Worship. The Crown is prepared to proceed.

SECOND ACCUSED: We've managed to get a lawyer, sir. But we can't get him here for another two weeks. We want to fight this case.

CROWN: The dates for trial are all in September by now, Your Worship. *(He shakes his head as he flips the pages of his date book.)* We've got the witness here. . . .

MAGISTRATE: When is your leave, officer? *(The officer leans toward the magistrate and speaks inaudibly.)* Well, we suggest trial on September 25 in 31 Court. *(He looks down at the accused.)* Counsel and witnesses must be there. You understand?

FIRST ACCUSED: Yes, Your Worship. Thank you, Your Worship.

CROWN *(with a little less enthusiasm than at the beginning of the session)*: Again two, Your Worship. A matter of throwing firecrackers. . . .
(Blackout.)

SCENE 7

A return to 23 Court. Magistrate Donald Graham is sitting, cheek in palm, while he deliberates evidence on a charge of indecent exposure. The accused stands near the dock.

MAGISTRATE *(speaking slowly)*: The woman witness said the accused had a newspaper in front of him when she saw him at the subway station. She only saw he was exposing himself from the side. The officer said the man was all zipped up when he arrived. I feel there is an absence of evidence that the man intended to assault anybody. I think the way the charge is drawn, we must dismiss it.

CROWN: Yes, Your Honour. Now, I've got this Vag C. *(A pretty blonde seventeen-year-old walks to a place in front of the bench.)*

CLERK *(in high-pitched, partly inaudible words):* You are charged . . . common prostitute or streetwalker. . . . How do you plead?

ACCUSED: Not guilty. *(A police officer walks to the witness box and is sworn in.)*

OFFICER: Your Honour, this girl is known to me as a prostitute. I observed her a total of thirty-five times on Avenue Road between June 4 and 22. I cautioned the accused, and she replied, "I'm starting to come up here because you morality guys don't worry us like you do in Chinatown." Later that night, she approached some men in a restaurant, then got into an automobile with them. She returned to the restaurant at eleven-thirty and got into a conversation with three other men. She walked out of the restaurant, saw the police, then walked back inside the restaurant. I identified myself and asked her for an account of her activities. She replied, "Listen, I only go out with guys when I'm hitch-hiking." It was not a good explanation, so I arrested her.

MAGISTRATE: Where did you arrest her?

OFFICER: In the hallway of the restaurant.

MAGISTRATE: And what did she say?

OFFICER: I only go out with guys when I'm hitch-hiking.

DUTY COUNSEL: What kind of good account do you require when you ask these questions?

OFFICER: I asked her to give an account of her actions!

CROWN: That's the case, Your Worship.

MAGISTRATE *(leaning back):* Well, I've heard the evidence, and I think it's an ambiguous charge. Case dismissed. *(The Accused breaks into an incredulous smile and leaves the courtroom.)*

DEFENCE: I appear for Miss . . . Your Worship.

MAGISTRATE: Arraign her.

CLERK *(partly inaudibly):* . . . charged inmate common bawdy house. How do you plead?

ACCUSED: Guilty.

CROWN: The facts are these, Your Worship. A police officer made a telephone call to an apartment on Spencer Avenue, and the accused invited him up to the apartment for the purpose of having sexual intercourse. The accused and her friend said they charged forty dollars each.

MAGISTRATE *(astonished)*: Forty dollars each?

CROWN: Yes, Your Worship. The police officer placed the accused under arrest.

DEFENCE: The facts are substantially correct, Your Worship.

MAGISTRATE: Okay, that will be $100 each or 30 days.

CROWN: Thank you, Your Worship. . . . charge of drunk.

MAGISTRATE: How do you intend to plead?

ACCUSED: Guilty.

CROWN: Nothing unusual in the case.

MAGISTRATE: Ten dollars or five days.

(Magistrate looks at his watch. It is 11:15 A.M., 105 minutes since the court opened. A total of sixty-five cases have been tried, disposed of, remanded, or directed to other courts for trial. He stands. The Crown attorney and the court staff also stand.)

CLERK *(loudly and clearly)*: Adjourned until tomorrow morning at 9:30 A.M. God Save the Queen and clear the court.

(Curtain.)

4 The Revolving Door

P. J. Giffen

One of the problems exacerbated by the urban environment is that of alcoholism, the refuge of the lost and forgotten. This article, which has been widely reprinted, draws attention to the way in which the police and courts in Toronto "process" chronic drinkers into the city's "notorious" Don Jail, where the alcoholic "dries out" before being released and returned on another drunk charge. The article's strength lies in its analysis of the way in which many chronic drunks have adapted to a way of life of which a stay at the Don Jail is an integral part.

The fact that the revolving door approach is still being used in 1970 testifies to the fondness for legislation and the continuing dominance of elements of Puritanism in Toronto. Both these aspects of the city's character are inherited from the nineteenth century, when "Toronto the Good" was ruled by traditional religious norms.

The author of this piece, P. J. Giffen, teaches at the University of Toronto, where he is interim head of the Department of Sociology. Data for this article was gathered while Professor Giffen was serving as director of the Ontario Addiction Research Foundation's study of the chronic drunkenness offender. Originally delivered as a paper to the Canadian Conference on Alcoholism in Toronto in March, 1966, the article was revised and first published in the *Canadian Review of Sociology and Anthropology* in August, 1966.

Anatole France has said, "The law in its majestic equality forbids the rich as well as the poor to sleep under bridges, to beg in the street, to steal bread." To this we may add: it also forbids the rich

241

as well as the poor to be drunk in a public place. The distinction between a private and a public place is an old and honourable one in our legal tradition. The institution of privacy, sanctified in law, has given us considerable freedom from coercion when under our own roofs. But since, in keeping with this tradition, the law has defined certain acts – such as getting too drunk to walk properly – as legitimate if done in private but illegal if done in public, it has loaded the dice against the lower classes. Social class and access to private places are closely related – particularly access to enough private places to cover most of one's social life.[1] And since the law has made imprisonment a penalty for the offence, it has in some measure helped to increase the offender's initial vulnerability by making it more difficult for him to keep a job, a residence, a family relationship, and other ties to private places. It is the end result of such a process that we are concerned with in this article: the chronic drunkenness offender, or what has become known as the "revolving door" problem.

The term "revolving door" is descriptive of the cycle of public intoxication, arrest, trial, incarceration, and release that dominates the life of the skid-row alcoholic. Since he is the very model of the recidivist and, once involved in this pattern, rarely escapes, it is obvious that an overriding consequence of the revolving-door phenomenon – the police, the courts, the jail, and skid-row drinking society – is the perpetuation of the proscribed behaviour. To understand how this is brought about, it is necessary to examine some of the functions performed for both the community and the offenders by these several systems.

The statements that follow are based on a study of chronic drunkenness offenders in Ontario that has extended over several years and was initiated and financed by the Addiction Research Foundation of Ontario. The chief sources of data have been:

– an interdisciplinary study of some 230 chronic offenders in the Toronto Jail, comprising extended interviews, a medical examination and laboratory tests, psychological tests, psychiatric examination, and documentary data from various sources;

– a shorter interview study of a sample of fifty first offenders;

– basic information on the 18,000 male public intoxication cases that appeared in Toronto's G Court over a period of a year, and some comparable information from the court of a smaller city;

– mailed questionnaires to chief constables and magistrates throughout Ontario; and

– participant observation of skid-row drinking groups and police arrest practices.

The police have considerable discretion in the use they make of public intoxication laws, as the offence of drunkenness in a public place itself is very common and the initiative in making an arrest almost always lies with the police officer. The choice of arrestees is a sampling procedure, but not a random one. The Ontario chief constables were frank in admitting that the power to arrest for this offence is used highly selectively, and our own observations substantiated this. The recurrent theme in the chief constables' replies was that the drunk must be creating a disturbance or be likely to do so, or he must be in some danger of coming to harm. One police chief stated, "A person may be under the influence, but if he or she appears to be able to look after himself and is not bothering others while making his way home, he is usually not molested." Another said,

> Our officers are instructed not to arrest persons who are able to navigate under their own power without interfering with other persons. We drive a large number of persons to their homes if they are co-operative and give their addresses.

The homeless, unattached drinker, as well as being more likely to appear in public when he is drunk, is also more likely to come to harm, since he frequently has no sheltered place to go to and nobody to look after him. However, the police in large urban centres usually do not take time to determine whether the man has a home. They are likely to make quick judgements based on such externals as dress, companionship, and location – and, perhaps, recognition of the inebriate as a regular customer. This appears in the replies of the police chiefs in such phrases as: "Usually persons who are homeless and bothering people . . . or drawing attention to themselves," and "The habitual offender is charged on every occasion." Data on the occupations, addresses, and marital status of offenders indicate that the public intoxication charge is, in fact, used most commonly as a means of dealing with homeless, unattached drinkers. Others are also caught up in the net, but they, too, are mostly from the lower classes.

An important constraint on the over-zealous, indiscriminate use of the public intoxication arrest is the opposition that would result from the interruption of role-performances if large numbers of productive citizens were punished for a trivial offence of no political significance.[2] It is instructive that in minor traffic offences, where the police sampling method inevitably nets many offenders with jobs and other responsibilities, the procedures for handling the cases differ markedly from public-intoxication cases. Traffic offenders are generally summoned to appear, allowed to avoid trial by advance payment of the fine, and even, in some communities, provided with a night court. In contrast, drunkenness offenders are usually arrested and held for trial rather than summoned, and they are forced to appear in court during working hours – a system obviously attuned to a clientele that is predominantly jobless and without duties to families or other organizations.

One interpretation of this role of the police is that of residual social control, a responsibility that is theirs because no others are concerned. Better-off drinkers, in addition to having homes in which to drink and taxis and cars in which to get there, are caught up in a network of relationships with others who will likely make efforts to protect them from harm and prevent their disruptive behaviour from becoming public. This role of law-enforcement agencies as a form of social control increases as one goes down the social scale and takes in other forms of deviance. Hollingshead and Redlich in their study of mental illness and class structure, for example, found that 52.2 per cent of the psychotics in the lowest class were brought or sent for treatment by the police or the courts, but that none of those in the two highest classes entered treatment by this route.[3]

In so far as public intoxication laws are used for the control of homeless, unattached men, they converge in function with vagrancy laws. The "idle rogues and vagabonds" at which such laws have for centuries been aimed have been seen as a threat to the community precisely because they are detached from normal social controls – aliens who are dangerous because they have nothing to lose. The drunk arrest may serve the police as the easiest means of keeping down the number of such men in circulation – easiest because conviction is almost automatic and the police are rarely called upon to testify.

It is significant that chief constables who were polled were over-whelmingly opposed to removing the offence from the statute books and that their stated reasons frequently included the idea that an increase in other crime would result. One of the more strongly stated responses was, "If these persons were allowed to roam the streets in an intoxicated condition without fear of arrest or punishment, I can see any number of crimes, rape, robbery, thefts, assaults, being committed as a result." It would seem, then, that the high arrest rate of homeless drunks is partly due to this police concern with preventative control. There is a slim empirical basis for this, in that some chronic offenders do commit occasional petty thefts when at large. But their criminal records also show that they very rarely commit assaults or other offences against the person once they become fully involved in the revolving door.

However, for the police, the responsibility for dealing with drunks is a mixed blessing. Their job is complicated by the fact that the offenders may be sick or semi-comatose and – perhaps more important – they may have injuries, some of them hidden, or be suffering from an acute illness. Since they are by definition criminal offenders and are by custom arrested rather than summoned, the presumption is that they should be put in the lock-up unless there are reasons apparent to a layman for taking them to a hospital. Every so often an alleged drunk dies or commits suicide while in custody, and the police are the subject of unfavourable publicity. This is one of the junctures at which the priority of the "criminal" over the "illness' definition of intoxication is clearly dysfunctional for the police.

The consequences of this arrest pattern for the chronic offenders are several. In terms of their physical welfare, and perhaps survival, the net result of having their drinking bouts terminated by arrest is beneficial.[4] However, recognition of this is not prominent in the reactions of the chronic offenders themselves. They express strong animus against the police – stronger than their feelings against the courts and in contrast to their generally accepting attitude towards the prison staff. They do not think that public intoxication should be an offence at all, and they regard the police as the people who in fact try and convict them, and that unfairly. More specifically, they complain that the police are much too zealous in arresting drunks who are harming nobody; that in doing so they discriminate on a class basis, particularly against men known to them as chronic offenders; that they are arbitrary and inconsistent, sometimes arresting men who are not drunk and at other times overlooking extreme intoxication; and that they tend to insult known drunks and physically abuse them. The validity of these accusations is not relevant here. What is important is that such beliefs, with a strong emotional component, reinforce the alienation of the chronic offenders. They become part of the common culture of skid row and contribute to its solidarity as a persecuted out-group.

THE COURTS

Drunk trials are probably the most simple, rapid, and routinized of criminal proceedings, usually taking less than a minute from beginning to end. The cast of actors is cut to a minimum: lawyers rarely appear for the accused (they appeared in less than one case in a thousand in G Court), the prosecution is usually handled by a police officer, witnesses are almost never called, there are no newspaper reporters, and the few spectators are likely to be idle onlookers rather than interested parties. Since the overwhelming majority of the accused plead guilty, the court has only to pronounce sentence, and this is usually done according to a standard scale of punishment established by usage. Except for the occasional brief interchange, usually initiated by the accused who wants to put forward a plea for clemency, no argument is heard.

Formally, the courts perform the same functions in drunk trials that they do in other criminal cases: what might be called the "sorting-out" function and the "legitimation" function. The sorting-out function is the outcome of various decisions that result in a specific disposition of the case: decisions as to whether a trial should be held at all, decisions as to guilt or innocence, and decisions regarding the penalty. The accused are put into categories that define what, if anything, may be done with them subsequently. When the trial has in theory been conducted according to the rules, and the disposition is based on the law, what is subsequently done to the accused is legitimated. The authority of others over the offender while he is still in custody or under supervision is now legal and therefore morally acceptable, and it may be backed by the use of force.

But the sorting-out function as it is performed in the drunk court is rudimentary and subject to conflicting expectations. The proving of guilt, as we have seen, is rarely necessary. Time-consuming weighing of alternative sentences tends to be discouraged by the triviality of the offence, by the limited choices open to the magistrate, and by the apparent lesson from experience that the recidivists are not going to be changed or deterred in any event.

The number of ways that the magistrate can dispose of the case is limited not only by the law but also by the lack of facilities that could be an alternative to imprisonment. Probation officers, scarce in relation to demand, are not often available for the supervision of drunkenness offenders. Alcoholism clinics or social welfare agencies dealing with this sort of man, if they exist, rarely have liaison with the courts.[5] In only a few jurisdictions is the magistrate given the option of sentencing offenders to a place of treatment. Some of the remaining sentencing choices open to the magistrates may be fictitious or inapplicable, especially where chronic offenders are concerned. A fine may in theory be an alternative to a jail sentence, but it is not an alternative in fact unless the offender can pay. We found that some 40 per cent of the first offenders in G Court were unable to pay their fines, and that the proportion increases to 96 per cent among men up for their sixth or subsequent offence within the year. If the law allows the magistrate to give the accused time to pay his fine, he is under an obligation to consent to this only where the accused is a good credit risk. Consequently, the privilege is rarely granted to chronic offenders, and usually only to those first offenders who have a job and an address. In effect, then, a fine is a jail sentence for most chronic offenders. The magistrate has little choice, and therefore he has little reason to spend time exploring alternatives in court.

In sending the chronic offender to jail, the magistrate is exposed to a value conflict whose nature has been expressed graphically by an American municipal court judge of long experience:

> In this environment, we have been driven to extreme frustrations, in part because we have been handed the two accepted tools of criminal penalization – the fine and jail sentence – to deal with what has appeared to us to be primarily a social and medical problem. We have found ourselves dissatisfied with these tools both on philosophical and practical grounds. On the one hand, we are cast in the role of the bully trampling down and further degrading those within our society who are already the weakest and most inadequate among us, ourselves frustrated by the realization that neither do we protect society by the prevention of law violations in this regard which, of course, is the basic function of all law enforcement.[6]

The generality of this conflict is to be seen in the following written conclusion from a 1959 conference of municipal court judges:

> The alcoholic is a compulsive offender who should be helped by the court rather than punished. . . . The municipal judge has the right, if not the duty, to inform his community that he is willing to continue to handle this health problem, but that he has not been given the tools to do the job. Until such tools are provided, a judge should not be required to incarcerate persons guilty of no offence other than their affliction with the illness of alcoholism.[7]

As these statements indicate, the current conflict in our society between the "illness" and "criminal" definitions of deviance may become a pressing one for the magistrate who is forced to be our agent in implementing one or the other. The illness definition, of course, implies that the proscribed behaviour is non-voluntary and that the appropriate response is treatment or some form of social repair rather than punishment. The traditional criminal definition assumes that the actor freely chooses to misbehave and that punishment according to a graded scale of seriousness and culpability is justified response. The conflict is likely to appear rather sharply in dealing with offenders whose behaviour is attributable to an addiction, since the illness definition has come to be widely accepted in this sphere.

Most magistrates are likely to subscribe in some degree to the illness definition, while being required by law in most jurisdictions to treat the drunken behaviour of the homeless alcoholic as a punishable offence. Even if the magistrate subscribes to the criminal definition, he is probably forced to recognize that the traditional claims for the appropriateness of punishment are weak where chronic drunkenness offenders are concerned. First, public drunkenness does not stand high in the scale of proscribed acts, and secular change undoubtedly has been in the direction of greater tolerance of inebriety. Second, he cannot believe that by sending the offender to jail he is protecting society by removing a dangerous felon from circulation. Third, he cannot long maintain a belief that punishment is a deterrent, although he may think that some first offenders learn a lesson. Moreover, the appropriateness of punishment is challenged by the many manifest claims to sympathy of the chronic offenders. They appear to be unfortunates who have already been punished by circumstances: lonely, homeless, without a future, perhaps old and ill.

In Ontario, the magistrate is allowed one way out of the dilemma. The Liquor Control Act enables him to sentence offenders to treatment within the reformatory system.[8] But here the paradoxes of combining clinical decisions with the judicial role become manifest. When it came into force in 1961, the provision gave the magistrate the right to sentence third offenders to compulsory treatment, thus designating the traditional standard of punishability – the number of offences – as a criterion for treatment. Since the act was amended in 1962 to allow courts to send for treatment any public intoxication offender "where it appears he may benefit therefrom," magistrates have, on the whole, continued to regard recidivism as a condition of elegibility. Our study of first offenders has shown, as might be expected, that being in court for the first time does not preclude the presence of alcoholism or other conditions for which a clinician might recommend treatment.

The magistrate is given no guidance beyond the vague wording of the law, and he is provided with no professional help in making the decision about treatment. We have found that, as a consequence, magistrates tend to develop their own individual rules of thumb that can quickly be applied, and that these differ considerably among magistrates. For example, some feel that it is useless to send the older skid-row alcoholics for treatment, and others feel that the treatment is appropriate only for men of this type. The research also showed that the courts throughout the province differ greatly in the proportion of offenders that they sent for treatment. For the treatment facility, this has meant an unpredictable flow of patients not of their own choosing. We have also found that magistrates, seeing their failures return, have tended to become pessimistic about the possibilities of treatment.

Despite their limitations as a sorting-out mechanism, the courts still formally perform the function of legitimation. But here, too, some qualifications are necessary. The legitimation provided by lower courts is provisional: the decisions can be challenged and upset in higher courts. On the two occasions in the last five years when proceedings in G Court have been challenged, the appellants have been successful. The grounds need not concern us here, but in both instances they involved practices or conditions common to most other trials in the court. We also found that in a period when the law prescribed minimum penalties, a large proportion of the sentences given chronic offenders were well below the statutory minimum. These distortions of the legal process can be interpreted as adaptations to the strains put on the courts by the requirement that they should deal with men of this type as criminal offenders. Undoubtedly, there are parallels in other jurisdictions.

The effect of the court experience on the offenders themselves is to add to their alienation. Their reactions to these trials are epitomized in the term "kangaroo court," which occurs so frequently in their conversation that it must be regarded as part of their common culture. In more detail, they complain that "you can't beat a drunk charge" (a conviction is inevitable); that they are herded through (like a "bunch of sheep," as one man put it); that they are given no chance to tell their stories; that the magistrate and the policeman who conducts the prosecution are in cahoots, and so on. They complain much more frequently about the demeaning way in which they are treated than about the sentences they are given – which is not surprising in men accustomed to jail but highly conscious of their lack of status.

In discussing the functions of the jail, we should make it clear that the "Don Jail" in Toronto, on which these observations are based, may not be typical. Many other jails may not possess in the same degree the conditions for the development of a stable and fairly complex occupational system manned almost entirely by drunkenness offenders. Since it is a large jail, and the more serious offenders awaiting trial or transfer to another institution are not required to work, the many routine housekeeping and maintenance jobs are done by the inebriates who constitute 30 to 40 per cent of the jail population. A condition for stability is unwittingly filled by the police and the courts who send the "regulars" (the term itself is significant and derives from the jail) to jail frequently and for fairly extended periods. The justification for using this case is that it brings out in exaggerated form characteristics of the adjustment of chronic drunkenness offenders to all prisons and also that it makes particularly evident certain potentials of these men in such a setting.

The effects conventionally cited as functions of imprisonment can be dismissed out of hand where the "regulars" are concerned. "Incapacitation" is of consequence only in regard to offenders who are dangerous when at large. "Rehabilitation" is a job the jails do not pretend to do, and the recidivism characteristic of our group indicates that it is not accomplished unintentionally. However, the jail does provide an excellent setting for physical recuperation, as the results of our medical examinations showed.[9]

"Deterrance" deserves more attention. Leaving aside the inappropriateness of this expectation where an addiction is involved, the jail experience is clearly not a painful one for the "regular." There is no need to linger on what are usually thought of as the deprivations of imprisonment; the chronic drunkenness offender is already stigmatized and already alienated from his family and respectable friends; since he rarely if ever has sexual relations with women outside, their absence is not experienced as deprivation (certainly not for thirty days) ; he has no job to lose; and the food, sleeping accommodations, and other creature comforts are probably better and certainly more predictable than he finds outside.

Of more interest are the ways in which the experience is rewarding, and the fact that it complements and thus helps to maintain his pattern of life outside.

To understand this we must examine, very sketchily, the jail system. Within the walls, there is a differentiated occupational structure made up of at least seventeen jobs or work crews, some of them employing up to twenty-five inmates. The guard (or it may be a civilian employee) in charge of each crew or job functions as an employer. When he recruits a new employee, the main requirement is that the man should be a "regular" – somebody who can be depended upon to return frequently and for a respectable time – and also, of course, that the man should not already be employed by another crew chief who wants to keep him. The men who make the grade acquire a recognized right to the job and can legitimately expect to be re-hired each time they are admitted. Formally, all prisoners are equal, but the jobs are informally graded in a rough hierarchy of prestige, related to the status of the people who are served, the freedom of movement the job allows, how close it is to the centres of communication in the jail, and the material rewards it carries. While there is no official payment, the jobs bring with them differences in the opportunities to get tobacco, extra food, changes in clothing, more frequent showers, and, in some cases, better quarters. Moving to a better job is possible for those who perform well, demotion is possible for those who abuse the opportunities of their jobs, and it is even possible, with time, to retire to the section of the jail reserved for the unemployables who have become too old to work.

The administration of the prison is judged largely on how well it looks after custody, internal order, and self-maintenance.[10] The "regulars" are an asset in all these respects: they do not try to escape, they are orderly and tractable, and they fill most of the work roles of the internal economy. Not surprisingly, the relationships that evolve are in some ways closer to those of an ordinary work situation than a prison. A sympathetic relationship tends to develop between many of the "regulars" and the staff, particularly within the work crews. Like foremen in industry, the crew chiefs are dependent on the co-operation of the men who work for them and must make numerous small concessions to this end. The men, from their side, have come to place a positive value on co-operation with the staff: they are allies in getting a job done, as well as in circumventing some of the more burdensome rules. It is revealing that the men who are unco-operative on the inside are usually those who have only a marginal relationship with skid-row drinking groups on the outside; men who have previously had serious criminal careers are also more likely to be unco-operative.

The relatively responsible behaviour of the "regular" in his job tends to extend to other aspects of his life in jail. He is, for example, likely to read newspapers and news magazines and even to engage in discussions of public affairs – things he rarely does outside. The pattern of "sharing" – which, on the outside, is likely to be confined almost entirely to alcohol – includes the other scarce material objects that are valued in jail and becomes a form of altruism in the common pattern of sharing smokes, extra food, and reading material with the old unemployables who cannot reciprocate. He, of course, abstains from drinking – external controls have made internal controls unnecessary – but he also states with conviction that he does not miss alcohol. Apparently, the relatively rewarding character of jail life has something to do with this absence of craving.

The jail life that we have described must be seen as complementary to the life the "regulars" lead outside, and the two lives are mutually reinforcing. The men seem to become adjusted to an alternation of confinement and freedom – of stable, responsible living and chaotic licence. Consciously or unconsciously, their motivation during life outside to eat regularly, govern their drinking, or get a job may be attenuated by the predictability of arrest. Their disciplined lives in prison may in turn be made bearable by the anticipation of the period of uncontrolled drinking. At an unconscious level, their exemplary behaviour in a situation of unjustified punishment may have the significance of a licence to transgress when they are released. Or, if they are highly ambivalent – as they give evidence of being – life outside may serve to satisfy their alienative need-dispositions, and life in prison, paradoxically, serves to satisfy their conformative need-dispositions. Many interpretations are possible.

Finally, a word about the function of jail in the integration of skid-row drinking society. It is in jail that men have the best chance to become acquainted with others like themselves, and the newcomer has the best chance to become acculturated to skid-row drinking norms. If you ask one of these men who he drinks with, he is quite likely to answer, "With guys I know from jail." The great majority of the men we studied served jail terms before they became full-fledged members of skid-row society. If there were no jail, skid-row drinking groups would undoubtedly exist, but they would probably be localized and fragmented, and recruitment to them would be much less efficient.

SKID ROW

Outside jail, membership in the society of skid-row drinkers tends to perpetuate deviant behaviour. Their peers reward deviance with social acceptance and, without malice, make social isolation the cost of going straight. It is a society of alcoholics oriented to collective drinking almost to the exclusion of activities that have no bearing on acquiring and consuming liquor and avoiding arrest. According to their norms of reciprocity, it is incumbent on the member to share his liquor, to pool his money with others to purchase it, to share his knowledge of safe drinking places, to allow friends to drink in his room if he has found a tolerant landlord, and so on. But the sharing of other material benefits is largely irrelevant, and responsibility for looking after one's fellows is not expected. As one man put it, "You have to look out for yourself unless you are sick from booze. I mean they are only interested in you to drink with."

Since little is expected of participants, membership is easily granted: social background, education, age, and appearance are irrelevant. The few unacceptable individuals are likely to be those who are known to endanger the drinking group by their aggressive, noisy, or bizarre behaviour, and those who persistently fail to reciprocate in furnishing wine. This form of company is temptingly easy to acquire for the man who has nobody else and who has limited personal resources to spend in the friendship market. In drinking together, the illusion of warm camaraderie may be sustained for a while. One "regular" put it this way: "When you're drinking, you're all close friends and buddies."

It also seems that what is easily acquired is little valued. The men are likely when interviewed to denigrate their skid-row companions, reflecting in some degree their own low self-esteem; they refer to their drinking friends as "bums," "drunks," or "skid-row characters." One man expresses it, "If you're one of the boys, you're O.K. in the District, but there are really no close friends in the District." They seem to be saying that these relationships are unsatisfying in that they differ from true primary relations found in the family or among close friends. What is lacking is the affection or emotion characteristic of primary relations and the diffuse obligation to help each other. The true primary relation is, of course, particularistic; individuals are not substitutable, whereas easy substitution is characteristic of skid-row interaction. Drinking groups are continually breaking up; members disperse to meet up with others and form new groups, sometimes going through several changes of companionship in a day.

The persistence of skid-row drinking society in its present form obviously depends on the modes of redistributing the affluence of the host society. Money for the purchase of alcohol must be forthcoming through panhandling and, to some extent, through pensions and welfare payments. The skid-row drinkers also depend from time to time on the numerous charitable organizations that furnish food, clothing, and shelter. Although the alcoholics usually eat little when on a spree and sometimes find other places to sleep, the hostels and missions make it possible for them to meet these minimum creature requirements at critical junctures and thus enable them to get by without changing their behaviour. Some of the organizations go further in unwittingly encouraging dependence by serving meals at times that conflict with holding a job, requiring the men to leave the hostel if they are employed, and in other ways making help and a regular occupation incompatible.

CONCLUSIONS

The criminal role, as many writers following Durkheim have observed, is inherently alienating. Since punishment serves as an occasion for reaffirming the importance of common norms, as well as for displacing aggression, the criminal is, in a sense, a scapegoat. The secondary result is that he tends to be isolated from claims on others and, under the appropriate circumstances, driven into the company of persons who are similarly stigmatized. In a modern society with elements of a puritan tradition and a fondness for legislating, the official machinery for stigmatization may continue to apply to forms of proscribed behaviour that are no longer popularly regarded as criminal or dangerous. If the proscribed behaviour is also susceptible to definition as the symptom of an illness, the conditions are created for value-conflict, compromises, and, eventually, fundamental changes that would make therapy or domiciliary care the dominant means of social control.

In the revolving-door system as it now exists, the alienating effect of criminal stigmatization is added to the effects of alcohol addiction and to other circumstances and personal characteristics that make for the isolation of the participants from kinship groups and from the occupational structure. Recruits to the revolving door find themselves in a system that supplies and rewards the addiction while adding to the reasons for seeking relief from tension. The distribution of scarce professional services and related resources is such that the skid-row inebriate is rarely involved in therapeutic relationships. If he is, the relationships are usually too superficial and short-lived to compete with the immediate gratifications that are easily available in the revolving door.

5 Crisis at the Victory Burlesk

Robert Fulford

It is a cliché of sociological analysis that many modern societies impose vigorous controls on nudity or near-nudity while
allowing evasions of such norms – within certain limits – in
such places as the burlesque show. This article treats in a
delightful manner the social atmosphere of Toronto's only
burlesque theatre and points to the role of pasties in "preserving" certain traditional norms regarding exposure of the
female breast.

It is a commentary on the changing sex norms of large
North American cities that the Victory Burlesque, during the
early summer of 1969, changed its policy. Pasties are no
longer used! With numerous go-go girls in local taverns bar-
ing all above the waist and the Mynah Bird in Yorkville running nightly nude movies – without police interference – it
would appear that the Victory had to change – or lose potential business. Whether Metro's Morality Squad will belatedly
raid such establishments – as they belatedly seized the film
*Can Heironymous Merkin Ever Forget Mercy Humppe and
Find True Happiness?* after a seven week run – is impossible
to say.

Robert Fulford is currently editor of *Saturday Night*. Previously engaged as a columnist for the Toronto *Star* and as
an editor of *Maclean's*, Mr. Fulford is widely respected in
Canada as a leading literary critic, writer, and broadcaster.
This article originally appeared in the book of the same name.

Shortly after 2:00 on a Monday afternoon, the strip show at the
Victory Burlesk Theatre in Toronto is nearing its climax. This
week there are five strippers, and now the last of them, the girl who
glories in the name Justa Dream, is out at centre stage, swinging.

255

There's a good crowd for Monday afternoon, maybe 300, and though nobody will laugh at the M.C.'s squalid little jokes, the audience seems pleased by the girls.

Everything is going well, but disaster is about to strike.

The Victory Theatre, I have to tell you first of all, is a very special burlesque house. This is not one of your Cleveland or Chicago passion-pit, pant-and-gasp strip houses, where the customers get all red in the face and shout at the girls, and the girls sometimes shout back. The Victory Theatre, Spadina at Dundas, Canada's only burlesque theatre, is a strip house that yearns for respectability.

Lou Landers, president of the company that owns the Victory, believes that burlesque houses should be patronized by both sexes. He's proud of the fact that since he took over a couple of years ago, the audience on weekends has been 40 per cent female. Men bring wives or girl friends. Mrs. Rose Bossin, who books the acts into the Victory, says the women admire the girls' costumes, enjoy the music, laugh at the vaudeville acts. They like the movies, too.

Landers is so conscious of respectability that he brags – yes, actually brags – about the fact that a couple of the Toronto morality cops (who regularly scrutinize the show) have told him they think the strippers are fine these days, very clean, very nice. This sort of testimonial would chill the blood of some burlesque managers. Landers thinks it's great. He doesn't like trouble with the cops.

And this is why, on Monday, shortly after 2:00 P.M., disaster approaches. The art of striptease in Toronto (it needs just a bit more background) is governed not by law but by custom. Over the years, the police have let it be known that they will tolerate just so much and no more. One of the essential limits is defined by Lou Landers in these words:

"It is not permissible to have a bare bosom in Toronto."

To prevent this illegality, girls at the Victory must at all times wear "pasties" – two little bits of cloth, usually coloured silver, one for each side. The legal minimum coverage. So now Justa Dream is on the stage and she is about one-third through her act. Suddenly her right-hand pastie falls to the floor.

Crisis! Disaster! Is there a cop in the house? Who knows? Justa Dream can't take a chance. She looks down nervously, sees the pastie just to her right, stoops down, scoops it up. Sticks it on. But of course the glue won't stick. (Glue failure was the problem in the first place.)

So Justa Dream, holding her hand to her bosom, looking for all the world like the heroine of a nineteenth-century melodrama, continues to dance. A few boors in the audience snicker at her plight. Justa Dream pays them no heed. She continues to the end of her act, stripping one-handed.

But she may be saved from the final agony. The band stops playing and now, according to routine, she's to take a quick bow and then begin a kind of scheduled encore.

She obviously hopes now that the stage manager will notice her problem, close the curtains, cut the encore. She looks off to stage left. No one closes the curtains. She shrugs – the biggest shrug of her lifetime – and goes through to the final beat of the big bass drum and final clash of the Chinese cymbal.

The day this happened I was in the theatre, and immediately afterward I began an investigation of life at the Victory. Upstairs, where balcony seats used to be, I found Landers and Mrs. Bossin in an office whose decoration spoke loudly of wild aspirations. The walls are painted black and white, in vertical stripes a foot wide. All the furniture is black with white trim, or the reverse. All ornaments are gold. There's a gold-painted Buddha, a three-foot high gold-painted sculpture of a greyhound racer, and on one wall an enormous gold butterfly made of wire mesh. Mrs. Bossin has a gold-painted electric typewriter. On the manager's desk sits a gold-painted adding machine.

Landers is a happy, expansive man. "We've tried to get mixed clientele at the Victory," he told me, meaning men and women. "We've tried to promote the theatre, too. We have group plans. Bowling clubs come here, sometimes service clubs. We find out what conventions are coming to town and we try to get groups of them coming here. It works pretty well.

"This week we have the amateur strip contest. We'll probably have seven girls competing, all real amateurs. There's one who's a horseback riding champion. The others include a nurse, a band singer, a lab technician, and a gym instructor. They use false names – everyday-sounding names, like Martha Wright and Carroll Stone."

The Victory has had amateur shows before, but most of its strippers are professionals from the American circuit. Their union minimum is $166.50 a week, for seven days, four a day. The average girl gets $200, the average headliner gets $350 or $400. The Victory has paid $1,040 for Libby Jones (the one with the college education) and $1,250 for Cup Cakes Cassidy. Landers is now talking about booking Lili St Cyr, who is still going strong and who asks $4,000 a week.

"The girls don't last too long," Landers told me. "In this business you're finished when you're much over twenty-five, unless you have something special. We put a suggestion box in the lobby, asking people what they want. Most of them say they want younger girls.

"A girl does well out of it. If she's anywhere near good, she makes $15,000 to $20,000 a year."

In order to do this, a stripper must adjust her style to local conditions. When she arrives at the Victory, she is confronted with "The Morality Regulations for Exotic Dancers," a mimeographed list of things the Toronto cops won't let you get away with. The list is such an exquisite combination of salaciousness and prudery that it seems to me one of the unique documents of Canadian culture. Here, for cultural historians, is the full text:

1. *Pasties and full pants are to be worn. Pasties are to be other than flesh coloured and securely attached. If you should lose a pastie, cover yourself appropriately and go off stage and the orchestra will cut your act. All panties will be other than flesh-coloured and have a two-inch strip of heavier material up the middle of the back.*

It will be noted that Justa Dream did not entirely comply with this rule. Her behaviour was governed, presumably, by a higher rule of show business: the show must go on.

2. *Once you start to remove your clothing, you cannot touch your body with your hands.*
3. *You cannot communicate with the audience: i.e., talking, noises, give-away items to patrons.*
4. *Do not touch curtains, walls, or proscenium.*
5. *You are not permitted to lie down on stage or runway.*
6. *You are not permitted to bump a prop.*
7. *You are not permitted to make any body movements that in the eyes of the public would simulate an act of sexual intercourse.*
8. *You cannot run any article of clothing between your legs.*
9. *After the first performance Friday, you must report to the mezzanine where your act will be analysed by the management. When your act has been reviewed, and any deletions are made from your routine, you will do your act as approved by the management for the balance of your engagement.*

In the lobby of the Victory there is a photograph of a star performer to come, and above it the sign: "Next Week's Thrill."

Part Four:

Deviant Behaviour and Deviant Groups

1

Middle-Class Rackets in the Big City

Pierre Berton

Some forms of deviant behaviour are rampant among those who define the norm: the middle class. In the following essays, the reader is treated to a fascinating account of the world of the fast- and phony-sell. Here are described the techniques, values, and norms of the companies and salesmen who try to "unload" shoddy goods on housewives in door-to-door selling. While some of the particular "operations" described here may have now disappeared, it is likely that ingenious "operators" will have created similar schemes which, among the thousands of newcomers to an anonymous city like Toronto, will bring similar results, at least in the short-run.

Pierre Berton, the author of these pieces, is both Canada's best-known TV interviewer and its leading journalist. The author of more than ten books, he is currently at work on an exhaustive study of the c.p.r. Railroad and its role in Canadian history. The following excerpts are taken from his book, *The Big Sell.*

One evening in the fall of 1959, Mrs. Donald Bant, a good-looking former model, newly arrived from England, received a telephone call at her home in Scarborough, a middle-class suburb of Toronto.

"Isn't this a beautiful evening, Mrs. Bant," said the cheerful voice, and Mrs. Bant had no idea he was reading from a script or that she was being sold a story.

"I called you this evening to ask your help with a couple of questions," the man on the phone said, "but first I'd better tell you whom I am with.

"This is the research division of International Health Products. We are the people who are introducing the fabulous new Health Maid electric servant – an entirely new concept in modern living.

261

This revolutionary new all-purpose kitchen machine is not yet available to the public, Mrs. Bant. We are conducting this research program as part of our educational program in order to show some of the wonders of tomorrow, and how the average Canadian family can have better nutrition and health from their food."

If Mrs. Bant had not been a newcomer to these shores, she would, in all likelihood, have hung up the phone at this point. Instead, she found herself nodding in agreement when the voice went on to say: "You *are* interested in better nutrition and health for your family if it's possible to get it, aren't you, Mrs. Bant? Most people who *think* are!

"Since you are interested in nutrition and health, Mrs. Bant, I would like to arrange your appointment to see this wonderful work and time saver and have you qualify for a chance to win one of these fabulous electric servants. In return, Mrs. Bant, all we ask is that after seeing this amazing machine, you will fill out a simple questionnaire giving your honest opinions about it – that's not asking too much, is it?"

Mrs. Bant had been ill for some time. Her husband was out of work. Both were heavily committed to payments for household goods. She told the man she could not afford to buy anything. He assured her he was not selling anything; he was merely asking for opinions.

"This preview that you'll be seeing is solely for research purposes, Mrs. Bant," he said. "We are not selling anything. . . . Health is something you can't *sell* – but must be *earned,* so we are only interested in those people who have a desire to do something for themselves."

Mrs. Bant said she didn't have much time.

"Well, Mrs. Bant," said the man on the phone, "we only have two things in this life to spend – time and money, and if both of these things are not spent wisely, we can neither have health nor anything else for long – isn't that true?" He didn't wait for Mrs. Bant to say whether it was true or not, but plunged on: "For that reason, Mrs. Bant, it is really in *your* interest to take a few minutes of your valuable time to see what we have. We won't try to sell you anything – that I promise."

Mrs. Bant succumbed, and presently, a man named Mr. McGregor arrived at her door. Mr. McGregor said that he was deeply and sincerely interested in the health of the nation. He had a letter from his company, whose office was identified as the Eglinton Health Centre. He read from the letter, which bemoaned the fact that "here we are living in a land of plenty with literally thousands of people suffering from malnutrition – the open door through which many other crippling diseases enter to destroy our health and rob us of our happiness." He talked knowingly about recent surveys which proved that the majority of school children were not properly nourished, because they ate meagre breakfasts. All this, he said, could be prevented by a few simple adjustments in eating habits.

Mr. McGregor stressed the importance of milk in diet, explaining that it was the greatest nutritional source of calcium and protein – something most children were not getting in sufficient quantity. He was gathering opinions, he said, on a new form of powdered milk. He brought a package of the milk powder into the house, and also a machine, which he said was necessary to mix the milk.

Mrs. Bant again explained that she could not afford to buy anything, but Mr. McGregor kept insisting he wasn't selling anything. He explained that the milk he was demonstrating was ten times better than milk available in the stores because of the process used to mix it. He demonstrated the marvellous machine which liquefied, blended, ground, whipped, mixed, pureed, and pulverized not only milk powder, but also vegetables, fruit, salad dressing, sauces, nuts, meats, cheese, cream, egg whites, batter, sherbet, baby food, and dried peas. It was the world's most sensible kitchen aid, said the knowledgeable Mr. McGregor.

Mrs. Bant said she could not afford to buy one. Mr. McGregor again explained firmly that the machine was not for sale. He would like her to fill out his questionnaire; that was all.

Mr. McGregor returned to the subject of milk as an important nutritional aid, and its cost to an average family. With two children, he said, Mrs. Bant must be paying $16 a month for milk; if she was not spending that much, he said, then her children weren't getting enough calories. And Mr. McGregor, who wasn't selling anything, reeled off some figures to prove his point.

"Why," said Mr. McGregor, "you're spending $2,000 a decade on milk, and all you've got to show for it is a lot of empty milk bottles.

"If I were to hold in my left hand all the empty milk bottles you wash in a month and in my right hand I hold the same amount of milk, plus this wonderful machine, which hand would you think was the greater value?"

Mrs. Bant was bewildered. She found herself saying the right hand. On hearing that, Mr. McGregor said he wanted to ask her a very special question:

"If I could do something very special for you, would you do something very special for me in return?"

It is a hard question to say "no" to. Mrs. Bant found herself nodding.

"It's obvious from your answer that you appreciate the importance of your family's health and realize it's something that must have proper care, if you are to maintain it. Right? Frankly, there just aren't enough people who appreciate this fact, but in introducing new health products, when we do find a family such as yours, we have something to offer them. . . . Now, if we are able to offer you one of these wonderful units as part of this program, without disturbing your weekly budget a penny, would you be interested?"

Mrs. Bant said that she supposed she would be.

Mr. McGregor then explained that, because of her interest in her family's health, his company was prepared to supply her with powdered milk; she would pay no more for it than she was paying for ordinary milk for her family. Furthermore, the company would let her have the machine free – if she would promise to use it.

Mrs. Bant's conscience had been stirred by all the talk of poor nutrition, and the way the salesman put it, she did not see how she could lose. She said she would like to have time to think it over, but Mr. McGregor said that was impossible; the offer was only good for the one evening.

Mrs. Bant asked what would happen if her children didn't like the milk. Mr. McGregor replied that his company would take the machine back immediately. He had a form for her to sign, he said; it was merely routine, but their lawyers insisted that they use it. Mrs. Bant, who thought she was getting a real bargain, signed. She signed up for fifteen pounds of powdered skim milk a month and promised to make nineteen payments of $16 each, together with a down payment of another $16. In other words, she committed herself to a debt of $320. The form she signed was a promissory note.

The next day, Mrs. Bant discovered that one of her children, who had a weak stomach, could not take the milk preparation. She also discovered that powdered milk, when bought at a grocery store, would cost her about $6 a month. She phoned International Health Products and tried to reach the salesman. He wasn't in. She left a message for him to call. He didn't call. When, after considerable difficulty, she finally reached him, he told her she must make her child drink the milk.

She called the manager of International Health Products and

asked him to take the milk and the machine back. She said she was willing to forgo the down payment, but wanted neither the milk nor the machine. The manager told her that she had signed a promissory note and was liable for more than $300. She could pay or go to court, he said. He advised her to get a loan somewhere.

Mrs. Bant said that in England ethical companies took things back if the purchaser wasn't satisfied.

"Well, you're not in England now," the manager said. "Things are done differently in Canada. Over here you don't believe anything unless it's written down and signed." She had signed a note, he explained; she would have to pay.

Mrs. Bant's husband took the machine back personally. A company representative refused to accept it. It was, he insisted, a second-hand machine now. He refused to give Mr. Bant a receipt for it, and so Mr. Bant took the machine home again.

When Mrs. Bant persisted in phoning again and again, the company changed its tactics. It offered to send her half the amount of milk contracted for and to reduce her payments to $13.50 a month; then it offered to suspend all milk-powder shipments if she would make payments of $11 a month for the machine. But she must pay for the machine, the manager said, or she would be taken to court. There was no further talk about the nutritional importance of milk, and it dawned on Mrs. Bant that it was the machine and not the milk the salesman was really peddling. At $11 a month, she was being charged about $220 for a combination blender, mixer, and grinder similar to those which retailed in department stores for less than $80.

Mrs. Bant made a final telephone call to International Health Products and was connected with a Mr. Keene. I listened to the conversation on an extension, and it was a tough one. Mr. Keene told Mrs. Bant flatly that "any arrangements the salesman makes won't stand up"; that "a man's word is something that's not accepted over here in Canada"; that Mrs. Bant had signed a promissory note, "which in actual fact has nothing to do with the merchandise; it's a loan"; that she was leaving herself wide open to court action, which would result in a garnishee of her wages; that the court would order her employer to turn one-third of what she earned over to International Health Products; and that, "if you're out of work, we'll just watch you until you get a job – there are organizations which will track you down."

The story, of course, has no end. That conversation, or one very like it, is being repeated over and over again in every large city on

the continent. Housewives are still answering doorbells and sign-
ing those innocent little forms that have so many teeth in them.
And some of them are waiting to be sued. . . .

In the world of the big sell, the customer is held in no more
regard by the salesman than the salesman is held by the customer.
They are engaged in a running battle of wits, and if the salesman
is a "shark" to his prey, the prey is variously a *mooch*, an *egg*, a
sucker, a *mark*, or a *peasant*. These are all terms which suggest
contempt; they are the salesman's and the con man's equivalent of
the word *square*.

I was given one day, in a darkened bar, a postgraduate course
in the art of being a mooch from an expert on mooches. His name
was Harry, and I met him through a mutual friend. He did not
call himself a salesman nor yet a sales representative nor even a
field representative; he called himself a con man. In this, too, he
was suffering from self-delusion since the select society of bona
fide confidence men would not admit him to their circle; his
methods were too crude, and, besides, he actually did sell the customer a little something. The classic con games are not designed to
sell; they are designed to take. The basic principles, however, are
always the same: the larceny and the ego of the customer are the
twin human frailties that must be played upon.

Harry, when I talked to him, was going back into the paving
racket, because, he said, almost everybody is a sucker for the
paving racket. It was a better racket, he said, than the chimney
racket, in which he considered himself the world's leading expert.

The chimney racket worked this way:

Harry would drive up to a doorway in a panel truck on which
was lettered an imposing name, such as ÉLITE CHIMNEY
REPAIR. "My company is checking all the chimneys in the area,"
he would say to the man at the door (or, as was more often the
case, the widow at the door, since widows are a prime target in
the chimney-repair racket). "We'd just like to make sure yours
is okay. There's absolutely no charge for the service."

As Harry said, the mooch cannot resist getting something for
nothing. If it's free, he'll usually say, "Go ahead." "And once
you've got the ladder up," said Harry, "you're in."

It was Harry's purpose to prove to the mooch that his chimney
was in a state of imminent collapse. He found it easiest, he told
me, to swindle professional people of considerable intelligence.
"They won't come down to your level," he explained. "They have
to pretend they know everything."

Harry offered them that chance:

"Looks to me like the cledes under the inner rim aren't in very good shape," he would say, squinting professionally at the chimney. He had long known that a real mooch cannot bring himself to ask what a "clede" is. The mooch would nod sagely and ask Harry to take a look.

Harry would scamper up the ladder and jimmy a few bricks off the chimney. He prided himself on partially destroying any chimney he inspected – knocking the bricks loose, actually smashing them, and then forcing the whole top of the chimney off with a crowbar. He would stay on the roof for some time, bustling about and tapping and peering down inside and smashing the occasional brick; then he would hustle back down the ladder.

"We were right," he would tell the mooch. "Those cledes are in terrible shape. Rusted right down to the hones. That could be dangerous – it's against fire regulations, as you know. The inner greels have pretty well had it, owing to smoke deterioration, but I think we can save the supporting skrims, the upper ones anyway, though the faces are badly tarnished. They may have to be burnished."

The intelligent mooch would nod knowingly as Harry fed him this gobbledygook.

"Come on up the ladder and see for yourself," Harry would say, shaking the ladder a little.

Nine times out of ten, said Harry, the nervous mooch would decline to mount the ladder. He would say that he preferred to leave it all to Harry; how much would it all cost? Not too much, Harry would tell him. He would know better when he got on with the job; a couple of hundred dollars at the most.

From then on, Harry would have the mooch in the palm of his hand. He would keep coming down to tell him things: just as he thought, the skrims would have to be burnished; that was going to add something to the cost. Harry could judge how much the traffic would bear, and he was generally right. Usually the sum came to about $1,000.

He insisted to me that he had once taken $3,000 from a prominent family simply for fixing the eavestrough on their home.

"They'll need to be leaded inside and out," he told the woman of the house, "but once they're leaded they'll last a lifetime." Then he painted them with ordinary red paint.

He is a psychologist, of course. Grouches are his meat. If he is warned away from a certain house by a colleague, he will attack the front door head-on as a matter of pride. If the mooch gets rough, Harry will simply say: "Boy, they told me you were a grouch, and they were so right! It's not worth doing business with you." Half the time, said Harry, he will get called back, and when that happens the mooch is properly trapped.

The paving racket, which Harry has since been engaged in, works this way:

He and his partner purchase a truck worth about $12,000. They make a down payment of $1,500 and drive it away (for they are adept at cozening car dealers, too). Then they go to the nearest paving company and hire as many men as they need simply by offering them better wages. They can afford to do this because they earn much more for paving driveways than legitimate firms do.

They buy cheap crankcase oil and other paving materials. They paint a company name on their truck; *any* name. The company isn't registered. Its phone number and address – if it has one at all – keep changing. The name itself changes every two weeks as Harry and his gang move swiftly from town to town. Thus, it is almost impossible for enraged householders to track them down. If they do, all they can launch is a civil suit. The chimney racket is out-and-out criminal fraud, but in the paving racket Harry has actually performed a service, albeit shoddy and expensive. You can sue him, if you can catch him, but he won't go to jail.

What he does is to charge outrageous prices – two or three times the going rate – for a job that will not last six months. At the end of the season he stops making payments on the truck, turns it in, and vanishes with his profit.

The mooches who listen to his smooth talk always believe that they are getting a bargain.

"Look," said Harry one day to an intelligent mooch, "because it's for you, I'm going to knock $50 off my price, but for God's sake don't tell anybody; I'd be out of business in a week at that rate!" And the two of them smiled a conspiratorical smile. Harry says he felt pleased about this because the man was a highly placed penal official. He paid $700 for a $290 job, the same as everybody else.

"But why are you telling me all this?" I asked Harry after he had explained it. "You know I'll print it. Won't that hurt you?"

"Not a bit," said he. "I'll even clip what you write and show it to the mooches. 'Look at this,' I'll say, shaking my head, 'isn't it awful what these fly-by-nights are doing? Why, they're ruining the business for legitimate corporations such as the one I represent.' And then I'll explain how much lower my prices are and how iron-clad my guarantee is. There'll be no trouble."

Harry's experiences with mooches who believe they are forcing down his prices supports the theory of my friend Buddy Abrahams that "the big gimmick in specialty selling is to appeal to the larceny of the customer." That is why so many sales today are disguised as private sales; the customer thinks he can get the better of a bargain if he is dealing with a non-professional. The newspapers, for instance, are full of advertisements for automobiles, furniture, rugs, electric ranges, and automatic washers, all of which seem to be for sale at a sacrifice by a private owner. I know of one man who consistently advertises various appliances for sale from his home, always at a "sacrifice." He is, in effect, an appliance dealer; but the prospects don't know this. When they phone, they are told his mother-in-law is moving in with him; she has brought along an extra automatic washer, which he must dispose of. His mother-in-law has been moving in with him for several years, but the customers are convinced that they are stealing him blind. They offer him $75 for a ten-year-old automatic washer that isn't worth $20, in the belief that they are getting a hot bargain on a recent model. He takes their money cheerfully.

Not far away there is a motherly little woman who uses a similar stratagem to sell furniture and rugs. *Bedroom suite, like new; private,* her advertisements read; and the mooches come flocking. Her story is that her mother has decided to move out, and she wants to get rid of the suite to make room for the new baby. Her home is crammed with such suites. Another motherly little woman advertises sacrifices on chesterfields and rugs "one month old, never used." I once studied her ads over the period of a month and estimated that she was spending $2,400 a year in the classified sections. Her story is that her daughter has just bought a house, that the mortgage rate is too high, that she has had to cancel the deal, and mama is stuck with the extra furniture. I sent somebody out to look over her place one day and discovered that there were a dozen new rugs stacked in her hallway. Various larcenous mooches buy them over the phone in the belief that they are getting the better of the motherly little woman; they would save money if they bought the rugs in a rug shop.

The car dealers, of course, have understood the private-sale technique for years and used it to their advantage. A good proportion of the ads for used cars that appear to be private sales are actually inserted by dealers who operate from their homes. The stories are always ingenious. *The wife doesn't like the colour of this car; you know how women are; I've just got to get rid of it and take a beating. . . . My daughter bought this and lost her job, and now I'm stuck with the payments; for God's sake do me a favour, Mac, and take it off my hands; I'll let it go for cost. . . . I got a new job in Vancouver, and I can't fool around bargaining; the car has to go; it's yours at a sacrifice.* I have checked out dozens of licence numbers on these so-called "private sales." About one in three turned out to be owned by a car lot. But the mooch is always convinced that he has got himself a live mooch of his own to work his will on; when he is in this kind of a mood, the mooch is a mooch indeed. . . .

One needs a translation guide, sometimes, to understand all the euphemisms now being employed to hide that awful word "salesman."

> Chosen applicant to be trained in special field of family service. This position offers prestige and security, sound income (on commission). Profit-sharing nation-wide organization. Applicants must be neat in appearance. Personal interviews only. (Phone number)

TRANSLATION: this is an ad for salesmen to sell cemetery plots for Resthaven Memorial Gardens, door-to-door, high pressure.

$475
GUARANTEED SALARY

> Promotional aspects will appeal to mature men who know the price of success and are willing to pay for it. Adult educational program, new to Canada and strongly financed by parent company.
>
> For appointment, call personnel manager. (Phone number)

TRANSLATION: you will be selling "Great Books of the Western World" door-to-door. "Adult education program" almost always means encyclopaedias or books of some kind. The odds are you will not get a guaranteed salary but will be paid straight commissions depending on how many sales you make.

> $12,500 PER ANNUM GUARANTEED ON SALARY AND BONUS
> We want an executive salesman for field representative in Toronto to service present accounts and to enlist new members for Canada's oldest and largest retail association.

Those who answered this ad found that it, too, did not deliver what it promised. The pay was actually $50 a week, plus $10 commission for each new client signed up, with no guarantee of anything.

The ad was placed by the Retail Merchants' Association, which that very month had been conducting a campaign against dishonest and misleading advertising.

2 YOUNG MEN, 16-22
To assist office manager of national publishing company. Salary. Miss Francis. (Phone number)

TRANSLATION: you will be selling magazine subscriptions door-to-door. You will not find that out by phoning, however.

When one of my agents phoned this number, he was told his duties would be typing. When he went to the office, he was sent out to sell magazines. Nothing was said about salary.

MEN AND WOMEN
Full Or Part Time
TO DO TELEPHONE SURVEY WORK
SALARY AND BONUS
(Phone number)

TRANSLATION: you will be making appointments for salesmen to call on prospects to sell them storm windows. The words used on the phone during this so-called "survey" will not be aluminum storm windows; you will talk about "health-giving products."

10 young men to do interview work in Public Relations Dept. of large publishing concern.

TRANSLATION: we want salesmen to peddle Collier's Encyclopaedia from door to door.

Due to expansion, leading food products corporation with offices in principal cities requires several clean-cut men to train as Driver Salesmen to cover established routes.

TRANSLATION: International Health Products, Inc., wants door-to-door salesmen to sell mixing machines to housewives while pretending to introduce an economy line of powdered milk. . . .

The Disinterested Surveyor is a favourite disguise in the world of the big sell. Indeed, the role has been used so often that it has worn a little thin (and bona fide survey companies are having difficulty completing their sampling as a result). A more recent and more effective disguise has been that of the Friendly Advisor.

"Good morning, Mrs. Worsley. I am from the Comprehensive Family Security Counsellor Division of Archmount Memorial Service Ltd. This department has been newly formed because of the very large number of families who, when they have had a death in their family, have turned to us for advice and guidance in connection with the many problems that arise in making final arrangements for a loved one. . . ."

This man was peddling pre-paid funeral plans, and the pitch that followed was designed to flatter the subject into thinking he had been specially selected to participate in a real bargain offer. Actually, it was considerably more expensive than regulation funerals in the same city.

A third disguise is that of the Enrollment Officer who wants to make a searching inquiry to see if you are eligible for the exclusive club to which you have been nominated. In 1961, for instance, young married couples in Canada began receiving in the mail a beautifully engraved card. The gold lettering informed them that they had recently "been nominated to membership in the Young Parents' League of Canada" and that "one of our Enrollment Officers on the nominating committee will be contacting you in the next few days to explain the functions of the League or reject your nomination according to your wishes."

One prospective member reported this brief conversation when the Enrollment Officer dropped around:

ENROLLMENT OFFICER: Good evening, I am here to explain to you that membership in the League is only made possible by one member nominating another. We assume that one of your friends who is a member feels that as young parents you are deeply concerned with the welfare of your children and would be interested in becoming members of the League.

YOUNG PARENT: What are you selling?

ENROLLMENT OFFICER: Just give me half an hour of your time. . . .

YOUNG PARENT: No! (Slams door)

What he was selling was $210 worth of child guidance books for the General Reference Research Company. Yet it is quite possible that he genuinely believed himself to be an Enrollment Officer and not a salesman, and it is fairly certain that, when his friends asked him what he did for a living, he reported proudly that he was an Enrollment Officer for the Young Parents' League of Canada. There is a certain amount of self-mesmerization here. After talking to the practitioners of the big sell and reading some of their literature, one is led to the conclusion that large numbers of them operate by a weird kind of double-think, which makes it possible for them to believe everything they are saying, yet, at the same time, to understand that it isn't true. . . .

The contest gimmick is a favourite door-opening device for companies pushing vacuum cleaners, floor polishers, cookware, and sewing machines. A Mr. L. Hartney, of 103 Parkside Drive, Toronto, was one such winner in 1959. This is the letter that was mailed to Mr. Hartney:

> Congratulations! You have been awarded a Consolation Prize by our Board of Judges. Enclosed you will find a $25.00 consolation certificate which can be deducted from the price of any of the items illustrated. For your convenience we have enclosed a card which entitles you to a free home demonstration.

In this case, it was no contest. Mr. Hartney had been dead for seven years.

Atlas Sewing Centres actually named "winners" of the first and second prizes on its mailing piece, and I was curious enough to check into one of these, since he appeared to be a man of the cloth. The Reverend J. J. O'Leary, of Sault Ste. Marie, Ontario, was listed as a first-prize winner in one Atlas contest, but, when Father O'Leary was reached by phone, he explained that he had not entered any contest. The firm had tried to give him a free vacuum cleaner, and he had returned it immediately. That did not stop them from using his name. But later on, this company and a similar firm, Super Master Appliances (which sent out almost identical letters), dropped the names of first- and second-prize "winners."

The technique continues to be successful in spite of the many ironies that these mass mailings produce. Inconsistencies do not bother the sales managers any more than public exposure does, since they have learned that a certain percentage of the public will always reply once it has been named a "winner." It does not matter that the contest is not specified. It does not matter that the winners didn't enter the contest – and know it. It does not matter that these letters are shamelessly mimeographed forms. They have won $25 somehow, somewhere, for something; why question it? One gets the feeling that it might be possible to walk down the street passing out envelopes to people, pumping their hands in congratulation, and crying, "You've won! You've won!" without having any of them ask: *Won what?* People expect to win something these days; it has become part of Our Way of Life. Only occasionally do they question the motives of the contest manager when the prize seems a little outlandish. There was, of course, the case of Mary Axford, in Toronto, who was telephoned on innumerable occasions by the Patricia Stevens Finishing School and given the news that she had been chosen the city's ideal debutante. The school offered to give her a free analysis in order to improve her speech, her beauty, her figure, and her deportment. The lucky girl tried to make it clear that she did not want to be the ideal debutante, but Patricia Stevens kept calling and doing her best to thrust the award upon her. Mary Axford never did succeed in getting across the point that at the age of eighty-one she felt a little old for such frivolities.

In some cases, there actually is a contest for sorts. Elna Sewing Centres (Canada) Ltd., for example, sponsored an "easy word game," which it sent through the mails. A kindergarten child would have had difficulty failing this test of wit, but thousands who were told they had won acted as if their ship had come in. The contest listed ten first prizes of $100, twenty second prizes of $50, and forty third prizes of $25 – well, not money actually – gift certificates. A man I know who worked for this firm told me that as fast as the contest entries poured into the Elna office, $50 certificates were mailed out – for everyone. It was his job at one point to call upon the lucky winners, break the news of their good fortune, and sell them a sewing machine. The basic price at the time was $299, and this was the price that both the lucky winners and the regular customers invariably paid. But the lucky winners were told that the retail price was $349 and that they could have the machine for $299 plus their certificate. My man told me a little sadly that many of them burst into tears of joy when the news of their fabulous winnings was broken to them.

The technique of some of these companies – Super Master Appliances was one – is to depict, on the letter to the lucky winners, the actual merchandise that they can buy at bargain rates by using their gift certificates. There is a sewing machine shown at $49.95 (or a mere $24.95, with the gift certificate), a floor polisher at $44.50, and a vacuum cleaner, with "all attachments necessary for a thorough job of house-cleaning," at a mere $39.50. With a gift certificate, of course, this vacuum would sell for the impossibly low sum of $14.50. I have yet to meet anyone who was actually able to buy one. The technique is to sell a much more expensive product. . . .

Another aspect of the big sell is the you-be-a-salesman scheme that removes the middleman entirely and threatens to turn half the populace into hucksters peddling electric organs, fire-alarm systems, and food supplements to one another.

In December, 1960, this advertisement appeared in the Toronto *Telegram* under "Construction Workers":

> Steady, year-round employment with Safety Equipment Company. Salary and bonus. Must be over 21, married and own a car and prepared to start work immediately. For personal interview, telephone ——.

This ad was placed by Vanguard Systems of Canada Ltd., a company that sells fire alarms, but those who applied did not learn this until much later. First, they found themselves closeted in a small room with several other men for their "personal interview."

A long, ambiguous sales lecture followed. There was talk about a sales-training course. There were flattering references to an enormous parent corporation that worked with jet aircraft. There was the usual mumbo jumbo about surveys, tests, public service, and, finally, the need for fire protection. There was a fifteen-minute tape-recorded sales talk. There were display cards, brochures, photographs. Finally, the men were allowed to see what they were supposed to sell – a set of six chromium-plated bells that worked on the thermostatic principle. They were told they would sell these bells to the public for $229.95 a set – an incredibly high price.

Then came the dénouement: to qualify, these lucky "salesmen" would themselves have to own a set of these alarms. The price, it was indicated, was a mere $14.95. The contracts revealed, however, that each man would pay $14.95 in cash and sign up to pay the remaining $215 in eighteen monthly installments. However, they were assured, they would not have to pay the rest because they could easily get nine of their friends to buy alarm bells too. They would get $25 credit for each sale, and, after the ninth sale, the money would start to roll in. And they could use the same sales gimmick on their friends! Their friends could become salesmen too, and sell their friends! The possibilities were endless.

A similar advertisement, placed about the same time in the "Help Wanted, Female" column, was slightly more direct in its message:

> Women, part-time, to do telephone soliciting at home for console chord organs; 1-2 hours a day and you can own one and earn extra money; commission basis.

The women who answered this ad discovered they must each buy a "demonstrator" organ for $149 before the company would give them the job. Having done this, they would be paid $10 commission for every organ they sold, but, until they bought an organ, they could not go to work.

These operations are small-time, however, when compared with the wave of food-supplement schemes which began to sweep the continent as early as 1958 and 1959 and which were built up on the pyramid concept. There have been several, but the best known, perhaps, was that of Nutri-Bio.

Like the other food-supplement schemes, Nutri-Bio managed to combine two of the wackiest traditions in the social history of North America: the universal get-rich-quick scheme and the universal get-healthy food fad. In its latter aspect, this certainly rivaled Dr. McCoy's orange-juice mania, *circa* 1925, and Gayelord Hauser's molasses-and-yogurt craze, *circa* 1949.

When Nutri-Bio moved into Toronto in 1960, after sweeping the United States and the Canadian west coast, it was said to have reached total annual sales of $100 million. Within twelve months there were few people who were not aware of it: those who weren't actually selling Nutri-Bio were on the receiving end of phone calls from people who were trying to sell it.

Nutri-Bio was supposed to contain almost every known vitamin, in addition to other nutritional aids. The idea of an all-in-one pill that compounds minerals and trace elements, as well as vitamins, has been received by nutritionists with as little enthusiasm as has the general thesis, promulgated by the food-supplement hucksters, that the populace is generally underfed and undernourished and will continue to be so unless it spoon-feeds itself with daily doses of the universal panacea.

Food faddism, however, has its own evangelism, and when this is attended by the evangelism that seems to accompany most modern-day salesmanship, the results can be awesome. In Nutri-Bio's ingenious scheme of things, every customer was automatically a salesman, and, since every customer believed (or supposedly believed) in the bodily advantages of the product – believed it, indeed, with a fierceness that resisted all cynicism – the effect was augmented. Nutri-Bio sales meetings, which were held all over town, had a religious fervour to them. The light of pure faith shone from the eyes of the sales apostles as they preached the twin gospels of Perfect Health and Unlimited Wealth.

In addition, the company marshalled an enviable troika of Hollywood stars to trumpet the merits of its product. Mr. Robert Cummings, toothpaste smile firmly in place, was high on the pantheon as a vice-president. His role was quite plainly that of Mr.

Eternal Youth. Mr. Harry Von Zell was rung in, via film clips, as the Average Bumbler, who takes Nutri-Bio "just in case." Mr. Marvin Miller, of *The Millionnaire,* enacted his TV role on a sound track played at the revival meetings. "If I've ever heard of a million-dollar proposition, this is it," said Mr. Miller's recorded voice. A glance at the expensive Nutri-Bio literature suggested that, of the two concepts Nutri-Bio was promoting, Wealth was proving to be somewhat stronger than Health.

The men at the top of the complicated Nutri-Bio structure did not appear to be taking any undue risks. Their technique was to corner customers by advertising for salesmen. Since every salesman was pledged to buy a year's supply of Nutri-Bio, "in order to believe in the product," and since every salesman had to pay, initially, the full retail price of $26 before he could start making money, it is difficult to see how the insiders could lose.

More than 60 per cent of the retail price of this food supplement went into sales costs. In addition, the salesmen had to pay for their promotion kits as well as for other sales literature. One wondered, sometimes, whether Nutri-Bio wasn't also in the publishing business. A slender twenty-one-page pamphlet entitled *Your Financial Opportunities,* which explained the sales set-up, was sold to the disciples at fifty cents a copy. Many a paperback novel sells for less.

The scheme itself, when reduced to its bare essentials, was fairly simple. The more Nutri-Bio one ordered in a batch, the less one paid for it – hence the profit margin increased for those who bought in large quantities. A man who bought a mere $276 worth a month, for instance, received a 40 per cent discount. In Nutri-Bio's quasi-military establishment, he was called a corporal. But those who climbed to the dizzy heights of generalship were awarded a 60 per cent discount. These people had to invest $13,000 a month in Nutri-Bio. Some of them had basements full of it.

The logic of the sales story, as enthusiastically explained at the revival meetings, was somewhat more shaky. Housewives were told, for instance, that if they made three calls on their friends each week they could earn $110 a month – and for only three hours' work. Three calls a day could bring in $828 a month. This presupposed that every call would produce a sale, that each call would take only one hour, and that the list of one's accommodating friends was unlimited. The evangelists airily dismissed this problem, however, and blandly went on to show that, when the repeat orders started pouring in, a housewife who worked three hours a week could make $2,200 a month.

But this was small potatoes in the Nutri-Bio Vision of Health and Wealth. It was much more lucrative to become an armchair wholesaler or "sponsor" by persuading one's friends to go out to sell Nutri-Bio, too. These friends would buy from you in job lots, thus allowing you to order larger and larger quantities of Nutri-Bio. When one of these friends hit the $13,000 mark and became a general in turn, then he could order directly from the factory – but you would still receive a 2 per cent commission on every sale he made. The implication was that the time would come when you could just sit at home and let the money roll in.

Once again, the laws of mathematics suggested that before long everybody in the land would be selling Nutri-Bio to everybody else. This is, in effect, what began to happen. By the spring of 1961, classified ads were appearing in the Toronto papers offering consignments of Nutri-Bio to any taker at half price. The saturation point had been reached. By 1962, the company was in financial difficulties in Canada. The pyramid idea, however, had by no means run its course. Even as the basements began to be glutted with Nutri-Bio, a new set of get-rich-quick letters started to circulate in the mails. A friend of mine received one from Vancouver.

"Look at this letter from George and Joan," he said, pulling a crumpled billet-doux from his pocket. "It's in George's handwriting, but it doesn't sound like either of them. . . ."

> Dear Tim and Mary:
> This is just a short note to let you know of "something to your advantage." I can't tell you much in a letter about this – the name I will give you to contact will give you the details. We were very fortunate in finding out and going into this ourselves.
> There is an opportunity of making over $1,000 a month. . . . There is no actual selling involved. . . . Sorry to be so mysterious. . . . You have nothing to lose. . . .

The phrases had a familiar ring to them, for they were remarkably similar to the ones that others had been given at other times to use on their friends. The firm in this case turned out to be Nutri-Foods of Canada Ltd., and it was apparently following in the footsteps of its various predecessors. As long as friendship is considered a saleable commodity, like vitamins, letters like this will continue to clog the mails as they did during the dime-letter craze of 1935.

2 Gambling Isn't Necessarily Gaming in Ontario

Carl Garry and John Sangster

In the eyes of the middle-class, gambling is a reprehensible activity unless carried on at the race track, stock market, or at home around the card table. To many lower- and working-class people, however, gambling is a fundamental part of their life-style – and they carry out their activities in very different settings than gamblers of the middle class. This article illuminates some of the gambling that goes on in Toronto and suggests some of the important social functions it provides for working-class society.

The two authors, Carl Garry and John Sangster, are currently teaching at Centennial College of Applied Arts and Technology, in Scarborough, where Mr. Garry is chairman of the Department of Social Sciences and Mr. Sangster is an instructor of sociology. Graduates of Atkinson College at York University, both men are working on post-graduate degrees. Their essay appears in this form for the first time in this anthology.

Contrary to popular belief, gambling is not illegal in Ontario, and it is more widespread in our society than generally recognized or accepted.

Despite those among Ontario's middle and upper classes and the church groups in the province which rail against gambling or attempt to deny its existence, gambling flourishes, and Ontario has long been known as a relatively wide-open place for people seeking the "action."

While there are many informal sanctions against gambling in the province, there are no *official* ones. But Ontario does have specific sanctions against *gaming* under Section 176 of the Criminal

Code. This Section provides that everyone who keeps a common gaming house or betting house is guilty of an indictable offense and liable to two years imprisonment. Among gamblers this is known as a charge of "keeper." Persons found in such houses – generally referred to as "found-ins" – are guilty of an offence punishable on summary conviction. A common gaming house is defined as a place kept for gain to which persons resort for the purpose of playing games.

Also under the Criminal Code, bookmaking is an indictable offense liable to two years imprisonment.

Therefore, this Section deals specifically with *games* or *gaming*. Thus, the *legal* definition of gaming distinguishes between participating in gambling games and gambling as a business venture. But Ontario police departments, in enforcing the Gaming Law, frequently fail to make this distinction. Consequently, many small house games are raided while the larger, well-organized games operate with little or no interference five and six times a week.

This fact was highlighted by the Hon. J. J. Wintermeyer in a speech to the Ontario Legislature in November, 1961. Mr. Wintermeyer, calling for an immediate Royal Commission to investigate organized gambling in Ontario, alleged that gambling on the scale reported at the time could only occur "with the collusion of the police and other officials."

This type of collusion or "protection," we later discovered, is referred to by gamblers as "the patch."

As a result of Mr. Wintermeyer's allegations, a Royal Commission headed by Justice Roach was set up. After a lengthy investigation into organized gambling in Ontario, a weighty volume of the Roach Commission's findings was published. Despite its size, the enormous number of words it contained, and its undoubted sincerity, it said very little. It seems, as it has happened on other occasions in places other than Toronto, that faced with a charge of graft and corruption in high places, society was obliged, through some public display, to affirm its clean social face. The published findings provided society's rationalization and the means, emulating Pontius Pilate, to carry out a symbolic washing of the hands.

However, the pertinent information to be gleaned from the Roach Commission's findings was the admitted fact that gambling clubs ran virtually wide open and *without* conviction in Ontario for many years – and that bribes were offered, whether accepted or not.

The essential objects of our study were not to make any value judgments such as "gambling is evil" or "gambling is good," but to discover the extent of gambling in Toronto, the type of people who gamble, the effect it has on them, the way in which it is conducted, and its social ground rules and demands.

For our main research area we selected Toronto's Lower Ward. This is a district bounded on the north by College Street, on the south by the waterfront, on the west by Bathurst Street, and on the east by McCaul. In the main, the Lower Ward is composed of low-priced dwellings which are, for the most part, neglected by absentee landlords. Tenants are attracted by low rents, familiar surroundings, and the usually available employment in the area's factories. While a good number of the residents of the Lower Ward, such as new immigrants and unskilled labourers with large families, are hard-working, honest people, ex-convicts, drifters, and deviants of all types find haven there.

In this section of Toronto, there is a network of interlocking lanes and alleyways – a maze which provides a multi-escape route for gamblers in the event of a police raid. In general, the physical structure of the district tends to nurture and even encourage deviant behaviour.

Moving into our selected area for on-the-spot observation and research, we decided, for the purposes of our study, that the distinction between gaming and gambling was irrelevant. Besides, the number of convictions for gaming are not a satisfactory index of the incidence or amount of gambling. Convictions are merely a labelling process and act as little more than a convenient device for counting heads.

During the next week in the Ward, we talked with taxi drivers, police – on the beat and at headquarters – area social workers, juvenile and adult residents, restaurant countermen, and "blue" bookstore proprietors. While gaining some recognition in the area, and some little understanding, we were not experiencing the acceptance we needed from the "group" and its leaders.

It was then that we had our first big break – without which the project would never have been completed. Through Dr. W. E. Mann of York University, we were introduced to Brother Lee at the Neighbourhood Coffee House and Mr. Derek Holloway of the St. Christopher House.

Both organizations – St. Christopher's sponsored by the United Church of Canada and the Coffee House provided for by the Anglican Church – stress social welfare rather than religious ideologies. They provide a kind of refuge and meeting place for the area's isolated and socially deprived residents.

With the consent of these two earnest men, we made their houses our bases of operation. With approval from these trusted individuals, we started to make our first "real" contacts. This allowed us to extend our area of operation and establish sub-bases at a well-patronized restaurant, an area hotel, a tavern, and various billiard rooms. At the same time, we visited pool rooms, bingo games, card games, and every other group social function or recreation outlet the district provides.

Now, almost into the third month, we were in a position to establish the start of a basic framework. Of thirteen young men interviewed around the St. Christopher house, none earned more than $3,500 a year and nine made below $3,000. Yet all these young men had gambled, in one way or another, and a number of them gambled frequently.

Within the next two months, we realized we had caught a glimpse of a world that is almost completely alien to the average Torontonian, who generally views the gambler as a deviate from the accepted middle-class Christian ethic of gain by hard work alone.

A heterogeneous society which tolerates a variety of ethnic, religious, and social groups tends to nurture small clusters of individuals who come together either along ethnic or racial lines. They may live in ghetto-like areas, speaking a vernacular and generally following many customs of their previous environment.

These groups never become fully assimilated, are frequently only partially acculturated, and are sociologically termed "subcultures." A subculture may be stratified on class lines as well as ethnic or racial lines. A subculture may be described as a group of people who come together with a common purpose that thwarts the will of the majority and furthers their own ends without much regard for the norms, mores, or folkways of the larger culture in which they are situated.

This was the type of "world" we were more or less privy to. A collection of separate subcultures, yet interwoven to build a whole – a solid front that shut out the curious and uninvited. A "world" that presented a reasonably submissive façade, behind which it lived according to its own laws; it had its own heroes and myths and legends – and it was within easy walking distance of Bay Street, the bastion of the main culture.

The youths we talked to at the St. Christopher House and a good many of the adults in the area were all agreed upon the desirability of gambling as a means to achieve an end. They attributed their low incomes to lack of marketable skills and periods of voluntary unemployment due to the tedium or menial nature of the jobs open to them.

By now we were acquainted with scores of stories – nearly always second-hand – about the friend or the "friend of a friend" who made the big "hit." Typical of these stories was one offered by a twenty-two-year-old named "John":

> Boy, if I could only hit a win like Danny's cousin did at Hialeah two years ago. That Danny's cousin – boy! There's a sharp guy for ya. He's on easy street now. Don't have to work no more.

Toronto's gambling fraternity – like any other subculture – has its store of myths and legends. Nick the Greek and King Farouk are looked up to with awe and admiration. Endless stories about the feats of these champions are listened to, exchanged, expanded, and repeated over and over again – and every version is accepted each time with avid interest.

We also discovered that the district respected a gambler versatile enough to take part in any game and his ability to wager large amounts without exhibiting undue emotion or anxiety. This was adequately borne out one night when we were permitted to watch a "duel" between two hustlers of the area in a pool room (The "Challenge" Bowling and Billiards) on Queen Street West.

When we entered, the two contestants were the only ones playing. The game was snooker. News of the duel had apparently spread, and the room was almost full of spectators who sat or stood according to their mood, avidly watching the action. Side bets ranging from twenty-five cents to $10 and more were being made among the onlookers.

The proprietor scrutinized each newcomer. Although in danger of losing his licence, he stood under the "No Gambling Allowed" sign and made no effort to interfere.

Finally, the game rested on who pocketed the eight ball. One of the contestants, whom we'll call "Lou," a nattily-attired twenty-four-year-old, apparently of Italian descent, picked up his cue and walked confidently around the table inspecting the possible angles. The calling of side bets and general comments from the spectators stopped as though somebody had thrown a switch.

Lou, seemingly unaware of the expectant silence, nonchantly chalked his cue. Straightening up from an examination of the table surface, he casually flipped the chalk to a shabbily dressed contemporary and made some humourous remark at which they both laughed.

The spectator who had been singled out by this gesture looked quite smug and glanced left and right to make sure the others were aware of the "honour."

Without any more posturing, Lou aimed his cue and made a spectacular shot. The black ball rocketed into the pocket. But before he could claim his victory, his cue ball, spinning precariously on the lip of the pocket, dropped in after the black.

Within the space of seconds, Lou had won and lost. With a calmness any professional would admire, if not envy, Lou walked to the rack and hung up his cue. Then, in one easy movement, he stepped back to the table, pulled a large roll of bills from his pocket – holding them so all could see – and peeled five twenties onto the green table, simultaneously exchanging flippant remarks with several onlookers.

Lou was obviously performing for his audience, showing them what they expected from him: to lose without griping. He added further to his stature by also exhibiting his ability to withstand loss.

As the bills hit the table, the winner was immediately surrounded by four or five of his cronies who put the "touch" on him for a few dollars. The loans were made quickly and without fuss. This was expected of the winner, as we later learned. A winner who was unwilling to lend money is condemned as either a "cheapskate" or a "grinder." The label is an onerous one in the Lower Ward, and a person so tagged can expect no help when his luck changes. A man's status in the initiated group depends largely on his borrowing and lending power. Loans are expected to be repaid without the lender asking. Anyone who takes longer than two weeks to repay a loan is labelled as "slow pay," and his borrowing power is greatly reduced.

By now we were in a position to form some opinions. We had some evidence that gambling is a significant status symbol in a large section of the lower-income structure. We also found that gambling was prevalent among the various ethnic groups in the area – although the types of gambling preferred by each group differed.

However, there was no evidence to suggest that the gambling subculture was stratified along either racial, ethnic, or class lines. The gamblers, those who lived mainly by gambling, represented all the groups, straddling the ethnic and racial subcultures.

The type of games played in the area – and listed in their apparent order of popularity, according to our observations – were:

1) *Pool rooms*
a) Pea Pool
b) Skittles
c) Black Ball
d) Snooker
e) Golf

2) *Cards*
a) Five and seven card stud poker
b) Five and seven card draw poker
c) Hearts
d) Euchre
e) Cribbage
f) Gin Rummy
g) Baccarat
h) Bridge
i) Klubbriash

3) *Horse Racing*
a) Local flat horse racing
b) Local harness racing
c) Out-of-town flat horse racing
d) Out-of-town harness racing

4) *Dice*
a) Fade game
b) Bank game

5) *Bingo*

We were now discovering that participation in these games was neither haphazard nor random, but patterned and organized. Gamblers of the area, and those who visited it, were usually at ease in any of the games listed.

A fairly typical example of the attitude of the real gambler in the area towards his life and his family responsibilities was thirty-two-year-old "Ken," who told us he had been gambling since he was fifteen. He was complaining one night about a bad streak of luck, but, like all veteran gamblers, he kept looking for his luck to change. "Somethin's gotta break pretty soon," he said, speaking to himself as much as to us.

My old lady is startin to give me a hard time. I barely been able to produce the grub money. I just gotta have a win pretty soon.

Then I can at least give her half a bill or a bill [$100] to shut her up. As long as she can go downtown with her old lady [her mother] she's happy and don't bother me. But right now she's on my neck an' I gotta straighten things around.

At least she knows I ain't boozin' or gashin' [drinking or going to bed with other women] it up like some guys. Mind you, I ain't goin' to pass it up, but I don't go lookin' for it.

When I'm out at night, I'm in action [gambling], an' she knows if I make a hit I'll piece her off [share the winnings]. Some guys H.O. [hold out] on their wives, but not me.

Like many of his veteran contemporaries, Ken saw his family strictly in terms of dollars. While he felt the obligation to bring money home to keep his wife quiet, he felt his duties as a husband and provider more or less ended there; his role as a husband and father was secondary to his role as a gambler.

While Ken was of Anglo-Saxon descent – as were many of the dedicated gamblers we met – it was not necessarily the native born Canadians who had the "fever."

However, we would like to make a distinction here between gambling among friends and a gambling subculture. Although there seems to be some natural overlapping – some individuals are members of both groups – for the most part they are separate and represent two different kinds of social phenomena.

In the gambling subculture, the "members" are all agreed that the only success which is valued is success through gambling. In this group, gambling permeates every phase of the individual's life. Such is not the case in the ethnic subculture. The two groups, in this respect, are clearly distinct and separate, although some interaction between them does occur.

Most of the gambling within ethnic and racial groups in the area is done among friends. For example, we made the acquaintance of a twenty-three-year-old Italian immigrant who was then employed as a ladies' hairdresser. Every Friday night he and his young, single Italian friends gathered in one of their homes to play baccarat. The game started about 10:00 P.M. and continued sometimes until 5:00 the next morning. Newcomers gain access to the baccarat-playing group only through the recommendation of one or more of the members. A girl was allowed to participate only if socially linked to one of the players. The big winner of the night was expected to contribute liquor to the next gathering and failure to do so meant virtual ostracism.

Of course, gambling among racial and ethnic groups in the area does occur outside the home games, but it is mainly restricted to small-take games in billiard rooms and a few hotels that provide games of skill. In the Lower Ward, each ethnic and racial group has its own favourite spot. For example, a place of recreation (The "Axis" Billiards) on Spadina north of Dundas was patronized by Negroes. A similar place on Augusta Avenue was predominantly Portugese (The "Faro" Billiards). Ukrainians met and played at a place on College ("Terrace" Billiards), while Italians dominated another place ("Roma" Billiards) on Augusta.

However, when a member of one of the ethnic or racial groups begins to deviate from the accepted order of values and begins to give gambling a higher priority, he is moving away from his subculture. When this happens, he will find a new group where his new values will be accepted. The group he joins cuts across racial, ethnic, social, and religious backgrounds.

Apart from the recreation centres dominated by ethnic or racial groups, there are many establishments in the area that are completely heterogeneous. After one penetrates the façade, the types that are on their way to becoming veteran gamblers can be spotted.

The age of the males frequenting these places and participating in gambling ranged from sixteen to seventy years. The former were completely indifferent to the law forbidding persons under eighteen to be on the premises.

These billiard rooms were always crowded in the evenings, especially on Fridays. One establishment we visited had six pea-pool games going on simultaneously with six to eight players at each table. Stakes varied from table to table, from a low of ten cents per ball to a high of $1 per ball; the average wager appeared to be about a quarter. This scale of bets held true for virtually all the billiard rooms we visited.

Most of the players we spoke to were either unemployed, part-time workers, or seasonal or unskilled labourers. A few were semi-skilled, but none could be classified as skilled labour. When asked why they left school before graduation, most of them said that their families could not afford to keep them in school. In most cases, the father's wage was insufficient to maintain the family.

Our talks with these boys suggested to us that the idea of upward social mobility is, to them, a myth. Although it is theoretically possible for these individuals to move upward, it is not practically realizable. Neither the financial means nor the role models are available to them. Without the money and the teachers, to speak of upward mobility for such people is entirely unrealistic.

By this time we had virtually lived among these people long

enough to be acutely aware of certain possibilities. "Ricky," whose $41-a-week salary helped to support his mother and five younger brothers, was intelligent enough to know that he could not survive in a conventional middle-class group. He sought an alternative and more realistic route through which he might achieve his ambitions. The particular subculture he had attached himself to provided him with a ready medium in which he could function, compete successfully, and achieve some kind of status among his contemporaries.

Having been successful as a spotter for the card games in the parks, it is more than probable that Ricky could graduate to more responsible and remunerative positions in the subculture. It is possible that as he learns his way around, he will be invited – even expected – to participate in ever more risky undertakings. For, in addition to its possible remunerative aspects, gambling also serves the lower classes as a form of recreation which more or less replaces other legitimate middle-class forms of recreation.

At this stage of our project we were anxious to be introduced to the big-money gambling. This, however, was no easy matter. It had taken us long enough to penetrate the lower echelon of the gambling subculture, and although we were now accepted at that level it appeared we would have to start from scratch again to reach the upper gambling bracket.

For about another six weeks we pressed, with discretion, all of our better contacts in the Lower Ward for an introduction to one of the big games. But our efforts proved unsuccessful. The best help we could get was the advice to "hang around Spadina and College an' talk to the guys up there."

For the next few weeks, we "hung around" the intersection, talking to bartenders, waiters, and countermen. All these men were willing to talk, and, in this respect, they proved to be valuable sources of information. But none seemed willing to take the chance of introducing us into one of the big-money, private crap games that occurred in the vicinity. One night, however, "Bob," a local cabby, finally agreed to take us to a game and pass us off to the "keeper" as his friends.

But his agreement had certain strings attached. Apparently he was one of the in-group, but he was down on his luck and was looking for a stake. This fact was undoubtedly the only reason he agreed to our proposal. He told us we would have to pay him $5 to cover the cost of the ride to the game and provide him with another $50 with which to bet. He would also have complete freedom in betting. Any winnings would be split three ways, but any losses would be carried entirely by us. He had us over a barrel; we agreed to his terms.

It was then about 11:45 P.M., and Bob told us the game generally got under way about 11:00 and carried on until 4:00 A.M. After making a quick phone call, he gave us an affirmative nod and got into the cab. We travelled about ten blocks into the Queen-McCaul area and pulled up in front of a totally dark house. As we approached the front door, however, it opened, and we walked into the hallway to be confronted by the doorman-lookout. After a few words of assurance from Bob, we were allowed to continue into the interior of the house.

We had to navigate a set of narrow cellar steps before reaching the room in which the game was run. About forty or fifty men were gathered around a baize-covered, rectangular table. One man was standing at each end, and one midway down the side. These were the dealers employed by the house. Their duty was to collect the losing wagers and pay off the winning bets. Each man had a box of coloured poker chips in front of him, the different colours denoting different values.

In the middle of one side of the table was a man called the "centreman" who held a plastic stick which he used like a broom to sweep the dice back to the "shooter." Only the centreman and the current shooter were allowed to touch the dice. The centreman called out "the point" (the number rolled) after each throw of the dice – and his decision was final.

Opposite the centreman (or "stickman" as he's sometimes called) was the only man in the room who was seated. This was the "keeper." On the table in front of him was a wooden cigar box. As the dealers converted cash to chips, they passed it to the keeper, who placed it in the box. Anyone wishing to leave had to see the keeper to cash in his chips. We were interested to note that these transactions took place in a cordial atmosphere. Winners were paid promptly and with a smile. Losers were given $2 for transportation home – and the keeper's condolences.

By now Bob had bought $50 worth of chips and was completely engrossed in the fast-moving action of the game. Like the others, as he placed his bets and followed the passage of the dice, he joined in the incessant humourous small-talk. It was amazing to watch some of the men place very complex bets on each and every throw of the dice while simultaneously keeping up a conversation in which housemen and players all participated.

Some players, when luck seemed to be running against them, would request a new pair of dice. Despite protests from players who were enjoying a run of luck, the centreman complied with every request. He would sweep the old dice towards the player who asked for the change, saying, "Take these home with you." In this way any suspicion of cheating was eliminated.

Each change of the dice was accompanied by elaborate ritual. The keeper would hand the dice to the centreman, who removed the foil wrapping, examined the dice, and carefully noted the manufacturer's identification number. Any player was free to examine the dice before they were put into play. Many would rub the dice on their sleeves or the fronts of their coats. Others would cup them in their hands and blow on them as if to establish some kind of communion. It was fascinating to see skilled players obviously emotionally involved in this ritual; they clearly needed reassurance and the feeling of power over the dice it provided.

The players ranged in age from twenty to sixty-five, but the majority appeared to be between thirty and forty-five. Some were dressed in casual sportswear, while others wore expensive business suits. Few were shabbily or unfashionably dressed. Good clothes were noticed and appreciated.

Bob complimented one stylishly dressed player on his suit. "I don't know how you do it, but it must be nice," he added.

"Don't tell anybody, but I've got a part-time job," the player replied with a grin.

This brought a laugh from everyone at the table. This and other derogatory remarks about work strongly suggested to us that this style of life, symbolized by the expensive clothes, could only be supported on earnings from an executive position or, failing that, an illegal enterprise. Remarks passed in conversation around the table suggested that a lot of the players belonged to the latter income group. We got the distinct impression that the group expected a man to be able not only to survive but to prosper without working.

Bob, our cabby friend, was in the minority. But hacking was seen as a kind of stop-gap or temporary position. It was as well for Bob that he had a job, for he appeared to be a poor hand at dice – or luck was still running against him. Within an hour and a half, he had lost our money. He stood around the table for a little while watching the run of the dice, apparently making mental bets. It was during this time that we noticed a number of men who had apparently lost their stakes asking the keeper for more money.

In some cases, the keeper would simply shake his head. In others, he would ask, "How far do you want to go?" In this manner the keeper puts the onus on the player for the limit on losses. When they had agreed on the amount, the keeper would make a point of asking the dealer for the specified amount of chips and counting them out before turning them over to the player.

Bob told us later that credit of this kind had to be repaid the next morning; there was no charge as long as the player paid promptly. A player who reneged on this type of loan could never again expect credit.

Bob picked up his $2 and a consoling word from the keeper, and we left. It has cost us $55, but the experience was well worth it.

By now we had spent many months in and around the Lower Ward and were accepted by a number of the "in" gambling groups. We had come to know them and were familiar with their attitudes and outlook on everything from family responsibility to off-track betting.

Off-track betting was a sore point with the majority of the gamblers in the area. They cannot understand "the privilege of sacred ground." A number of bookmakers operate in the area and are respected by their clients, who feel as though they have been personally insulted if the bookmaker is arrested.

"Joe," a veteran horse player, summed up the general feeling this way:

How silly can people get? If you pay the admission price to E. P. Taylor at Woodbine or Greenwood, then it's legal to bet. But if you're not standing on Mr. Taylor's ground, then it's not legal. Have you ever heard of anything so ridiculous?

Clearly, in the eyes of Joe and his many associates, the bookmaker served a useful function. At the same time, the off-track betting laws were held in utter contempt. To us this indicated a very real need for Ontario to consider carefully the possibility of introducing government-controlled, off-track betting shops similar to those in Great Britain. In our opinion, a step in that direction would be a much more positive move than the suggested introduction of Sunday horse racing; Sunday racing would tend to aggravate the problem of off-track betting – certainly it would offer no solution.

However, at that stage of our project, we were not so much interested in answering questions as asking them. We approached the Metropolitan Police Department and the Metropolitan Toronto Juvenile Court. At both these places, we attempted to obtain statistics regarding social variables and their relation to gambling.

Mr. Lane of the court was unable to provide any statistics whatsoever – not by choice, but simply because such information was non-existent. As far as we could learn, the court feels little or no need to compile such statistics, despite the role such a court plays in society.

Our meeting with police officials was more congenial, although equally unenlightening. We spent a good part of a day with two officers of the morality squad (Inspector Pilkington and Sergeant Wilson). They seemed willing to co-operate, but they were of little or no help.

The police are concerned, as is the Juvenile and Family Court, with apprehension and conviction rather than with prevention and/or rehabilitation. The police could do little more than confirm what we had already uncovered. However, it is interesting to note that they told us, "To our knowledge, there are no floating crap games in Toronto. We've cleaned them all out."

Mr. Lane told us that gambling was not a significant contributor to family disorganization. He ranked the causes of family disorganization in order of their priority as alcoholism, promiscuity, and failure to provide. Yet the police told us:

> Family disorganization due to gambling and alcohol are approximately the same. We get two or three calls every week from angry wives whose husbands gamble their pay away. These women insist we raid the games and often provide us with the address.

Obviously, some contradictions exist between these two official bodies.

For every "two or three calls every week" (the police did not specify any particular area from which the calls came), it seems logical to assume there are scores of wives with gambling husbands who, for any one of several reasons, choose not to divulge their predicament.

Further, the Juvenile and Family Court fails to differentiate statistically the causes for failure to provide. One reason could be gambling.

Our experience with the gambling fraternity of Toronto proved conclusively that the general incidence of gambling is far greater than officials admit publicly, and that gambling begins at a much earlier age than popularly believed. Another point of interest is that gambling, or even gaming, is not generally considered criminal. Certainly not in the same sense as drug trafficking and prostitution – and there is more public permissiveness of gambling, at least in the Lower Ward.

Our lengthy research made it clear to us that present gambling laws are somewhat inadequate and nurture evasion. And in this respect, there is a very real danger that laws which are held in contempt by a large segment of the population can lead to a weakening of the whole normative structure.

We would not suggest legalized gambling in the Las Vegas manner, but a closer examination of the present situation. Every generation has produced its not inconsiderable crop of gamblers – dedicated and otherwise – and always will.

Therefore, some intelligent recommendations regarding gambling legislation suitable for Toronto in the 1970's will be necessary in the near future.

3 Functions of Argot Among Heroin Addicts

Lloyd G. Hanley

The defences raised by heroin addicts to preserve the sanctuary of their subculture against the intrusions of outsiders are as guarded and as little understood as the secret initiation ceremonies of a religious cult. The special virtue of this article lies in its insight into the values and communication processes that obtain among some of the "regulars" of Toronto's underworld.

"Lloyd G. Hanley's" knowledge of the underworld is the fruit of years of service as an undercover agent for the police; for obvious reasons, his by-line is a pseudonym. Under the same name, he has co-authored articles about the Mafia in Canada and the use of marijuana in Toronto, both of which appeared in *Deviant Behaviour in Canada*, edited by W. E. Mann. This article first appeared in W. E. Mann's *Sociological Profile of Canada* in 1968.

The argot spoken by the criminal subculture has interested and excited social scientists for many years. It is related to the "underworld."

In general, the members of the underworld call themselves "rounders." More specifically, they are labelled as "Heavies" (robbery and strong arm specialists), "Pete men" (safebreakers), "Hypes" (drug addicts), "Boosters" (shop lifters), "Grifters" (confidence men), "Whizz" (pickpockets), "Clout men" (shopbreakers), and "Hookers" (prostitutes). These designations are as real as those of doctor, mechanic, or salesman.

The names that many rounders acquire are called "monickers," and they are as unusual as the language itself. Imagine a close continuing personal relationship with people who are known to you merely as "Snitch," "Suitcase Simpson," "Harry the Hat" (who is not to be confused with Harry the Horse), "Blond Norma," "Fat Eddy," "Eddy the Wop," "The Frenchman," "Frankie Skitch," and so on.

In this world of rounders, nearly any name will do, and the monicker usually has very little connection with the set of names acquired at birth. Rounders are apt to be rechristened as they become a part of the subculture, and their original names are lost along the way, only to show up from time to time on police arrest sheets.

While this enquiry concerns the functions of argot among heroin addicts, there appears to be a core of argot common to the whole criminal element, so my remarks will have a general application.

To prepare a glossary of argot terms as David W. Maurer did in *The Big Con*[1] would be an exhaustive effort, and the result would be as incomplete and limited as Dr. Maurer's was. He was treated to an extensive period of being "tried on"; that is, the con men he dealt with told him the stories they thought he wanted to hear, possibly to win his good will. It might be cynical to remark that knowing a university professor, well enough to use him as a reference, would probably have its advantages.

Rounders enjoy nothing better than "cutting up old scores," or talking of their past adventures, much as sailors are reputed to do. The actual event in question is not too important; it is the skilful telling of the story in good company that matters, and con men are trained story tellers. These observations are not intended to detract from Dr. Maurer's book; in fact, I share his fondness for a lie well told in the colourful rounder argot. In this respect, I am reminded of the line in *My Fair Lady* which goes: "The French don't care what they do actually, as long as they pronounce it properly." Such is the case with rounders.

I have reviewed Dr. Maurer's glossary (1958), as well as those prepared for drug addicts (1954) and safebreakers (1942) by the New York City Police Department.[2] The words in each of these glossaries could be used in this area without any problem in meaning; I suspect that criminal argot is relatively uniform in North America.

The criminal subculture adopts words already in common use, then redefines them to suit its own purposes or needs. As an example, I will construct three fairly typical sentences and give their translation. Either argot is a parsimonious way of describing criminal events or my translation is rambling, but I think that the former is the case.

A bull dagger/cracked wise/with her Man/
A lesbian was flippant with her source of narcotics –
who was kinky.
who was treacherous.
He could get her straightened out/
He might have hired someone to beat her or even kill her –
but he traded her/
 but he gave information which led to her arrest –
to piece off/a clout beef/with the Heavies.
to have shopbreaking charges withdrawn by the Break & Enter
Squad.
#He's got static all over town now.
His part in this affair is well known, and the subculture is
opposed to the action he took.

Who becomes a rounder? Slum dwellers seem to get some
priority, but the subculture is open to people from other backgrounds.

Dr. Eysenck suggests that criminals tend to have a high "stimulus threshold"; that is, tolerance to levels of excitation from the
stimuli that surround them. We are probably familiar with people
who attempt to locate themselves in quiet surroundings to read,
listen to classical music, or simply think quietly. This atmosphere
might be extremely unpleasant to another person who prefers
crowds, alcoholic excesses, drug abuses, loud jazz bands, and
smoky night clubs. According to Eysenck, this latter description
applies to the criminal. Whether this high "stimulus threshold"
is inherent or acquired is not satisfactorily resolved. At any rate,
it seems true that members of the criminal element may be found
in the older bars, jazz night clubs, and restaurants in the downtown
area.

There are approximately 125 heroin addicts living in Toronto.
Generally they live in hotels and rooming houses in the area
bounded by Parliament Street in the east, Bathurst Street in the
west, Queen Street along the south, and Bloor Street in the north.
They collect in several restaurants in the Jarvis and Dundas area,
but they do not spend much time in the bars and beer parlours in
the same area (many have been excluded from these bars for one
infraction or another). The lesbian addicts gather in the Elizabeth
and Dundas section of Chinatown.

I interviewed fifteen addicts in the course of this research. The
interviews were tape recorded with a concealed machine. I also
used tape recordings of twelve interviews with different addicts

296   *The Underside of Toronto*

which were obtained on another occasion. I made no effort to select a random sample but chose the respondents simply by watching an area they frequent until I saw one leave the area alone. I then approached the subject as if the meeting were accidental.

The subjects have known me for at least eight years, but I have not had any contact with them for about two years. I selected this method because I thought that the addicts would be suspicious of a deliberate confrontation followed with what might appear to them to be idle chatter.

What is the addict's conception of the dimensions of Toronto? They seldom leave the downtown area and appear to be oriented toward the centre of the city. They appear to regard any place which is not within this familiar section as being a considerable distance away. In a very rigid sense, the Dundas and Yonge Street intersection represents the centre. Spadina Avenue, a half mile away, is "out in the West End." Sherbourne Street is "in the East End." I asked one respondent what had become of an old friend of his and he replied,

> I don't see much of Bill anymore. He's packed it in [stopped using]. I hear he still does a little boosting [shoplifting], but nothing serious. He's gone square [reformed]. Living way the hell out in the west end somewhere. Around College and Bathurst with his sister [about three-quarters of a mile away].

"The corners" (Jarvis and Dundas) attract old addicts long after their close associates have died or left the area for other reasons. I had occasion to talk with an old ex-addict who has lived seventy-eight years the hard way and shows it. She used to sit in one of the restaurants for several hours a day, so I asked her why she kept coming back to "the corners." She said,

> I haven't touched shit [heroin] for ten years. You know that [I didn't but nodded agreement anyway]. I'm too old to hustle now [be a prostitute], and I never was any good as a thief, so I just packed it in. I get the old age [pension]. I don't know anything but the corners, so I come down to look for the old timers [old addicts] and cut up a few old scores, have a few beers, and then go home. I got a room. The corners aren't what they used to be. Did you ever see so goddam many punks in all your life?

She made this last remark in a very loud voice and referred to four people sitting in a booth ahead of her. They were known addicts who appeared to be "coasting" (under the influence of heroin).

If language shapes reality, as Benjamin Wharf claims, we are confronted with an interesting situation. This is a subculture that makes use of the same words as the society that bred it, but the words have quite a different connotation, often irrelevant to the original one. They speak English but not the same English as the population at large. A sort of paralanguage.

It might be logical to suggest that the conditioning processes involved in acquiring a deviant outlook and an appropriate language also involve a redefinition of the norms and values of society. This learning situation has taken place within a fused social context which is neither completely typical nor atypical. The total view of reality may also be a fusion which can confound the understanding of people who have only internalized the standards of "normal" society. Thus I overheard two addict prostitutes talking in the lobby of a hotel. Their conversation seemed to concern the problems of working wives, which is a fairly mundane topic in middle-class society, but their orientation was striking.

> Poor Fran, why she sticks with that man of hers is a mystery. She has to hustle her ass all over town to keep things going, and when she gets busted [arrested] he won't even stir himself to make bail. Why that lazy bastard won't even steal. She's too good for him, I say.

W. E. Lambert *et al* in the essay, "The Influence of Language-acquisition Contexts on Bilingualism," concludes,

> Experience in separated contexts comparatively increases the associative independence of translated equivalents in the bilingual's two languages. If the bilingual has learned his two languages in culturally distinctive contexts, the semantic differences between translated equivalents are comparatively increased.[3]

The novice might acquire associative knowledge of the argot by the simple expedient of memorizing a printed vocabulary, without taking part in the activities of the subculture. By comparison, connotative meaning is acquired by actually taking part in the culture as the language is being learned. In this way, words become symbols or cues, which can elicit some sort of complex emotional response, not just the exercise of memory. Certain perceptual sets have been formed.

The habitual user of argot will have well-developed sets of expectations rooted in his language. These expectations will be largely absent in the novice. For example, "a good score" does not mean that the Ottawa Rough Riders gained a safe margin over the Hamilton Tiger Cats; it means that someone was able to execute some sort of criminal operation with a lucrative yield. The argot user is in some sense bilingual. He "knows" the criminal argot, while the novice may "know about" it.

How does one go about being accepted and learning the mysteries of this very loose but coherent subculture? Is it necessary to rob and plunder in order to gain acceptance? No, I don't think so. Being a criminal involves having a certain perspective, but this perspective can be shared without the necessity of committing a criminal act. There are a number of hotel managers, entertainers, and shop keepers in the downtown area who are popular with the criminal subculture. Rounders often gather in a particular store or hotel to talk. The proprietor is known to them as "good people"; that is, he is to be trusted. He is "in." This person continues to earn his living in a socially acceptable manner and does not take part in criminal activities.

On the other hand, I spoke with a known "heavy" shortly after Matthe K. Smith (The Beatle Bandit) was convicted of robbing a bank and killing a man who tried to stop him. This informant had taken part in a number of bank robberies in the past and supports himself now mainly by collecting money from reluctant gamblers. He seemed to be annoyed when I mentioned Smith and said, to the best of my recollection,

> I hope they hang the bastard. He's bugs [insane]. There was no need to do what he did. It was stupid. I don't know him, and I asked around, so he's no rounder. Somebody will straighten him out when he gets to the joint [Kingston Pen].

Smith committed suicide shortly after he arrived at the penitentiary.

Crime is the domain of the rounder, and certain acts of violence are a violation of the norms, at least in the Toronto area. The simple commission of an offence will not insure entry into the subculture.

If you want to know "what's really going on," how do you find out? "What's really going on" involves a wide variety of criminal activities, including techniques and the personalities involved in crime, described by people who were supposed to be there, or who know people who were. The accounts are given in the argot and interpreted in line with the criminal perspective. These stories seem to be told more for the enjoyment of the audience than for their education, although I suppose a person might pick up tips to improve his performance.

In the course of a research paper on marijuana use, another sociologist and I contacted five people who were well-known to us as rounders and marijuana users. We were familiar with each of these people, and the matter of their marijuana use was never in question. When we were able to get the group together for a discussion, we were frustrated because they would not discuss marijuana use. They talked about articles on the subject which they had read in magazines. They talked of marijuana use as it might be talked about by non-users in the living room of their homes – that is, from sources that were generally available. It appeared as if they were relatively uninformed on the subject. This seemed rather incongruous, since each person at the interview session knew that this was not the case. What went wrong?

During the disgruntled post-mortem that followed this so-called interview session, the other student and I realized we had confused our subjects. We had failed to speak any argot at all. We had failed to provide them with the cues necessary to indicate that we wanted to know "what's really going on."

Each of the subjects knew that we spoke the argot fluently, and most of our previous conversations with them were either carried out in argot or laced with it. On this occasion, we were in a place where argot is not spoken. When the informants arrived, we both continued to use language that was normal in those surroundings. We frustrated their expectations. As a result, the subjects "chilled" on us and responded in what seemed to them to be a suitable manner. The session lasted less than an hour.

Another interview was arranged at the same location, and this time the oversight was corrected. We discussed marijuana, heroin, and crime generally for nearly four hours on this occasion. The results were entirely satisfactory.

It is probably important that the personal reactions of the subjects to both of the experimenters was nothing short of ambivalent. While they had no reason to dislike us, they had small cause to think of us as friends. They were not a captive audience, but I think they felt a strong obligation to come as we requested them to. The same situation existed in the following case and might be borne in mind.

This incident caused me some concern, even after the research had been completed. I had become accustomed to easy access to the events and rumours current around "the corners," gained through conversations with addicts and other rounders. For the first time, I had been cut off from "what's really going on" when I had expected to hear it.

It is a fairly common practice among addicts to continue to associate with people who have offended them, but any conversation in the presence of the offender is guarded. The miscreant doesn't take long to get the point. He may leave the area until his misdemeanour has been forgotton, or else he may try to make amends.

Two alternatives presented themselves in this case. In the first place, our failure to use argot when we knew it (it may have been a key to communication), might have been interpreted as a misdemeanour. Did they think we were trying to act in a superior manner? Secondly, did the omission to use argot have the same effect as actually offending our subjects?

I have discounted the first possibility because the second interview was arranged without any trouble very shortly after the first one aborted, and this one went well. Since I could detect no traces of animosity among the respondents, although they certainly seemed wary, I accepted the second alternative.

It appears as if we failed to pass a verbal screening process which none of us was conscious of. If such a process exists, it might serve to exclude a naïve stranger from making contact with people who would reveal themselves as members of the criminal element. Conversely, the screening would facilitate meeting members of the criminal element. I cannot extend the hypothesis beyond this point since the depth or extent of the eventual relationship would likely depend on personality factors peculiar to the individuals and distinct from language.

I attempted to use my familiarity with argot to test the frequency of argot use by respondents, which in turn should affect the content of a conversation. My hypothesis was that if I used argot with the respondent, he would respond in a similar manner and would discuss criminal activities. If I did not use argot, the respondent would not, nor would he talk freely about crime.

The interviews were of a twelve minute duration and tape recorded. I used argot with eight experimental subjects and didn't with seven control subjects. My remarks were fairly noncommittal, in that I did not attempt to lead the course of the conversation. I addressed the experimental subjects by their nicknames and said, "What's shak'n?" which is a form of salutation. When some sort of response seemed to be required, I might say, "Jeez, ya don't say."

With the control subjects, I addressed them by their given names and said, "How are you tonight?" When I thought it was necessary for me to make some remark, I would say, "I see, that's interesting." From time to time, it was necessary for me to make some comment or answer questions addressed to me during the conversation. I attempted to do this in line with the original scheme. In Table I, we see the results of an analysis of the fifteen conversations.

TABLE I

MEAN AVERAGE FREQUENCY OF ARGOT WORDS USED BY SUBJECTS PER MINUTE

Time: (Min.)	/ 1	2	3	4	5	6	7	8	9	10	11
Control Grp:	/ 3.3	2.0	1.7	1.3	1.4	1.7	1.1	0.7	1.3	1.0	0.4
Experimental	/14.9	16.7	15.9	12.0	10.9	10.7	10.7	9.5	9.8	10.8	10.6

Total Mean Average Per Minute:
1) Control Subjects: 1.4 argot words.
2) Experimental Subjects: 11.7 argot words.

The control subjects did not use argot to any extent, nor did they discuss the current events of "the corners." It may be of interest that four of these subjects said they had stopped using drugs and were looking for work, while none of the experimental subjects made this claim. Although it is just a subjective impression, the control subjects seemed to be at a loss for something to say. The interview session seemed to drag along. The method of interviewing was employed in such a way that I interviewed the first person in argot, but not the second, etc. Thus it was a random decision in each case as to whether or not argot would be used.

It may be more than a chance event that four of the control subjects claimed to have reformed. I find this particularly questionable since I observed each of the fifteen subjects coming from an area where heroin is usually sold. I made no effort to verify these accounts by examining their arms for needle marks or by asking other people who would know.

It seemed to me that the experimental subjects over-reacted. I chose a busy intersection as a place to carry out the interview, so there were a number of people passing by as we talked. None of the interviews was carried out in private, but the traffic varied with each interview. Five of the experimental subjects elected to use what is known as McGarvey Slang during the first few minutes of the interview. This slang is a mixture of argot and pig latin; for example: *"I weazas on my weazay up teazown to a meazeet."* That is, "I was on my way up town to a meet [rendezvous]."

A conversation carried out under these conditions can be virtually private, regardless of who may be nearby. At first, I had some difficulty understanding what was being said, but I adapted after a few minutes. The conversations with the experimental subjects moved along well, and there didn't appear to be any shortage of topics to discuss or lack of interest in the meeting itself.

I do not think that the number of subjects is adequate to draw any scientific conclusions, but the interviews seem to indicate that argot serves as a screening device in verbal exchanges. It would not be difficult to devise more valid testing procedures.

The table above indicates increased use of argot during the introductory period of the interviews. As the interview progressed between one and five minutes, the use of argot dropped off and stabilized. This same phenomenon can be seen with even three of the control subjects, although the effect is not as pronounced. It may be that the control subjects were attempting to use the argot since they knew from previous experience that I spoke it. It would be of advantage to use an experimenter who was unknown to the subjects in an attempt to reduce the effect that prior familiarity might have.

The experiment also had an effect on the expectations of the experimenter. As I listened to the control subjects, I felt satisfied that they were *not* using argot at all; with the experimental subjects, it seemed that they were making very liberal use of argot. In short, there appeared to be a considerable disparity between the conversational contexts of the two groups of subjects.

When I played back the tapes, I found that the control subjects had, in fact, used argot, while the experimental subjects used less of it than I had expected. The ratio between the control and experimental subjects was about one to ten; yet during the period when the experimental subjects were using between twenty to twenty-one argot words a minute, it was necessary to listen very carefully in order not to lose the text of the conversation. This was in spite of the fact that I have been familiar with argot and the McGarvey Slang for about twenty years.

I replayed the tapes and counted the number of words per minute used by the eight experimental subjects. They spoke at a rate between forty and sixty words a minute. The mean average was approximately forty-seven words a minute. The control subjects spoke at a slightly slower rate, forty-five words a minute, compared to about fifty-two words a minute for the experimental subjects. Does this faster rate of speech coupled with the increased use of argot have a specific function in the relationship?

It occurred to me that there were at least two distinct possibilities. In the first place, if the listener were not completely familiar with argot – that is, not capable of gleaning connotative meaning from the conversation – he would be required to translate each word as he had learned it from a vocabulary and apply it to the conversation.

Some argot expressions have a wide range of meaning, so a translation often depends upon how the word is used in a phrase or sentence. For example, "The Crow" is a lookout to warn his accomplices if someone is approaching. The lookout may also be called a "Six Man," "Sixer" (possibly referring to a sixth sense), or "The Nose." "The Crow" may also be a fake or cheat with a reputation for stealing from his partners in crime. I can see the logical connection between the two interpretations. Who has the best chance of getting away from the scene of a crime and leaving his friends to be arrested? – it is "The Crow."

There are a variety of similar words that could cause the conscientious vocabulary student to become lost in a forest of verbiage. He would be quickly identified as a pretender – a ringer. The argot then allows his hosts to adjust to the situation and decide openly what to do with this "mark," even while he is present. This poor fellow will probably go home a little poorer but a lot wiser.

The second possibility is that the listener feels an urge to move closer to the speaker in order to hear everything that is being said. The spatial distance between the speaker and his audience decreases, and the speaker may talk more softly. The opportunity to eavesdrop is drastically reduced. During the interview sessions, I often moved to within a foot of the speaker in order to hear him more clearly.

Edward T. Hall, in *The Silent Language,* states that being eight to twelve inches from a speaker is regarded as "close." This distance is reserved for "very confidential" matters and is carried out in an "audible whisper." Hall points out,

> Not only is a vocal message qualified by the handling of distance, but the substance of a conversation can often demand special handling of space.

It may be recalled that the contents of the conversations in argot dealt mainly with current events in the world of crime. The message is only for those who "know what's really going on." Outsiders are excluded not only by the message construction, but by the effect of its delivery.

The control subjects and I maintained a distance of three to six feet between us while we talked. They did not look at me frequently or use my name, but kept glancing at the people passing by or looking down at the sidewalk. On the whole, they gave signs of being uneasy – by shifting position, by putting their hands in their pockets and taking them out again. They did not use hand gestures to any extent. Their overall deportment gave an impression of humility. They may have thought that I was acting out of character and been confused by it.

The experimental subjects were generally more animated in their conversations. One of them was openly antagonistic. Many of his remarks were directed against me; however, he spoke fluently, and that was what seemed to matter at the time.

These subjects did not retreat if I moved close to hear them, nor did I feel inclined to back away if they approached me. They directed most of their remarks to me, often called me by name, and looked at my face from time to time. They also glanced around at the traffic and the people passing by. Three or four of them touched me with their hands to stress the importance of some remark they were making. On the whole, they did not give me the same impression of humility or shyness. They seemed to be more comfortable in the situation, more open and more familiar with the conduct that was expected of them.

The hostile respondent did not touch me but stood with his hands firmly in his pockets, leaning slightly toward me. This man had been drinking, but his hostility toward me had been a chronic attitude for at least six years.

Each of the respondents had a fairly well-developed set of prior attitudes toward the experimenter. Our roles had been distinct, yet we shared an abiding interest in crime. Their personalities and activities had been a matter of genuine interest to me, as my personality and activities had been to them.

It might provide some focus on this relationship to mention what I will call the "tourist syndrome." On a number of occasions I have met members of the criminal element from Toronto who are in another city or well out in the suburbs of Toronto. Invariably, they seem genuinely happy to see a face from "the corners." This is followed by a long conversation concerning "what's going on" in Toronto, of course. This takes place despite the fact that our relationship might have been something less than cordial in Toronto's downtown area. Other people in similar circumstances have mentioned this phenomenon to me, so it seems to be a common one.

SUMMARY

Jack Vance, in his book *Languages of Pao,* gives an account of a fictitious civilization in which languages were developed intentionally to reinforce a division of labour. Language coincided clearly with a social class. It epitomized the functions, specialities, and goals of that class. Words which conflicted with the single-minded purposes of the class had been omitted, so ambiguity within the class was unlikely. Language prevented each class from an exchange of ideas. In effect, the classes were divorced from each other while operating in the same society. They lacked common ground, a common set of connotative meanings.

Argot as it is spoken by the criminal element presents us with a similar, but a far more subtle consideration. Whatever distinctions I might make between the criminal element at large and the drug addict subculture will dissolve when it comes to a discussion of argot. They speak the same language.

It is a form of speech which has developed in the densely populated, heterogeneous core of large cities, amid bustling crowds, the hard sell, and the fast buck. It has been fairly stable over a period of time and is uniform throughout North America, but it is not a written language.

Criminal argot has been moulded by a subculture which is not in opposition to society; actually, its members are indifferent to society, amused by but disdainful of society's sacred values. In the mind of the rounder, society and its values are phoney. Society is a façade. The rounders themselves are real and basic. This is a simple philosophy, but it is basic to them. Their philosophy is a secret which they must keep to themselves. It welds them together.

Argot, like the subculture which speaks it, has the appearance of normality. Words that look like those which comprise the argot can be found in most dictionaries, but their criminal connotations can't be found in dictionaries. The people who speak argot can't be picked out of a crowd on the basis of their physical appearance. There are few obvious signs of deviance.

The drug addict, the thief, and the confidence man have been spawned in crowds. They prey on crowds, but they have a secret to keep from that crowd. They known "what's really going on." Fluency in criminal argot allows them to keep their secret.

Society deplores crime and makes laws to deal with it. The rounders celebrate ingenuity, cunning, and excitement. The law is an inconvenience. A good escapade must be retold to people who will appreciate its intricacies, people who conceptualize the event. It must be told to people who can revel in the suspense of near certain detection and the climax of a successful escape. But there are hard times too: the sorrows of addiction, the angry bewilderment of betrayal, and terror of the one-way ride. They are part and parcel of the same subculture.

The vocabulary of society is inadequate, so they have fashioned their own out of necessity to maintain privacy and to obtain a vehicle to carry their myths, rumours, and achievements to other parts of the underworld, just to let them know "what's really going on."

4 The New Nudity Exposed

Jack Batten

As the trend towards increasing exposure of the female figure accelerates in the large North American cities, the curious are bound to ask, "How far are they going to go in Toronto?" The following article is not without its facetious and sardonic overtones as it outlines the examples of the new nudity that were to be found in Toronto in February, 1969. One sees the operation of both social and aesthetic norms and something of the ambivalence that surrounds our increasing liberalism. It should be noted that when *Futz* came to Toronto in May, 1969, its chief promoters were hauled into court and fined: Toronto's attitudes towards the public display of the human body could hardly be described as consistent.

Jack Batten, columnist for the Toronto *Star* and associate editor of *Saturday Night,* has had his articles published in most of the major magazines of Canada, including *Chatelaine, Saturday Night,* and *Maclean's.* The following article first appeared in *Toronto Life* in February, 1969.

10:30 A.M. I warm up for the ordeal ahead (or will it be a joy trip?) with an in-close inspection of recent issues of *Playboy, The Village Voice,* and *The Realist.* Why? Easy – this is the day I embark on an expedition to uncover evidence of the New Nakedness in Toronto. It's supposed to be all over North American society, this New Nakedness. People shucking their clothes. Includes topless waitresses, topless go-go dancers, topless *and* bottomless ballet dancers.

Young matrons wear see-through fashions. Movies give us Jane Fonda's nipples *(Barbarella),* Alan Bates' buttocks *(King of Hearts),* a groupie's pubic hair *(Blow-Up).* On Broadway, kids cavort in the musical *Hair* absolutely bare. And it's artistic. Same thing in plays *Futz* and *Tom Paine*. Off Broadway, players in the Living Theatre production of *Paradise Now* chant in the aisles: "We're not allowed to take our clothes off," and then take their clothes off.

Some musicians follow similar practice. Charlotte Moorman, lady cellist, performs works by composer Nam June Pak for topless cellist. San Francisco rock group, The Allmen Joy, is noted for nude rock. It's not just a gimmick. Nudity is becoming a social concept, apparently imperative, or at least attractive, in many arts. No longer a mere voyeuristic device, but an accepted value. Does it go even further? Is all this stripping actually a new celebration of the human form? Are we losing our clothes hangup? Have we discovered love of our bodies? I set off to investigate the existence of New Nakedness in Toronto to resolve all questions.

11:00 A.M. Continue perusal of magazines. Decide *Playboy,* with its rubbery, shaved bunnies and its treatment of undressed women as part of man's furniture, belongs to Old Impotence, not New Nakedness. *Village Voice* brings news of Cerebrum, a new New York discothèque, a discothèque of the future for all cities, where the first step for patrons is the shedding of all clothes in favour of diaphanous white gowns. Ahh, the *Realist* – its spirit of general free-form irreverence and its blunt shots of boy and girl hippies in their unbrushed, unadorned natural buff state seem to be drawing me nearer to the New Nakedness. Or so I speculate.

12:01 P.M. I'm first in line for the buffet at the Drawing Room, Toronto's first and, so far, only topless dining room. Well, almost topless. Waitresses wear brief costumes featuring filmy, black, see-through blouses. I carry a plate of so-so lamb stew and salad to one of the Drawing Room's couches, then attempt to see through. I succeed. My waitress is a small, lovely thing with a cool expression and breasts that are decidedly saucy. The sight enhances the meal. Most waitresses in the Drawing Room seem attractive – no tough faces, pendulous breasts, or expanding rears – and the place fills rapidly with lunching businessmen. Very straight crowd – hardly any sniggering, and the ogling is decidedly covert. All quite genteel, but it yields no real clues to New Nakedness. My waitress tells me that, for her, it's a good job, that she feels modest in her blouse and that she wouldn't care to go any barer.

12:55 P.M. Stop by Times Square Book Store and linger over its rows of sunbathing magazines, French post cards, photo collections of girls wearing high heels and garter belts and snapping whips. Note traces of spittle at corner of a fellow male customer's mouth and decide I am in the wrong place.

1:08 P.M. Enter Zanzibar Tavern, which advertises "topless go-go from noon to four every afternoon," and quiz assistant manager about the attitudes of his topless dancers to their work. "Well, we're the only place in town that ever advertised in the paper for topless dancers," he says, "and we had dozens of girls in here asking for an audition. Some of them were just curious, like they didn't know whether they'd have to dance in their bras or what, and some turned out to be just too big. We like our girls thirty-six or thirty-eight. But with all of them, all the kids who auditioned, what I think is they just like to show off their bodies to the crowd."

I check the afternoon's two performers. *My God*, they're awful! They're *homely!* What have they got to show off? Their breasts droop, their figures are describable in straight lines, their bellies tend to swell. It's an anti-sexual experience I'm enduring. The New Nakedness? Oh hell! Girls, please put your clothes back on. I flee the Zanzibar in horror.

3:36 P.M. I retreat to the Central Library on College Street to hunt out the words of experts on New Nakedness. Come across a charming comment by the large, lumpy, hairy poet, Allen Ginsberg, on his affection for the portrait by painter Wynn Chamberlain depicting Ginsberg and his friend Peter Orlovsky in the raw: "Why am I interested in seeing myself nude? Because for years I thought I was ugly, and now I see beauty." Also like quote from *Vogue* magazine: "In our time, like a clear wind blowing, it is Pride of Body that has ripped away the barriers of the past and thrust us wondrously into the present. Today – in the pictures we look at, in the music we dance to, in the clothes we wear – we know we've come toward an era of the healthiest and most liberating self-awareness." One pop philosopher I discover, examining the trend to public nudity, decides it springs from 1) unrest among the young; 2) general disillusionment with the Puritan Ethic; 3) a new freedom among women symbolized by the Pill; and 4) the influence of the hippies.

6:10 P.M. Telephone actor friend: "Nude theatre in Toronto? Well, I dunno. But I can take you to this stag tonight where some girls. . . ." No nude theatre in Toronto.

6:32 P.M. Return to the Drawing Room where a Paint-In is in progress. Canvas for the painting is a smiling, buxom young lady in bikini pants and pasties. An artist has drawn designs on her body and patrons pay $1 each for privilege of colouring in the designs. At first the men in the room seem gripped by nervous hilarity. But as each approaches his turn at painting, he grows calm and involved with girl's body. Nothing sexual here. More a kind of spiritual communication. And the girl seems to become lovelier as the evening moves along. It's a joyful experience. Am I on to something?

8:00 P.M. First show of the night at the Brown Derby Tavern for the Humming Birds, all-girl, topless rock quartet. Girls are attired in leather micro-skirts, white boots, black net stockings, and silver pasties, and when they begin to sing and play (three on guitars, one on drums), their ample breasts quiver ferociously. It strikes me as, at best, an unsettling sight. Things career downhill when one guitarist, who doubles as M.C., takes over the microphone. "This the first time you fellas have seen topless?" she bellows at a table of three men who, I judge from their greying, distinguished looks, are brain surgeons or Supreme Court justices. They cringe. I cringe. "I hope you fellas keep your glasses on – it helps the show. Yeah, you're lookin' at our best assets."

8:30 P.M. I drop into the Coq d'Or where Rompin' Ronnie Hawkins and his band are blasting merrily while two topless go-go girls, bathed in flickering psychedelic lights, gyrate on their elevated platforms. One dancer, a luscious West Indian girl, presents the most beautiful body I've come across so far. After the band finishes its set, I ask Rompin' Ronnie about his attitude as a muscian to the topless phenomenon. "Lord Gawd Almighty," he begins (he's from Arkansas), "those sweet young *hors d'oeuvre* surely take the weight off the band. The crowd's so busy lookin' at them that they don't pay much mind to what we're playin'. We can take it nice and easy. New Nakedness? Why man, it looks awful familiar to me."

9:10 P.M. Decide to pass up the topless go-go at the Brass Rail, Bermuda, Friars, Concord, etc. and to ignore the topless show-girls at the Blue Orchid and the Caravan in favour of a visit to the Mynah Bird on Yorkville Avenue. I pay $4 at the door, and for my money I'm treated to one topless dancer (with pasties) in a cage and two topless mannequins (without pasties) posed on two slowly revolving pedestals. They're attractive, but I feel no artistic vibrations. Upstairs, another room offers a continuous presentation of stag-type movies. Tonight's feature is *The Nude World of June Palmer*. "We were the first topless club in Toronto back in 1966," the Mynah Bird's owner advises me, a young, slim, self-possessed man named Colin Kerr. "When we started, other club owners told me I was in for police trouble. But I'm still doing capacity business every night. And do you know where I get my topless girls? From the police. Patrolmen are constantly coming to my door with girls they've found wandering around Yorkville. They ask me if I'll give the girls jobs and keep them off the street, and I do."

10:00 P.M. I reach the Victory Burlesque Theatre at Spadina and Dundas in time for the final show in the "Giant Amateur Strip Tease Contest." Girls allegedly without any previous stripping experience take off their clothes (street clothes, not spangled costumes) in a competition that lasts for four weeks, and the winner is decided by audience reaction registered on an applause metre. The Victory lobby is a cavalcade of signs: "Who knows? You may see the girl next door!" "Girls from all walks of life! Nurses. Students. Hair dressers. Models." "Positively no photographs to be taken inside!" "If you belong to a club, legion, union, bowling league, charitable organization, or neighbourhood group, special group rates are available!"

The first contestant is interviewed on-stage by the M.C. before she begins her routine. She's a plump, sweet-faced girl with long blonde hair and a pink mini-dress, and she says her name is Bonnie Scott, she's from London, England, and she works as a bar maid. She launches into her strip. It falls into three acts. First she dances around the stage and down the runway in her dress, then follows the same procedure but takes off her dress while she dances, leaving bra and bikini panties; finally, more dancing as she removes her bra and trips around the stage and runway in her pants and pasties. She dances awkwardly but proudly. She looks guileless and vulnerable. What she is doing up there isn't related to any professional stripping I have ever seen, not to Sin Tana or Miss Una Vack or Ineeda Man, not to them and their posturing, their struts and bumps and grinds. This is, I realize, a kind of innocence I'm watching.

The second girl brings more of the same. She's forgotten to leave her wrist watch in the dressing room – or maybe she needs it, like Linus's blanket. The third girl has a beautiful body with smallish breasts and she takes her bra off while the band plays *"My Lean Baby."* It's charming. The fourth girl tells the M.C. her occupation – "brain surgeon" – and the medical students in the audience, all of whom have arrived in their white meds smocks, cheer wildly. The girl dances slowly and sensuously, like she's enticing someone. Who? I look at her and decide it must be her husband. Girl No. 5 is stunning. Her name is Helga Erskine, she is a swimming instructor, and her face is beautiful. She smiles shyly. She begins to dance and a magic stillness strikes the place. This is the crummy Victory Burlesque Theatre, accustomed to audiences of dirty old men and raucous U. of T. students, and this girl is mesmerizing us all. We've crossed some mysterious line from mere leering to open admiration. Her body – down to white panties and white pasties – is as spectacular as her face. I sense a new emotion inside me. It's something like envy! This girl is showing off the way she really is. Her body is beautiful, and she is actually showing it off to other people. I envy her. Here I am trapped inside my clothes. I push out into the aisle, heading for the door, and I chant: "We're not allowed to take our clothes off."

11:35 P.M. Driving home, I think I'm on to the meaning of the New Nakedness. I forget all the ugliness I've seen, those crude broads at the Brown Derby and the homely ones at the Zanzibar. Vogue, Allen Ginsberg, and Helga Erskine are right – it's pride in your body. I feel good. I feel pride in my body. It's catching – this New Nakedness.

11:56 P.M. I hear on the car radio that Helga Erskine has won the "Giant Amateur Strip Tease Contest."

5 Toronto's Pornography: Disease or Symptom?

Albert Coleclough

The gradual relaxation of legal controls on blatant exploitation of sex in print and on celluloid, along with the "sexual
revolution," has made pornography a big business in many
modern metropolises. Toronto is no exception to this; in fact,
more than one observer of the pornography phenomenon has
described Toronto as the largest pornography production
centre on the continent. How this "business" operates, who
its customers are, and what the police are doing about it are
questions raised by both social critics and the public at large.

The author of this article, Albert Coleclough, is a teacher
of sociology and law enforcement at Humber Community
College, Toronto; he was previously a detective with the
Toronto police force, and his experiences in that position
give him a unique viewpoint on his subject. In co-operation
with Lloyd G. Hanley, he previously co-authored an article on
marijuana users in Toronto which appeared in W. E. Mann's
Deviant Behaviour in Canada. The following article appears
in this anthology for the first time.

A British newspaper, *The Spectator,* has labelled Toronto "the
pornography centre of North America." Several years of police
experience in downtown Toronto caused me to doubt the accuracy
of *The Spectator's* charge. Opinions obtained from a small group
of people made up of police officers, lawyers, members of the
press, teachers, and a representative of the Clarke Institute of
Psychiatry also indicated *The Spectator's* claim to be an exaggeration. These people had some knowledge about pornography in
the Toronto area, and each agreed that the amount of material
has been increasing, but their estimates as to the extent of the

increase ranged from slight to great. None were willing to state that a full-scale pornography industry had formed in this area.

In order to understand the significance of pornography in Toronto, it would be well at the outset to examine the following four questions:

What is pornography? Pornography is an evaluative term meaning different things to different people. Section 150 (8) of the Criminal Code states:

> For the purposes of this Act, any publication a dominant characteristic of which is the undue exploitation of sex, or of sex and any one or more of the following subjects, namely crime, horror, cruelty and violence, shall be deemed to be obscene.[1]

Pornography is not illegal unless it is obscene, and it does not become obscene unless there is "undue exploitation" of sex, or of crime, horror, cruelty, or violence with sex. But what does the phrase "undue exploitation" mean? Is it "undue exploitation" of sex and violence, for instance, to advertise the film, *Laughter In The Dark*, as "A chic exercise in sex and sadism for the voyeuristic public!"? This example was taken from the entertainment page of the *Toronto Telegram*, Friday, September 19, 1969. It would be naïve to deny that this ad, to which the general public (including children) is exposed, exploits sex, but is this undue exploitation? It is possible that the advertisements come closer to the definition of obscenity in the Criminal Code than the products they advertise.

For the purposes of this paper, pornography will be regarded as material having sexual content which is intended to arouse strong sexual emotion.

How extensive is its use? Police efforts to discourage the growth of pornography in Toronto have apparently failed. On Yonge Street between Dundas and Bloor, there are now more "porno" shops than ever. Store windows display row after row of paperback skin-books with titles such as *Erotica and the Teenager, The Gay Lords, Sex Cheat, Affair, Orgy, Warm and Willing, Sex Mate, Woman Patient, Bartered Flesh, The Erotic Revolution*, and many more. The titles and illustrated covers of such books are self-explanatory; they cater to every erotic whim from "straight" sex to bestiality.

For the person whose sexual appetite is whetted by the window display, directional signs reading "We dare you to walk in the back," "Seeing is Believing," and "Adult Books" guide him to more expensive "imports," sealed in plastic wrappers and selling for $5 and up.

For those whose tastes extend beyond the literary, some book stores have movie rooms for "Adult Movies." The movie fan in search of erotica, however, is not limited to backroom movies. Many films which have been passed by the Ontario Board of Censors give stiff competition to even the best quality stag-type, blue movie on the market today. One such film is a British production called *If*, which takes place on the campus of a tradition-steeped English public school. *If* vividly depicts sado-masochism, nudity (including male and female genitalia), intercourse, homosexuality, and bloody machine-gun killings.

Certain movie houses located on Toronto's Yonge Street are known in homosexual argot as "meat racks," known homosexual hangouts where members of the "gay" world go to "cruise for trade." A short walk on the east side of Yonge from Dundas to Gerrard will inform the observer that these theatres provide their fair share of commercial sex.

While one theatre advertises "Violence, Hate, Way-Out parties," a nearby competitor is pushing a delightful junket all about "beautiful, young and moonlighting wives" who "rock and shock a city with unprintable scandal." The billboard proclaims that "Every man was their tool for pleasure," and the management achieves with twenty-four words what a multitude of pictures could never do by adding a black-bordered apology: "Sorry. . . . We cannot show you scenes from this movie in our ads as we do not want to offend shy or prudish people." Frequently, the most creatively erotic or pornographic part of these films is the billboard advertising. Inside the theatre, more action takes place in the men's washroom than on screen.

Weekly tabloids which are on sale at most newsstands perform a vital communications role in the world of off-beat sex. They inform the interested about the latest in pornographic literature and the newest inovations in deviate paraphernalia – crotchless underwear for the male homosexual or exhibitionists, or battery-operated, phallic-shaped personal vibrators that can be used by men and women anywhere, with or without oil or cream.

The personal columns of *Tab International, Justice Weekly, Confidential Flash,* and *Hush* offer a variety of social arrangements for the deviate, ranging from heterosexual mate-swapping or volunteering one's wife for lesbian relationships to sadistic homosexuals advertising for masochistic partners as in the following ad from *Flash Confidential:*

Transvestite, white, very well built, bizarre, exotic, neat, educated, extremely dominant, strict disciplinarian. Wears high heel boots, spurs, leather garb and other bizarre attire! Will train males and females. Write now!

It is virtually impossible to obtain accurate statistics on the flow of pornographic material in Toronto. What I have discussed to this point has been in reference to commercially produced and distributed material. Needless to say, there is also a large amateur source of pornography. Recently, an employee of a reputable publishing firm in Toronto was found to be producing pornographic comic strips on his firm's printing equipment. Polaroid photography has been a boon to the home pornographer. Before instant processing, he was obliged either to process his own film or to accept all the risks of having someone else do it.

What are its functions and effects? Superficially, the function of pornography is to induce sexual arousal. However, it has a deeper sociological significance. Pornography can serve as an accommodative device by providing a fantasy situation within which social conflict may be reduced. It functions not unlike the secret lives of Walter Mitty; when social pressures become unbearable, the individual who resorts to pornography may find escape and possibly some measure of fulfillment.

In an adult whose sexual development has not been influenced in his formative years by pornography, it is unlikely that even the worst hard-core material would have any detrimental effect. This would seem to be the consensus of opinion of medical practitioners and psychologists. It is supported, in fact, by the number of normal heterosexual policemen and censors who, in the course of their jobs, have viewed all manner of materials which depict various form of sexual activity.

A Toronto expert in psychosexual problems, however, claims that for those people whose sexuality has not been consolidated by full and normal sexual activity – in other words, the very young – there is a danger. The viewing of such material prior to normal heterosexual contact could cause self-induced perversion arising out of the faulty emphasis depicted in that which is viewed. Fredric Wertham, a New York psychiatrist, relates the following incident:

> I carried out an extensive psychiatric examination of the leader of the so-called "Brooklyn Thrill Killers," a group of four boys aged fifteen to seventeen. They had tormented girls by whipping them with bull whips on their bare legs.

They burned, beat, whipped and tortured men whom they attacked, mostly in parks. They were finally arrested after killing a young Negro whom they had found sleeping on a park bench. They dragged him away, burned, hit, beat and tortured him, then pushed him – still alive – from a pier into the river where he drowned. These boys had read *Nights of Horror,* which they used as a textbook. They even imitated the detail of forcing the victim to kiss his tormentors' feet. The fashionable theory that such reading matter helps children to get rid of their aggression evidently did not work with them.[2]

Does it threaten the moral fibre of our society? This is a very difficult question to deal with because both pornography and obscenity are evaluative terms. Obscenity and obscene pornogaphy fall under the jurisdiction of the Criminal Code, which is a federal statute. However, what is considered to be obscene in one town or locality may not be considered obscene in another because of the social ethos which determines the meaning of "undue exploitation." The climate of opinion in Toronto regarding pornography fluctuates between tolerance and condemnation.

Many authorities, including the police, argue that if stringent enforcement and severe penalties were meted out to purveyors of pornography, two purposes would be served – it would rid the city of a pornography industry and reduce the incidence of sex crimes. Others, notably the professional associations of lawyers and physicians, point out that we will not cure the illness simply by eliminating a symptom.

A Toronto-based writer of pornographic manuscripts informed me that the pornography market is carefully surveyed and caters to a highly segmented readership. For instance, an agent will contact a writer and suggest the theme of a psychosexual problem such as homosexuality, lesbianism, sado-masochism, bestiality, wife-swapping, or some other topic which will have a good market value at a particular time. The writer commented, "Even if you could conceivably get rid of all the commercial outlets, the kooks are still going to be here, and when you get some deviate going out to prepare his own stuff, that's when you've got troubles." The paedophile, for instance, if deprived of commercially prepared pornography, may turn to using children as models in the production of his own material. The social consequences of this are obvious.

It has been said that today "sex is becoming a spectator sport." Certainly sex is portrayed in many ways in our communications media, which are extremely important socializing agents in the modern world. It may well be that we are becoming a society of voyeurs.

Toronto, because of a strongly entrenched, church-supported taboo, is officially resistant to pornography. This resistance attempts to exert control through customs regulations, censorship boards, and the police. The result is that these agencies are placed in the untenable position of having to interpret a law regarding obscenity which we have already described as being almost impossible to interpret objectively. The primary responsibility for control of questionable material lies with the Metropolitan Toronto Police. A Detective/Sergeant with the Morality Squad recently told me,

> We haven't even scratched the surface. We may win the battle, but we're losing the war. We find ourselves in a funny position. The [Criminal] Code specifies one thing, but community standards are more permissive.

There is substantial evidence to indicate that the use of pornographic material is particularly prevalent among highly educated people in business and the professions. Typical of the personal ads placed in the Toronto-published tabloids is the following from *Tab International:*

> Tall, attractive, sophisticated couple, early forties. New to area, would like to meet other sincere and swinging couples and ladies for interesting times. We enjoy all kinds of fun. What is yours? Discretion assured. Can travel. First ad. All answered. Phone a must. Photo optional.

Such carefully worded ads are charged with between-the-lines significance for those who either are or wish to be participants in "swinging" (mate-swapping) activities. The crux of the "swingers" ethos is that its members are highly motivated toward obtaining hedonistic experience in a variety of erotic circumstances. Nevertheless, because of their social circumstances, it is necessary for them to put on a front of conformity; one cannot safely appear to be immoral. It is paradoxical that while "swingers" stress discretion, they are usually willing to exchange polaroid photos of an extremely personal nature with total strangers. This is, however, an accommodating device whereby the participants enter into a "conspiracy of silence" with others. It is, in effect, a silent protest against, and an escape from, the restrictions of society.

The pornographer deals in fantasy – another form of escape. Nowhere is this more evident than in the exposé-type stories found in the local tabloids. One particular feature story with no date-line purports to reveal a shocking practice of sales training wherein salesmen and saleswomen are trained how to seduce the housewife in order to make sales. The article closes on a puritanical note and says,

> Tabloid x believes that there is no room for such immoral practices in business.
> There are enough temptations in our world today. Why add new ones?
> Let's bring back fair practices in business – and clean ones.

PORNOGRAPHY AND THE SEX OFFENDER

While there is evidence that persons convicted of sex crimes and offences are frequently users of pornography, there is no proof that pornography in itself motivates the sex offender. There are usually many sociological and psychological factors at work in the precipitation of such offences. For purposes of classification, it is convenient to think in terms of two distinct psychological groups. The neurotic offender characterized by such manifestations as voyeurism, fetishism, transvestism, and exhibitionism is generally a passive, relatively harmless individual. On the other hand, the psychopathic offender, who tends to be a greater threat to society, is characterized by the fact that he is usually egocentric, conscienceless, and selfish. His offences include such deviations as sado-masochism, pyromania, and paedophilia of the sort that involves serious child molestation. Again there is no clear indication that pornography is the primary motivator.

CONTROL THEORIES

There are three main proposals for dealing with pornography – prohibition, moderation, and licence.

Western society's experience with total prohibition in other areas would suggest that this is no answer. One suspects that this would open the flood gates of organized crime in the area.

The theory of moderation, with all of its semantic difficulties, is the process that we are trying to employ at the present time with less than entirely satisfactory results.

In light of the recent Danish experience, it is fashionable to speak in support of licence or complete freedom as being the best possible alternative. Statistics emerging from Denmark showing dramatic decreases in sex crimes and sales of pornographic material seem very encouraging. As yet, however, the experiment has not been in effect long enough to answer all questions. For example, is the material more accessible to Danish children now that restrictions have been lifted? If it is easier to obtain, what will the long-term effects be on youthful personality development?

CONCLUSION

While our present system of control seems less than adequate, it would seem foolhardy to rush headlong into a Danish-type experiment without more information. At present, the best solution seems to be the improvement of sex education in the home and at school. By fostering healthy, normal attitudes towards sex and sexual adjustment through more effective education, we will do much to cure the disease of which pornography is only a symptom.

6 The Gay World

William Johnson

As the controls of a former era are relaxed, the world of
the homosexual in Toronto is growing and becoming increasingly visible. This article mixes descriptions of "gay"
individuals and their problems with an account of the centres
of homosexual activity and the norms that regulate behaviour in them; it may dispel some commonly believed
myths about the appearance and life-style of those who shun
normal heterosexual activity.

The author of this piece, William Johnson, is currently a
senior reporter with the Toronto *Globe and Mail.* He has
also taught sociology at the University of Toronto while
studying for a PH.D. This article originally appeared in the
Globe Magazine in January, 1968, and was later reprinted
in W. E. Mann's *Deviant Behaviour in Canada.*

Toronto, haven for hippies and draft dodgers, may be on its way
to becoming the homosexual capital of North America.

"Toronto has changed in the last three years. Right now, it's
the best city in North America for the gay," a clerk told me in a
bookstore specializing in homosexual erotica. Around him were
rows of magazines offering pairs of smiling, naked male athletes
grappling, pairs of naked females in lesbian poses, pairs of naked
girls holding down and beating a third.

"Toronto is the Mecca for all of North America. You have
people who move here from New York, Detroit, or Chicago, because Toronto is the place to be if you're gay."

My confidant was a young Montreal professional man now
living in Toronto. It was 1:00 A.M. in an Avenue Road coffee shop

frequented by the gay. Some straight (heterosexual) people also go there to watch the drag show (a floor show put on by men dressed and acting like women), so the young man could safely venture an appearance. He could not risk being seen in an all-gay haunt and could not permit himself the dangerous luxury of friends who are gay.

The International Guild Guide, a kind of Baedecker for the gay, published each January, lists gay haunts in cities around the world and describes what is to be found at each. For California, with a population almost equal to Canada's, the Guide lists only three places where persons of the same sex can dance together. For Toronto alone, it lists two, and a third opened in June after the 1967 issue appeared.

The trend in this city was running strong long before the recently-proposed amendments to the Criminal Code which would legalize homosexual acts between pairs of consenting adults in private. In Toronto, according to inspector William Pilkington, head of the Metro morality squad, persons engaging in such private acts have not been prosecuted in the past decade, and, in the last case, the outcome was a suspended sentence.

New York, Chicago, and Los Angeles have larger gay communities than Toronto. And they have organizations, such as the Mattachine Society and the Daughters of Bilitis, dedicated to fostering more favourable public attitudes toward homosexuals. They publish their own magazines *(One, The Ladder)*.

Toronto has no protective organization for homosexuals, according to a man long prominent in homosexual circles, simply because none is needed. "The only people who get into trouble today are those who act like idiots."

Toronto used to have a magazine for homosexuals, published monthly throughout 1966. Called *Two,* it offered male pin-ups, documented and denounced discrimination against homosexuals, published essays ("The Homosexual and the Prison System"), ran short stories with a homosexual love motif, reviewed books *(Summer in Sodom),* and provided a forum for homosexual readers to vent grievances, discuss problems, and ask questions ("Is there any truth in the reports of cure cases in the United States?").

Two ceased publication because, according to its former publisher, "we made our point by publishing for a year. Besides, the field was adequately covered by American magazines."

One Yonge Street club is going full swing on a Saturday night.

Call it the 713 Club, not its real name, to protect it from the gawkers and troublemakers who descend on such places when they become known. It and another club up the street were established five years ago, the first of their kind in Toronto.

As you go down the steps to the basement, there is nothing to indicate that you are entering a club. All you see at street level is one of the many hair dressing shops strung along Yonge.

At the bottom of the stairs, where you pay your $1.75 admission, you are closely scrutinized. If you look as if you belong, you get in – no questions asked. If you look straight, or like a curiosity seeker or a troublemaker, you may be challenged and told that the club is private.

You emerge into a large room. It might be just another dance hall, but all you see are males. On the floor, about 200 males, closely bunched, are dancing the foxtrot. If the music is fast, they do the Watusi or a combination of all the steps of the past twenty years.

Some dance at arms-length, talking. Others, arms twined and eyes closed, cheeks together, sway back and forth. One couple in a dark corner ignores the management's prohibition and dances mouth to mouth.

Watching the dancers are another 200 to 300 men. Most are standing; some are seated at tables. The latter are generally older and look more sedate. There are pairs talking in various parts of the room. Groups of four or five stand about making desultory remarks, their eyes surveying the room as if they are bored with each other and hoping to discover a living doll.

Standing against the wall are the wallflowers. Their faces betray the same unmistakable look – a mixture of wistfulness and blankness, timidity, and hope. The look of the wallflower everywhere.

The club would surprise the average heterosexual. The first surprise is the number there. To see a roomful of perhaps 500 men who are almost without exception homosexual comes as a shock to anyone used to thinking that homosexuals are rare.

The most reliable estimate on homosexual numbers was made by the late Dr. Alfred Kinsey and his team of researchers from the University of Indiana during the 1940's and early '50's. They found that 4 per cent of the male population is exclusively homosexual throughout life. This means that there are more male homosexuals in Metro Toronto than there are male Jews. But if we also count as homosexual anyone who, for a minimum of three years after the age of sixteen, shows himself to be drawn sexually to men at least as much as to women, then 18 per cent are homosexual. For Canada, this means that the male homosexual population, active or latent, is approximately 1.8 million – larger than the combined populations of Prince Edward Island, Nova Scotia, and New Brunswick.

Furthermore, Kinsey discovered that 37 per cent of all men have a homosexual experience to the point of orgasm at some time after sixteen.

The figures for women are about one-third those for men. Together, they add up to such astounding totals that the researchers did not believe their own results. They started their investigation again with different subjects and repeated them again and again. Each time the answer was the same.

The figures bear out the Toronto homosexual who told me: "Society is going to have to come to terms with us sometime, because we aren't just going to go away."

A second surprise for the newcomer to a gay club is that the homosexuals don't look the way he thought they would.

The commonly held stereotype of a homosexual is called, in gay jargon, a screaming queen: a man, sometimes in female clothing, mincing about, hips swaying, hands loose at the wrist, fingers curled, lisping with sliding vocal modulations. Screaming queens are common among the female impersonators in a drag show. On Hallowe'en, they descend in full ultra-feminine glory on Yonge Street, parading from haunt to haunt to the cheers and jeers of passersby.

But screaming queens constitute a minority among homosexuals; experts estimate they comprise between 5 and 15 per cent. Moreover, transvestism (the desire to wear clothes and act the part of the opposite sex) is by no means limited to homosexuals.

One drag queen I spoke to said that he has wanted to wear girls' clothes since he was three. When he started school, he was allowed to wear girls' clothes for two years, but then his embarrassed parents insisted on male attire. To himself, he is a woman in all but external sexual characteristics. Every night, after work as a hospital orderly, he dons women's clothes.

Queens are looked upon with tolerant contempt by most homosexuals. During the drag show, they are heckled good-naturedly. The average homosexual does not think of himself as a woman, I was told again and again.

"I don't feel like a woman, I don't want to be like a woman, or act like a woman, and I certainly don't want to dress like a woman," said one homosexual who, in gay parlance, has been "married" for five years. He lives with a "femme" (a male with some feminine mannerisms) and in their menage he takes the aggressive, masculine role, while his partner takes the passive, obedient role.

Though they ordinarily despise swishy gestures, even masculine homosexuals will sometimes camp (exhibit feminine mannerisms).

A homosexual who is cruising (trying to pick up a partner) might make an effeminate gesture as a signal that he is a homosexual. Among themselves, homosexuals may camp in parody, poking fun at themselves by playing the stereotype. It becomes an in-joke.

The Toronto clubs are puritanical in their insistence on decorous behaviour. An inebriated person will not get past the door. Raucous conduct and blatant displays of affection are firmly discouraged by the management. Men may dance together, but they may not smoke while dancing.

There is one exception to the rule of gay respectability.

"Sit down, honey, you're not safe in here alone," the butch broad (a lesbian with mannish traits) told my wife, taking hold of her arm. My wife had walked alone into a bar, not far from the bus depot, which is notorious in Toronto as the chief hangout of a certain class of butch broad.

It was dingy, crowded, and smoky. Within half an hour, three fights broke out. The members might have modelled for a Hogarth or a Goya painting. The place itself could have been the prototype of a temperance poster's rum parlour.

My wife walked through the mixed wing. People stared at her. Then she walked into the all-female section. "Hey, look at that!" "Sit down, honey!" "Looking for someone, sweetheart?" "Wow –" Even a couple of wolf whistles. All from the girls seated at tables.

It was then that the blonde reached out and sat my wife down beside her. "I'm sort of waiting for someone," my wife said. "That's o.k.," the girl replied, "but you better sit down anyway and wait here. I'm not kidding when I say you're not safe walking through here alone. This section here is for butch broads, and that other section is for whores. In that section the men will jump you, and in this one the women. And they don't always take no for an answer."

According to the lesbian manager of one of the clubs which, unlike Club 713, caters to both males and lesbians, homosexuals do not go to clubs primarily to entertain companions or even to make pickups. "If I had something good, a club like this is the last place I'd want to bring her," she said. "There's too much competition around."

Where homosexuals are concerned, the clubs evidently function as places where they can drop their masks and be at ease among their own. ("You know, the only time when I really forget I'm gay is when I'm in a gay crowd.")

Many homosexuals look to one another for support against the disapproval – sometimes violent – which they know most heterosexuals feel toward them. Several I spoke to referred to the difficulties they experienced in "coming out" – realizing they *were* homosexuals.

One lesbian said her father accepts her, but her mother and sister won't speak to her. "I had a car accident last year," she said, "and my father came from Hamilton to see me in the hospital. For a while they didn't know whether I was going to live or not, but my mother didn't even send a postcard."

Not all have such difficulties. Some say they had no trouble simply accepting themselves.

An immigrant in his fifties says that whenever he returns to his native country and sees the friends he grew up with, who married and stayed where they were born, he becomes certain he has had a more interesting and satisfying life than they. Most homosexuals have, painfully, adjusted; to reject their homosexuality would be to reject themselves.

It is a common error to attribute to homosexuals a penchant for paedophilia (child molesting). One often hears that boys must be protected from seduction, the assumption being that homosexuals are attracted to young boys. Studies published by the Forensic Clinic of Toronto's Clarke Institute of Psychiatry refute the assumption. Paedophilia has nothing to do with homosexuality; it is a separate problem. Paedophiles may be homosexual or heterosexual.

A male homosexual of thirty indignantly denied the common assumption: "When I was twenty, I was attracted to boys of about twenty. As I get older the men who attract me are also older, close to my own age. I haven't the slightest interest in teen-age boys."

Homosexuals respond in different ways to the moral precepts of society, by whose standards they are at least sinful or sick, if not degenerate. Some try to inhibit their homosexual actions, even if they can't alter their tendencies: for example, a priest I know who has become a notable scholar. For him, inhibiting overt sexuality is similar to heterosexual priests who inhibit their overt acts of sexuality, even though their tendencies differ.

Another example: two Catholic girls, lesbians who have been living together for nine years. They allow themselves limited expressions of tenderness without feeling guilty, but when, carried away by passion, they engage in greater intimacies, they become conscience-stricken and confess to a priest.

Many homosexuals who cannot or will not accept continence as a solution to their own sexual tendencies try to approximate as closely as possible the heterosexual ideal dominant in society – marriage. Thus, several homosexuals mentioned with pride "married" couples – both male or both female – who had been living together for fifteen, twenty, or twenty-five years.

Several also said they hope some day to meet the right partner and get married – perhaps for life. Marriages are usually celebrated with an exchange of wedding bands, a party to which friends are invited, and sometimes even a religious service conducted by a friend.

One gay male, married five years, admitted he occasionally has affairs with other men, but considers himself no different from most heterosexual husbands, who, he believes, occasionally commit adultery. He added though that his partner, a femme, is strictly monogamous and very jealous if he shows an interest in other men – again, he feels, a characteristic feminine reaction.

Though most homosexuals dream of a homosexual marriage, the chances for a stable union are not good. All the factors which tend to make a heterosexual marriage stable work to destroy a homosexual union. The church considers a homosexual marriage sinful, if not sacrilegious. The family and friends of a heterosexual couple usually expect the husband and wife to stay together, but the family and heterosexual friends of a gay couple usually try to break up their liaison.

Marriage, especially where there are children, brings income tax deductions, and, with children, it becomes economically difficult to contemplate rupturing the family unit. But for homosexuals there are no children, and the economic bond usually means little.

Finally, heterosexuals generally consider it immoral to seduce a person who is married, whereas homosexuals, who have no formal marital bonds, frequently feel no scruple about seducing one another. Donald W. Corry, a pseudonym for a New York homosexual who has written a book on the subject, even maintains that "marriage" makes a homosexual more attractive to other homosexuals.

With respect to stability, there seems to be a clear difference between the unions of homosexual males and lesbian females. To females, the strictly sexual aspect of a union is not as important as to males, according to Dr. Johann Mohr of the Clarke Institute of Psychiatry. Thus, lesbians are less likely to cruise on the street, in the park, in bars, in steam baths, and in public toilets. Lesbians less frequently engage in one-night stands. When they do form a union, they are less promiscuous. Their unions seem to be more stable.

A lesbian suggested an explanation for such stability: in a relationship between two lesbians, one is usually a butch, the other a femme. But when neither is particularly butch or femme – which is the more common case between males – the union is unstable.

Because homosexual males are more numerous and more promiscuous, cruising is important to them.

A favourite place for some is the steam bath. The reason is obvious: men sit naked in the steam room, stand naked in the shower room, and lie more or less covered with a sheet in the rest room. For a homosexual, it is like a straight man being given licence to walk into a room full of naked females.

It is 3:00 A.M. in a steam bath known as an after-midnight homosexual hangout. The rest room has three groups of twenty-four cots, each about eighteen inches wide, crowded one against the other. There is only one unoccupied cot in the room.

Draped in my sheet, I lie down on the cot. My neighbours on either side are apparently asleep. I close my eyes, drowsy from the steam. Soon I feel a foot brush my foot – accidentally? I don't move. A foot touches mine more firmly. I don't respond. A knee rests against mine. I don't respond.

My neighbour, still "asleep," turns his back on me. He will have to cruise someone else.

Certain parks or certain sections of parks become known as favourite cruising grounds. Philosophers' Walk, behind Toronto's Royal Ontario Museum, is prime cruising ground. Winston Churchill Park, at the corner of St. Clair and Spadina, is preferred by some. Some say Queen's Park is as popular among homosexuals as politicians, but others maintain Queen's Park is passé.

Cruising homosexuals often walk a dog on a leash. The dog provides a plausible explanation for exploring remote and wooded sections of a park. It also becomes an excuse for striking up a conversation with a stranger, especially if he too has a dog.

The eye is the chief means of communication. Homosexuals

glance at men just a little longer than other men do. Exchanges of glances signal mutual interest and make way for an opening gambit such as, "Nice night." Conversation follows, with the ambiguity preserved. Then, sooner or later, one takes the decisive step: "Are you busy right now?" Or: "Do you live close by?"

Not all homosexuals cruise, nor do most who cruise do so in steam baths, on the street, or in public toilets. Most homosexuals look upon the man who cruises in public toilets as demented. I was told about a dress designer with a good business who had been arrested several times for gross indecency in public toilets, with his name appearing in the newspaper. He eventually lost his business and is now working for someone else. "He's sick, that's all. He wants to get caught. Why else would he be cruising in a place that he knows the police have staked out?"

Cruising aside, the ways homosexuals are brought together are much the same as for heterosexuals.

Said one homosexual: "When Jack came into town and was studying at the university, I had all kinds of friends who said we should get together. They threw a party where we met, and we hit it off," He is now "married" to Jack.

There are also office romances. One homosexual I spoke to had been dating girls until he fell in love with a male who worked in the same department. They lived together for three years.

When I met him – call him Karl – he had just broken up with his friend. We were at a gay coffee shop, and Karl had just come from a Christmas party where he had had several drinks. The alcohol had lowered his guard, but he was not drunk. There were tears in his eyes as he described his tragedy.

"I loved that boy, I loved him so much! I would have done anything for him. I would have died for him. I went $3,500 into debt buying presents for him. But then I discovered he was sleeping with other fellows while we were living together, so we broke up."

It had been six weeks since their breakup, but Karl was still miserable. He said he drives his car at 100 miles an hour and doesn't care whether he lives or dies. At the time I spoke to him, he was torn between an urge to go to his friend and the feeling that he would only be humiliated if he did.

There is a network of male prostitutes, called hustlers, who operate in bars known to be frequented by homosexuals. They also hang around parks and street corners waiting to be picked up. If a hustler is not himself homosexual, or maintains the belief that he is not, he is called "trade." "Rough trade" refers to hustlers who are liable to beat up or roll the homosexual, either after or instead of sexual relations.

One type of male prostitute in Toronto dresses as a female and picks up heterosexual males who think he is a female prostitute. One stood in court recently – a nineteen-year-old boy wearing a champagne-blonde wig, nylon stockings, high heels, and mouton fur coat. "She" was charged with keeping a bawdy house in her apartment.

Estimates of the number of such drag queens operating as female prostitutes in Toronto range from eight to fifty. How do they get away without being discovered by the trick (client)? By performing unorthodox sexual acts and by giving a plausible reason for avoiding normal sexual intercourse – for example, "It's that time of the month . . .."

Anyone who doubts that a young man could pass successfully for a girl has never seen a drag show. Certainly, the master of ceremonies at Club 713 looks as though "she" could win a beauty contest – as long as she didn't have to compete in the bathing suit category.

Female butches in drag are fairly common, but usually not as convincing. An exception is a leather-jacketed butch broad who works in a factory and is taken for a man by her co-workers. Though a number of butch broads dress in suits, they usually wear some feminine article of apparel. One, with a duck-tail haircut, who hangs around a downtown Toronto café, was wearing on a recent Saturday night a man's brown suit, a man's white shirt and black turtleneck sweater and men's socks – but a woman's suede oxfords.

Some lesbians engage in heterosexual prostitution. Prostitution is not considered respectable. But to be supported by one's partner is. A femme lesbian told me proudly she is supported by her lover, a female university student.

A survey of homosexuality inevitably focusses attention on the areas of difference between homosexuals and heterosexuals rather than on what they have in common. The average homosexual won't be found in a bar or a steam bath, does not consort with prostitutes, and does not spend his time cruising.

Like the average heterosexual, he works at his job as doctor or deliveryman, butcher or bus driver, policeman, producer, or clerk. He worries about the cost of living and about being respected and loved; he is concerned about air pollution and traffic jams, taxes, illness, and death. In fact, the closest thing to a homosexual is a heterosexual.

The past year has repeatedly thrust the issue of homosexuality upon the conscience of a Toronto – and Canadian – public long used to ignoring it.

A novel, *Place d'Armes* by Scott Symons, and a play, *Fortune and Men's Eyes* by John Herbert, have brought to somewhat shocked local audiences the artistic expression of undisguised homosexual passion.

The Supreme Court of Canada ruled in November that homosexuals likely to repeat even private homosexual acts with consenting adults might be declared dangerous sex offenders and sentenced to preventive detention, possibly for life. Then, last month, Justice Minister Pierre Trudeau introduced his amendments to the Criminal Code legalizing such private acts. The issue is now unavoidable.

The bewildered who turn to the experts for enlightenment will likely be disappointed. Despite long speculation, psychiatrists still do not really know what causes homosexuality.

The favourite current theory, advanced by Dr. Irving Bieber, a noted American psychoanalyst and researcher, is that homosexuality is associated with a possessive and dominant mother and an absent, ineffectual, or repellent father. This theory, though, was tested only on homosexuals sufficiently unhappy to seek psychiatric help. And the same theory has been trotted out to explain psychological ailments from alcoholism to juvenile delinquency to drug addiction.

California research psychologist Evelyn Hooker, by carefully controlled research involving homosexuals and heterosexuals not undergoing therapy, has been able to create serious doubt about the long-held view that homosexuals are neurotic or arrested in their emotional development. Today, many psychiatrists and psychologists believe that homosexuality is not itself a problem; it becomes a problem only when the individual is unable to accommodate it harmoniously in his personality.

Though little is known about homosexuality, fear of it lies like a scar upon much of the Western world. Sandor Ferenczi, one of Freud's chief disciples, wrote: "It is astounding to what extent men today have lost the capacity for mutual affection. . . ."

The cost of bearing an immemorial tribal legacy of fear and horror for homosexuality has been high for the heterosexual. Constraint, loss of spontaneity, and emotional impoverishment in his dealings with other males have, according to social scientists, all been part of the taboo.

Trudeau's amendments, by striking at the shackles of fear and hate which willy-nilly bind together the homosexual and the heterosexual, may yet free both.

Notes

INTRODUCTION

1 N. K. Dhalla, *These Canadians* (Toronto: McGraw Hill, 1967), p. 45.

2 *Ibid.*

3 These include Nels Anderson's *The Hobo: The Sociology of the Homeless Man* (Chicago: University of Chicago Press, 1935), Louis Wirth's *The Ghetto* (Chicago: University of Chicago Press, 1928), and Harvey Zorbaugh's *The Gold Coast and the Slum* (Chicago: University of Chicago Press, 1929), and other monographs on such subjects as the taxi dancehall girl.

4 A number of eminent Americans came and went; some Canadians stayed, but only one or two of the full-time professors in this period had a Toronto background.

PART ONE

CHAPTER 1

1 Michael Harrington, *The Other America* (Glencoe: Free Press, 1962), pp. 2-3.

2 Kevin Lynch, *The Image of a City* (Cambridge: M.I.T. Press, 1960), p. 141.

CHAPTER 2

1 His riding included the colourful Spadina district, covered in *Maclean's* (July 6, 1957). The slum areas to which he referred (Ontario *Hansard*, April 14, 1951) have yet to be cleared.

1b The Manpower Centre has since relocated.

2 This is less true of the district west of Bathurst Street.

3 In one school of three hundred pupils, two of the seven classes are opportunity classes, which means that the children in them have I.Q.s below 90.

[4] This area has just about the highest mental-illness rate for the Metropolitan area. See Diane Jaffey, "Ecology and Mental Disease in Toronto," M.S.W. thesis, University of Toronto, School of Social Work, 1956.

[5] W. L. Warner, M. Meeker, and K. Eells, *Social Class in America* (Chicago: University of Chicago Press, 1949).

[6] As piggy-back hauling becomes more popular, overtime is being cut down.

[7] It is impossible to get precise data from the appropriate authorities on this item. An analysis of the voters' list for the provincial election in 1958 indicated that from 5 to 10 per cent of the men in this area claimed unemployment at that time.

[8] E. W. Bakke, *The Unemployed Worker* (New Haven: 1940).

[9] Characteristically, the local ethnic churches are not recipients of many such requests.

[10] See "Anybody Eats Here Free," *Maclean's* (September 17, 1955).

[11] Jerome K. Myers and Bertram H. Roberts, *Family and Class Dynamics in Mental Illness* (New York: 1959).

[12] There is no settlement house in the Lower Ward, and the two which are a mere two or three blocks north of Queen Street are considered well outside the neighbourhood and draw very few young people from the Ward on a regular basis.

[13] Except for the Roman Catholics', church collections pay only a small fraction of clergymen's salaries.

[14] The hospital is about a third of a mile north of Queen Street, on Bathurst Street.

[15] Interviews with a random sample of residents indicated that very few read popular magazines, and less than 50 per cent take a daily newspaper.

[16] In 1959, fifty Roman Catholic and twenty-nine Protestant families were under Children's Aid supervision.

[17] See Morris Axelrod, "Urban Structure and Social Participation," *American Sociological Review* XXI (February, 1956), pp. 13-18.

[18] Except when the Woodbine racetrack is open; then they are half-empty.

[19] See D. Gottlieb, "The Neighbourhood Tavern and the Cocktail Lounge," *American Journal of Sociology* LXII (May, 1957).

[20] Banks of telephones in the hotel lobby make it easy for bookies to report bets.

[21] One publican, however, has a rule that politics must not be discussed, as he believes it leads to too many fights.

[22] The churches have nothing resembling a club or social program for such men.

[23] With a quarter they can, with the help of a buddy, soon make up $.75 for a bottle.

[24] This gentleman, who has lived in the area for thirty-five years and was formerly identified with legitimate church work, had many underworld connections in the area.

[25] Richard A. Cloward, "Illegitimate Means, Anomie and Deviant Behaviour," *American Sociological Review* (April, 1959), pp. 167-9.

[20] It appears that taking dope is fundamentally against the mores among the main Old Canadian group in the Lower Ward.

[21] If the police were to arrest all bootleggers in the Lower Ward and elsewhere in Toronto, the jails would be full to overflowing, and there would be an impossible congestion in the magistrates' court.

CHAPTER 4

[1] This was reflected not only in their greater involvement in community affairs but also in the joking references that were sometimes made: when a group of women were arranging for a bingo night, the question of prizes arose, and, when one suggested giving husbands away, the others considered these of little value. Someone else who suggested exchanging them was met with the quick retort "What's the point? One's as bad as the other."

CHAPTER 5

[1] Peter C. Pineo, "The Extended Family in a Working-Class Area of Hamilton," *Canadian Society: Sociological Perspectives*, eds. Bernard Blishen and others (Toronto: Macmillan, 1964, rev. ed.); Philippe Garigue, "French-Canadian Kinship and Urban Life," *American Anthropologist* 58, 6 (December, 1956), pp. 1090-1101, reprinted in *French Canadian Society*, eds. Marcel Rioux and Yves Martin (Toronto: McClelland and Stewart, 1965); Michael Young and Peter Wilmott, *Family and Kinship in East London* (New York: Humanities, 1957); Herbert J. Gans, *The Urban Villagers: Group and Class in the Life of Italian Americans* (New York: Free Press, 1962); Eugene Litwa, "The Use of Extended Family Groups in the Achievement of Social Goals: Some Policy Implications," *Social Problems* 7 (1959-1960), pp. 177-87; Frederick Elkin, *The Family in Canada* (Ottawa: Vanier Institute of the Family, 1964).

[2] Herbert Gans noted that "one of the distinguishing marks of a working-class group is its detachment from the larger society. . . . Because working-class culture is different from middle-class culture, the move from one to the other is a difficult one, requiring behaviour and attitude changes of considerable social and emotional magnitude. The most important changes are cutting the attachment to the family circle and the peer group society, and a concurrent shift from person- to object-orientation." *The Urban Villagers, op. cit.*, pp. 253-54. Bennett Berger found the auto workers in a new suburb participated in organizations to only a meagre extent. *Working-Class Suburb, op. cit.*

William F. Whyte's distinction between "corner boys" and "college boys" in the same Italian slum, the former stressing peer relations and the latter entering into wider associations such as the Italian Community Club, reflects more closely than the Gans or Berger studies the complexity of primary-secondary relations in a downtown, working-class community such as Riverdale. *Street Corner Society* (Chicago: University of Chicago Press, 1955, 2nd rev. ed.).

[3] Albert K. Cohen, *Delinquent Boys: The Culture of the Gang* (Glencoe: Free Press, 1955), p. 94.

[4] Cf. Whyte, Cohen, *op cit.*; Michael S. Olmsted, *The Small Group* (New York: Random House, 1959); George C. Homans, *The Human Group* (New York: Harcourt Brace, 1950).

[5] Cf. especially Eugene Litwa, *op cit.*, and "Geographical Mobility and Extended Family Cohesion," *American Sociological Review* XXV (June, 1960), pp. 385-394.

[6] Cf. Young and Willmott for other aspects of the changing roles of working-class women, in which they speak of them as being "liberated."

[7] Robert K. Merton's theory of the role-set is pertinent to the changing role of women in blue-collar society. There is a strain in the direction of integrating the expectations of those in the role-set which has implications for the social structures concerned. "The Role-Set: Problems in Sociological Theory," *The British Journal of Sociology*, 8 (June, 1957), pp. 106-120.

[8] Cf. A. O. Haller, "The Occupational Achievement Process of Farm-Reared Youth in Urban-Industrial Society," *Rural Sociology*, 25 (1960), pp. 321-333; P. Wilson and R. Buck, "The Educational Ladder," *Rural Sociology*, 25 (1960), pp. 404 ff.

[9] Anthony H. Richmond found that the level of education of immigrants into Canada since the Second World War was strongly related to the degree to which they were acculturated and integrated into Canadian society as a whole. About one-third of his sample belonged to associations mainly attended by the Canadian-born. *Post-War Immigrants in Canada* (Toronto: University of Toronto Press, 1967), p. 155.

[10] Marc Fried, *op. cit.*, p. 144.

[11] *Ibid.*, p. 145.

[12] *Ibid.*, p. 130.

[13] S. N. Eisenstadt, *The Absorption of Immigrants* (New York: Humanities, 1954).

[14] Herbert Gans attempts to distinguish the lower-, working-, and middle-class strata from one another on the basis not of any one factor, such as occupation, but of subcultures in which there are distinctive social relationships, behaviour patterns, and attitudes – all part of a social and cultural system. In effect, he bases his distinctions chiefly on family and kinship patterns. Because of the relative homogeneity of his population – in Italian, low-income areas – class differentiations are sharper between his working- and middle-class people than were apparent in Riverdale. *The Urban Villagers, op. cit.*, Ch. 11.

Although our Riverdale survey was confined to chief wage-earners, distinctions between their "subcultures" – both middle- and working-class – and that of lower-class neighbours were sharp. An unpublished random survey of the South Riverdale population as a whole, conducted by John Wayne for WoodGreen Community Centre in 1965, for the purpose of assessing needs for services, revealed wide divergencies between the cultural patterns of workers and non-workers in the community.

[15] *Ibid.*, Ch. 11.

[16] *Ibid.*, p. 89 ff.

[17] Marc Fried, *op. cit.*, p. 130.

[18] Albert K. Cohen, *op. cit.*, Ch. 3.

[19] Ideal type," a key term in Max Weber's methodological discussion, refers to the construction of certain elements of reality into a logically precise conception. It has nothing to do with evaluation. Weber "felt that social scientists had the choice of using logically controlled and unam-

biguous conceptions, which are thus more removed from historical reality, or of using less precise concepts, which are more closely geared to the empirical world." *From Max Weber: Essays in Sociology,* trs. and eds., H. H. Gerth and C. Wright Mills (New York: Oxford University Press, 1958), p. 59.

[20] Albert K. Cohen, *op. cit.,* Ch. 4, "Growing Up in a Class System." Cf. John Seeley, A. Sim, and E. Loosley, *Crestwood Heights* (Toronto: University of Toronto Press, 1956), esp. Chs. 7-9; Edward Gross, *Work and Society* (New York: Crowell, 1958), pp. 162 ff. (on the ambiguous role of education in opening and blocking entrance to high-status occupations); Theodore Caplow, *The Sociology of Work* (Minneapolis: McGraw-Hill, 1954), p. 220.

[21] Cf. Gideon Sjoberg, "Are Social Classes in America Becoming More Rigid?", *American Sociological Review,* 16 (1951), pp. 775-783; Talcott Parsons, "A Revised Analytical Approach to the Theory of Social Stratification," Ch. 19, *Essays in Sociological Theory* (Glencoe: Free Press, 1954).

CHAPTER 6

[1] W. Howells, *Back of History: The Story of Our Own Origins* (New York: Doubleday, 1963), p. 34.

[2] Ruth Benedict, "Anthropology and the Abnormal," *Journal of Genetics and Psychology,* 10 (1934), pp. 59-80.

PART TWO
CHAPTER 2

[1] Muzafer and Caroyln Sherif, *Exploration Into Conformity and Deviation of Adolescents* (New York: Harper & Row, 1964).

[2] Kenneth Keniston, *The Uncommitted: Alienated Youth in American Society* (New York: Harcourt, Brace & World, 1965).

CHAPTER 3

[1] W. E. Mann, *Canadian Trends in Premarital Behaviour* (Toronto: 1957), p. 59.

[2] *Ibid.,* p. 11.

[3] *Ibid.*

[4] The University of New Brunswick sample was below 70 per cent and thus not worth scientific discussion.

[5] At the time this article went to press, full computer analysis of the York study had not been completed.

[6] There were other revealing questions, but space to discuss them here is unfortunately unavailable.

[7] Metropolitan-raised youth in the study at the University of Western Ontario were in favour of intercourse upon engagement. See Mann, *op. cit.,* p. 50.

CHAPTER 5

[1] See Raymond Breton, "Institutional Completeness of Ethnic Communities and the Personal Relations of Immigrants," *The American Journal of Sociology* LXX, 2 (September, 1964), pp. 193-205.

² J. P. Fitzpatrick, "The Importance of 'Community' in the Process of Immigrant Assimilation," *The International Migration Review* I, 1, p. 6.

³ *Problem del lavoro italiano all'estero* (Rome: Ministero degli affari esteri, 1966). G. L. Monticelli, *I movimenti migratori italiani* (Rome: U.C.E.I., 1965).

⁴ This index was obtained from another study in the ethnic research program by A. Gordon Darroch and Wilfred G. Marston, *An Ecological Analysis of Ethnic Segregation in Toronto.*

⁵ See A. H. Richmond, *Immigrants and Ethnic Groups in Metropolitan Toronto* (Toronto: 1968), pp. 10-11.

⁶ *Ibid.*

⁷ Obtained from unpublished materials developed by Darroch and Marston.

⁸ N. Glazer and D. P. Moynihan, *Beyond the Melting Pot* (Cambridge: M.I.T., 1963).

CHAPTER 6

¹ The Municipality of Metropolitan Toronto, created by the government of Ontario in 1953, includes both the central city and its surrounding municipalities. All references to "Toronto" or "the city" can be understood here as references to the whole metropolitan area, unless otherwise stated.

² Recent figures indicate that there are approximately 300,000 Italians, 100,000 Germans, 50,000 Poles, and 50,000 Ukrainians among the total Toronto population of 2 million people. *Globe & Mail*, July 12, 1969.

³ Merrijoy Kelner, "The Elite Structure of Toronto: Ethnic Composition and Patterns of Recruitment," unpublished PH.D. dissertation, University of Toronto, Department of Sociology, 1969.

⁴ Suzanne Keller, *Beyond the Ruling Class,* (New York: Random House, 1963).

⁵ Such a socially homogeneous group of decision-makers closely resembles the élite group delineated by C. Wright Mills in *The Power Elite* (New York: Oxford University Press, 1956).

⁶ John Porter, *The Vertical Mosaic* (Toronto: University of Toronto Press, 1965).

⁷ These figures must be regarded as approximations only, due to the difficulties involved in assessing ethnic origins, particularly in cases where individuals have changed their names and otherwise attempted to pass into the Anglo-Saxon majority.

⁸ *The Telegram*, February 1, 1968.

⁹ Keller, *op. cit.*, p. 23.

¹⁰ E. Digby Baltzell, *The Protestant Establishment: Aristocracy and Caste in America* (New York: Random House, 1964).

¹¹ *Ibid.*, p. 8.

PART THREE

CHAPTER 1

¹ Aim of the project: "The aim of the education program is to provide an environment where indivduals and groups of people can create their own

educational experiences – experiences relevant to the individuals involved and fashioned by them in regard to both form and content."

Principles of the project: "Education at Rochdale will be democratic and community-oriented. Decisions regarding education within Rochdale will be made by the people directly involved in the education project. The degree of a member's participation in the making of a particular decision will be in proportion to how much that decision affects him.

"The character of education at Rochdale will not be that of isolation from society but, rather, that of involvement with the extended community in a manner to be determined by those participating in the program. The Rochdale member is necessarily a member of a larger society, and no rigid distinction is made between his role as 'student' and as a 'social being.' "

Approach to education: "Essentially, Rochdale will be a centre of imaginative intellectual and creative activity and will appeal to potential members on this basis. . . ."

[2] Objects of Rochdale college:

a) To advance learning and the dissemination of knowledge;

b) To promote the intellectual, social, moral, and physical development of the members . . . and the betterment of society;

c) To establish an education-residential institution in which participants determine the form and content of their own education and the direction and intensity of their involvement;

d) To establish and maintain a library;

e) To establish and conduct seminars, lectures and correspondence courses and to publish a journal and such other scholarly material as shall be relevant to the educational purposes of the Corporation. . . ."

[3] The sum of $5,038,200 was loaned to Campus Co-operative Residence Inc. by Central Mortgage and Housing. The remaining 10 per cent of the cost of the $5,713,000 building came from Rubin Corporation, the developer ($430,000 at 7 per cent interest), past earnings of Campus Co-op ($124,800), and from a college fraternity ($120,000). The long-term C.M.H.C. mortgage at 5.875 per cent interest requires equalized payments averaging $31,275 monthly. There are also other interest and repayment costs. The building budget for the 1968-69 academic year is $586,430. Income is mainly from rents from the building, which theoretically accommodates 850 persons. The financial picture is apparently fairly stable. All these figures concern the building and operating budget; the education budget is another story.

[4] There are five types of rooms or suites at Rochdale. Besides the Ashram Suites, other living units are Aphrodite Suites (living room, bedroom, kitchen, and bath), Franz Kalka Units (a single room and double room, sharing a common bath), Gnostic Chambers (the same as Franz Kafka units, but with a kitchen) and Zeus Suites (a huge living room, two bedrooms, kitchen, and bath). Costs range from $250 a month for a Zeus Suite down to $17 a week if you double up in a Gnostic Chamber.

CHAPTER 4

[1] Arthur L. Stinchcombe, "Institutions of Privacy in the Determination of Police Administrative Practice," *American Journal of Sociology*, LXIX (September, 1963), pp. 150-160.

[2] Abraham Flexner argues that the customers of prostitutes for this reason are rarely charged with an offence. *Prostitution in Europe* (New York: 1920), p. 108.

[3] A. B. Hollingshead and F. C. Redlich, *Social Class and Mental Illness: A Community Study* (New York: Wiley, 1958), p. 187.

[4] The medical study indicated that the health of the chronic offenders was surprisingly good. The main explanation seemed to be the role of the police in terminating sprees and the effect of incarceration in providing enforced recuperation and spacing sprees.

[5] Although the Salvation Army is an exception, its emphasis on spiritual regeneration through religion is in contrast to the methods of professionally manned agencies and appears to limit the type of person whom it can influence.

[6] Judge William Burnett, *Proceedings: Conference on the Alcoholic and the Court* (Portland: Oregon State System of Higher Education, 1963), p. 5.

[7] *Proceedings: Processing the Alcoholic Defendant: Rocky Mountain Regional Conference of Municipal Judges* (Washington: U.S. Government Printing Office, 1969), p. 90.

[8] Revised Statutes of Ontario, 1960, Chapter 217, with amendments.

[9] Most of the men were found to gain weight in jail. Since they were in jail frequently, this tended to prevent the sequelae of malnutrition associated with prolonged heavy drinking.

[10] Gresham M. Sykes, *The Society of Captives* (Princeton: Princeton University Press, 1958), pp. 18-30.

PART FOUR

CHAPTER 3

[1] David W. Maurer, *The Big Con* (New York: 1958), p. 232.

[2] H. Becker, *Outsiders* (New York: Macmillan, 1963), fly-leaf.

[3] Proshansky and Seidenberg (eds.), *Basic Studies in Social Psychology* (New York: Holt, 1965), p. 265.

[4] E. T. Hall, *The Silent Language* (New York: Doubleday, 1959), p. 162.

CHAPTER 5

[1] J. C. Martin, Q.C., *Martin's Annual Criminal Code* (Toronto: 1959), p. 98.

[2] Ralph Slovenko, editor, *Sexual Behaviour and the Law* (Springfield: 1965), p. 846.

Bibliography

BOOKS

ARTHUR, ERIC *Toronto, No Mean City* (Toronto: University of Toronto Press, 1964).

BERTON, PIERRE *The New City: A Prejudiced View of Toronto* (Toronto: Macmillan, 1961).

CLARKE, S. D. *The Suburban Society* (Toronto: University of Toronto Press, 1966).

_____ *Urbanism and the Changing Canadian Society* (Toronto: University of Toronto Press, 1961).

CORNISH, JOHN *Sherbourne Street* (Toronto: Clarke, Irwin, 1968). A novel.

GARNER, HUGH *Cabbagetown* (Toronto: Ryerson Press, 1968). A novel.

INTERNATIONAL INSTITUTE OF METROPOLITAN TORONTO *Newcomers and New Learning: A Project of the International Institute of Metropolitan Toronto, 1964-1966* (Toronto: 1966). By Edith Ferguson.

KAPLAN, HAROLD *The Regional City: Politics and Planning in Metropolitan Areas* (Toronto: Canadian Broadcasting Corporation, 1965).

_____ *Urban Political Systems: A Functional Analysis of Metro Toronto* (New York: Columbia University Press, 1967).

ONTARIO. ROYAL COMMISSION ON METROPOLITAN TORONTO. *Report.* (Toronto: 1965).

ARTICLES

ARCHER, D. B. "Public Housing in Toronto," *Canadian Labour* 11 (March, 1966), 13-16.

BATTEN, J. H. "Underworld Toronto," *Canadian Forum* 41 (October, 1961), 149-51.

JONES, M. V. "Urban Focus and Regional Planning," *Canadian Public Administration* 9 (June, 1966), 177-80.

KAPLAN, HAROLD "Politics and Policy-Making in Metropolitan Toronto," *Canadian Journal of Economics* 31 (November, 1965), 538-51.

MANN, W. E. "Adult Drop-outs," *Continuous Learning* v, 2 and 3 (March-April, 1966; May-June, 1967), 55-67 and 127-43.

ROBB, G. A. "Counter-Revolution in Urbanism," *Canadian Architect* 8 (August, 1963), 45-50.

ROSE, A. "Changed City," *Canadian Welfare* 39 (January-February, 1963), 6-11.

ROSS, A. "Status Guide to Toronto," *Maclean's* 81 (November, 1968), 36-7, 75-9.

SHEPHERD, H. L. "A Centre Where Hippies Can Drop In, Turn Off, and Think About Going Home," *Maclean's* 81 (August, 1968), 2-3.

SMALLWOOD, FRANK "Report of the Royal Commission on Metropolitan Toronto," *Canadian Public Administration* 9 (June, 1966), 268-9.

Acknowledgements

These pages constitute an extension of the copyright page. For permission to reprint copyright material, grateful acknowledgement is made to the following:

Excerpts from *These Canadians* by N. K. Dhalla, © 1967 by McGraw-Hill Company of Canada Limited. Reprinted by permission of the publisher.

"Anthropology on the Town" by Charles Tilly. Reprinted by permission of the author.

"The Lower Ward" by W. E. Mann. Reprinted (with slight alterations) from *Urbanism and the Changing Canadian Society* edited by S. D. Clark, by permission of University of Toronto Press, © University of Toronto Press, 1961.

"Family and Kinship in Riverdale" by Stewart Crysdale. Reprinted by permission of the author.

"Blacks in Toronto" by Martin O'Malley. Originally titled "A Tolerant People? Nice to Believe. We're Really Just Polite Racists." Reprinted by permission of *The Globe and Mail*.

"Alienated Youth" by Dr. John Byles. From *Youth, Deviance and Social Control*, published by the Ontario Department of Education. Reprinted by permission of the author.

Excerpts from *The Globe and Mail* (November 14, 1968) in "Sex at York University" by W. E. Mann. Reprinted by permission of *The Globe and Mail*.

Excerpts from the *Toronto Daily Star* (April 2, 1969) in "Sex at York University" by W. E. Mann. Reprinted with permission *Toronto Daily Star*.

"Student Radicals" by Steven Langdon. Originally titled "Why Student Activists Are Zeroing in on a New Target." Reprinted by permission of the author.

"Unity and Disunity in Two Ethnic Groups in Toronto" by Clifford J. Jansen and J. Gottfried Paasché. Originally presented as a paper at the 1969 meeting of the Canadian Sociology and Anthropology Association. The research upon which the findings are based was supported by grants from the Canada Council and the Central Mortgage and Housing Corporation. The studies were carried out under the auspices of the Ethnic Research Programme of the Institute for Behavioural Research, York University. The Co-ordinator of the Programme and Principal Investigator is Dr. A. H. Richmond, Department of Sociology, York University. Published by permission of the authors.

"Changes in Toronto's Élite Structure" by Merrijoy Kelner, P.H.D., a revised version of "Ethnic Penetration into Toronto's Élite Structure," a paper presented at the annual meeting of the Canadian Sociology and Anthropology Association, York University, June, 1969. Published by permission of the author.

"Rochdale: the Ultimate Freedom" by Barrie Zwicker. Originally published in the November-December, 1969, issue of *Change* Magazine. Reprinted by permission of *Change* Magazine and the author.

"Life and Death on the Telephone" by Elizabeth Kilbourn. Reprinted by permission of the author.

"A True-Life Drama" by Betty Lee. Reprinted by permission of *The Globe and Mail*.

"The Revolving Door" by P. J. Giffen. Originally titled "The Revolving Door: A Functional Interpretation." Reprinted from *The Canadian Review of Sociology and Anthropology*, 3:3 (1966), by permission of the author and the publisher.

"Crisis at the Victory Burlesk" by Robert Fulford. From *Crisis at the Victory Burlesk* by Robert Fulford, © 1968 by Oxford University Press, Canadian Branch. Reprinted by permission of the publisher.

"Middle-Class Rackets in the Big City" by Pierre Berton. From *The Big Sell*, copyright 1963 by Pierre Berton. Reprinted by permission of McClelland & Stewart, Toronto; Alfred A. Knopf Inc., New York; Collis-Knowlton-Wing Inc., New York; and the author.